The Lectionary 2019

First published in Great Britain in 2018

Society for Promoting Christian Knowledge
36 Causton Street
London SW1P 4ST
www.spck.org.uk

British Library Cataloguing-in-Publication Data
A catalogue record for this book is available from the British Library

ISBN 978-0-281-07910-0
ISBN 978-0-281-07911-7 spiral-bound

1 3 5 7 9 10 8 6 4 2

Designed by Colin Hall, Refined Practice
Typeset by Fakenham Prepress Solutions, Fakenham, Norfolk NR21 8NN
Printed in Great Britain by Ashford Colour Press

Produced on paper from sustainable forests

CONTENTS

UNDERSTANDING THE LECTIONARY

Common Worship on left-hand page

July 2019 ***Common Worship***

		Sunday Principal Service Weekday Eucharist	Third Service Morning Prayer	Second Service Evening Prayer
21 Sunday	**THE FIFTH SUNDAY AFTER TRINITY (Proper 11)**			
G	*Track 1* Amos 8. 1–12 Ps. 52 Col. 1. 15–28 Luke 10. 38–end	*Track 2* Gen. 18. 1–10a Ps. 15 Col. 1. 15–28 Luke 10. 38–end	Ps. 82; 100 Deut. 30. 1–10 1 Pet. 3. 8–18	Ps. 81 Gen. 41. 1–16, 25–37 1 Cor. 4. 8–13 *Gospel*: John 4. 31–35 *or First EP of Mary Magdalene* Ps. 139 Isa. 25. 1–9 2 Cor. 1. 3–7 **W ct**
22 Monday	**MARY MAGDALENE**			
W **DEL 16**		Song of Sol. 3. 1–4 Ps. 42. 1–10 2 Cor. 5. 14–17 John 20. 1–2, 11–18	*MP*: Ps. 30; 32; 150 1 Sam. 16. 14–end Luke 8. 1–3	*EP*: Ps. 63 Zeph. 3. 14–end Mark 15.40 - 16.7

Column 1

- **Date**
- **Colour:** An upper-case letter indicates the liturgical colour of the day. A lower-case second colour indicates the colour for a Lesser Festival while the Lectionary upper-case letter indicates the continuing seasonal colour.
- **DEL:** Week number of Daily Eucharistic Lectionary.

Column 2

- Name of the Principal Holy Day, Sunday, Festival or Lesser Festival;
- a note of other Commemorations for mention in prayers;
- any general note that applies to the whole *Common Worship* provision for the day;
- one of the options where there are two options for readings at the Eucharist or Principal Service.

Readings: Readings occur in this column only in two circumstances.

1. **On Sundays after Trinity** where there are two 'tracks' for the Principal Service readings (where there is a choice of first reading and psalm, but the second reading and Gospel are the same in both tracks), Track I appears in this column.
2. **On Lesser Festivals throughout the year** where there are readings for that festival that are alternative to the semi-continuous Daily Eucharistic Lectionary, these also appear in this column.

Column 3

On Principal Feasts, Principal Holy Days, Sundays and Festivals this gives the Principal Service Lectionary, intended for use at the main service of the day (in most churches the mid-morning service), whether or not it is a Eucharist.

On other weekdays this gives the Daily Eucharistic Lectionary for those wanting a semi-continuous pattern of readings and a psalm for Holy Communion. It is most useful in a church where there is a daily celebration and a core community that worships together day by day, though its use is not restricted to that.

Column 4

On Principal Feasts, Principal Holy Days, Sundays and Festivals this gives the Third Service Lectionary. Many churches will have no need of it, for it comes into use only if the Principal and Second Service Lectionaries have been used. Its most likely use is at Morning Prayer (when this is not the Principal Service). Where psalms are recommended for use in the morning, these also appear in this column.

On other weekdays this provides the psalmody and readings for Morning Prayer. Where two or more psalms are appointed, the psalm in bold italic may be used as the only psalm. Psalms printed in round brackets ( ) may be omitted if they are used as an opening canticle at Morning Prayer. Where † is printed after the psalm number, the psalm may be shortened if desired. For those wishing to follow the Ordinary Time psalm cycle throughout the year (except for the period between 19 December and the Epiphany and from the Monday of Holy Week to the Saturday of Easter Week), this is printed as an alternative to the seasonal provision.

Column 5

On Principal Feasts, Principal Holy Days, Sundays and Festivals this gives the Second Service Lectionary, intended for use when a second set of readings is required. Its most likely use is in the evening, when the Principal Service Lectionary has been used in the morning. Sometimes it might be used at an evening Eucharist. Where the second reading is not a Gospel reading, an alternative to meet this need is provided. Where psalms are recommended for use in the evening, these also appear in this column.

On other weekdays this provides the psalmody and readings for Evening Prayer. Where two or more psalms are provided, the psalm in bold italic may be used as the only psalm. Psalms printed in round brackets ( ) may be omitted if they are used as an opening canticle at Evening Prayer. Where † is printed after the psalm number, the psalm may be shortened if desired. For those wishing to follow the Ordinary Time psalm cycle throughout the year (except for the period between 19 December and the Epiphany and from the Monday of Holy Week to the Saturday of Easter Week), this is printed as an alternative to the seasonal provision.

Book of Common Prayer and space for notes on right-hand page

Book of Common Prayer

July 2019

	Calendar and Holy Communion	Morning Prayer	Evening Prayer	NOTES
	THE FIFTH SUNDAY AFTER TRINITY			
G	1 Kings 19. 19–21 Ps. 84. 8–end 1. Pet. 3. 8–15a Luke 5. 1–11	Ps. 82; 100 Deut. 30. 1–10 1 Pet. 3. 8–18	Ps. 81 Gen. 41. 1–16, 25–37 1 Cor. 4. 8–13 *or First EP of Mary Magdalene* Ps. 139 Isa. 25. 1–9 2 Cor. 1. 3–7 **W ct**	
	MARY MAGDALENE			
W	Zeph. 3. 14–end Ps. 30. 1–5 2 Cor. 5. 14–17 John 20. 11–18	(Ps. 30; 32; 150) 1 Sam. 16. 14–end Luke 8. 1–3	(Ps. 63) Song of Sol. 3. 1–4 Mark 15.40 – 16.7	

Column 6

- Liturgical colour (*see column 1*).

Column 7

- The name of the Principal Holy Day, Sunday, Festival or Lesser Festival;
- any general note that applies to the whole Prayer Book provision for the day and an indication of points at which users may wish to draw on *Common Worship* material on the opposite page where the BCP has no provision;
- the Lectionary for the Eucharist on any day for which provision is made.

Column 8

This provides the readings for Morning Prayer, together with psalm provision where it varies from the BCP monthly cycle.

Column 9

This provides the readings for Evening Prayer, together with psalm provision where it varies from the BCP monthly cycle.

A letter to indicate liturgical colour in this column indicates a change of colour for Evening Prayer. The symbol in bold lower case, **ct**, indicates that the Collect at Evening Prayer should be that of the following day.

Column 10

Space for notes.

ABBREVIATIONS OF BOOKS OF THE BIBLE

Old Testament

Gen. (Genesis)
Exod. (Exodus)
Lev. (Leviticus)
Num. (Numbers)
Deut. (Deuteronomy)
Josh. (Joshua)
Judg. (Judges)
Ruth
Sam. (Samuel)
Kings
Chron. (Chronicles)
Ezra
Neh. (Nehemiah)
Esth. (Esther)
Job
Ps(s). (Psalms)
Prov. (Proverbs)
Eccles. (Ecclesiastes)
Song of Sol. (Song of Solomon)
Isa. (Isaiah)
Jer. (Jeremiah)
Lam. (Lamentations)
Ezek. (Ezekiel)
Dan. (Daniel)
Hos. (Hosea)
Joel
Amos
Obad. (Obadiah)
Jonah
Mic. (Micah)
Nahum
Hab. (Habakkuk)
Zeph. (Zephaniah)
Hag. (Haggai)
Zech. (Zechariah)
Mal. (Malachi)

Apocrypha

Esd. (Esdras)
Tobit
Judith
Wisd. (Wisdom of Solomon)
Ecclus. (Ecclesiasticus)
Baruch (Baruch)
Song of the Three (Song of the Three Children)
Susanna (The History of Susanna)
Prayer of Manasseh
Macc. (Maccabees)

New Testament

Matt. (Matthew)
Mark
Luke
John
Acts (Acts of the Apostles)
Rom. (Romans)
Cor. (Corinthians)
Gal. (Galatians)
Eph. (Ephesians)
Phil. (Philippians)
Col. (Colossians)
Thess. (Thessalonians)
Tim. (Timothy)
Titus
Philem. (Philemon)
Heb. (Hebrews)
Jas. (James)
Pet. (Peter)
John (letters of John)
Jude
Rev. (Revelation)

MAKING CHOICES IN *COMMON WORSHIP*

Common Worship makes provision for a variety of pastoral and liturgical circumstances. It needs to, for it has to serve some church communities where Morning Prayer, Holy Communion and Evening Prayer are all celebrated every day, and yet be useful also in a church with only one service a week, and that service varying in form and time from week to week.

At the beginning of the year, some decisions in principle need to be taken.

In relation to the Calendar, whether to keep The Presentation of Christ (Candlemas) on Saturday 2 February or on Sunday 3 February, and whether to keep the Feast of All Saints on Friday 1 November or on Sunday 3 November.

In relation to the Lectionary, the initial choices every year to decide in relation to Sundays are:

- which of the services on a Principal Feast, Principal Holy Day, Sunday or Festival constitutes the 'Principal Service'; then use the Principal Service Lectionary (column 3) consistently for that service through the year;
- during the Sundays after Trinity, whether to use Track I of the Principal Service Lectionary (column 2), where the first reading stays over several weeks with one Old Testament book read semi-continuously, or Track 2 (column 3), where the first reading is chosen for its relationship to the Gospel reading of the day;
- which, if any, service on a Principal Feast, Principal Holy Day, Sunday or Festival constitutes the 'Second Service'; then use the Second Service Lectionary (column 5) consistently for that service through the year;
- which, if any, service on a Principal Feast, Principal Holy Day, Sunday or Festival constitutes the 'Third Service'; then use the Third Service Lectionary (column 4) consistently for that service through the year.

And in relation to weekdays:

- whether to use the Daily Eucharistic Lectionary (column 3) consistently for weekday celebrations of Holy Communion (with the exception of Principal Feasts, Principal Holy Days and Festivals) or to make some use of the Lesser Festival provision;
- whether to follow the first psalm provision in column 4 (morning) and column 5 (evening), where psalms during the seasons have a seasonal flavour but in ordinary time follow a sequential pattern; or to follow the alternative provision in the same columns, where psalms follow the sequential pattern throughout the year, except for the period between 19 December and The Epiphany and from the Monday of Holy Week to the Saturday of Easter Week; or to follow the psalm cycle in the Book of Common Prayer, where they are nearly always used 'in course';
- whether to use the Additional Weekday Lectionary (which begins on page 118) for weekday services (other than Holy Communion). It provides a one-year cycle of two readings for each day (except for Sundays, Principal Feasts, Principal Holy Days, Festivals and during Holy Week). Since each of the readings is designed to 'stand alone' (that is, it is complete in itself and will make sense to the worshipper who has not attended on the previous day and who will not be present on the next day), it is intended particularly for use in those churches and cathedrals that attract occasional rather than regular congregations.

The flexibility of *Common Worship* is intended to enable the church and the minister to find the most helpful provision for them. But once a decision is made, it is advisable to stay with that decision through the year or at the very least through a complete season.

All Bible references (except to the psalms) are to the New Revised Standard Version, Anglicized edition (1995). Those who use other Bible translations should check the verse numbers against the NRSV. References to the psalms are to the *Common Worship* Psalter.

BOOK OF COMMON PRAYER

A separate Lectionary for the Book of Common Prayer is no longer issued. Provision is made on the right-hand pages of this Lectionary for BCP worship on all Sundays in the year, for the major festivals and for Morning and Evening Prayer. The Epistles and Gospels for Holy Communion are those of 1662, with the additions and variations of 1928, now authorized under the *Common Worship* overall provision. The Old Testament readings and psalms for these services, formerly appended to the Series One Holy Communion service, may be used but are not mandatory with the 1662 order.

Readings for Morning and Evening Prayer, which are the same as those for *Common Worship*, are set out in the BCP section for Sundays and weekdays. The special psalm provision of the BCP is given; however, where the *Common Worship* psalm provision is used, verse numbering may occasionally differ slightly from that in the BCP Psalter, and appropriate adjustment will have to be made (a table of variations in verse numbering can be found at www.churchofengland.org/prayer-and-worship/worship-texts-and-resources/common-worship/daily-prayer/psalter/psalter-verse). Otherwise the Psalter is read in course daily through each month.

The Calendar observes BCP dates when these differ from those of *Common Worship*; for example, St Thomas on 21 December. Additional commemorations in the *Common Worship* Calendar are not included, but those who wish to observe them may use the *Collects and Post Communions in Traditional Language: Lesser Festivals, Common of the Saints, Special Occasions* (Church House Publishing).

The Lectionaries of 1871 and 1922, to be found in many copies of the BCP, are still authorized and may be used, but - with the exception of the psalms and readings for Holy Communion mentioned above - the Additional Alternative Lectionary (1961) is no longer authorized for public worship.

Although those who use the BCP, for private or public worship or both, are free to follow any of the authorized lectionaries, there is much to be said for common usage across the Church of England, so that the same passages are being read by all. It is of course appropriate that BCP readings should be taken from the Authorized or King James Version for harmony of style, with the daily recitation of the BCP Psalter.

The integrity of the BCP as the traditional source of worship in the Church of England is not in any way affected by the use of a common lectionary for the daily offices.

CERTAIN DAYS AND OCCASIONS COMMONLY OBSERVED

Plough Sunday may be observed on 13 January 2019.

The Week of Prayer for Christian Unity may be observed from 18 to 25 January 2019.

Education Sunday may be observed on 8 September 2019.

Rogation Sunday may be observed on 26 May 2019.

The Feast of Dedication is observed on the anniversary of the dedication or consecration of a church, or, when the actual date is unknown, on 6 October 2019. In *CW*, 27 October 2019 is an alternative date.

Ember Days. *CW* encourages the bishop to set the Ember Days in each diocese in the week before the ordinations, whereas in BCP the dates are fixed.

Days of Discipline and Self-Denial in *CW* are the weekdays of Lent and all Fridays in the year, except all Principal Feasts and festivals outside Lent and Fridays between Easter Day and Pentecost. The eves of Principal Feasts are also appropriately kept as days of discipline and self-denial in preparation for the feast.

Days of Fasting and Abstinence according to the BCP are the forty days of Lent, the Ember Days at the four seasons, the three Rogation Days, and all Fridays in the year except Christmas Day. The BCP also orders the observance of the Evens or Vigils before The Nativity of our Lord, The Purification of the Blessed Virgin Mary, The Annunciation of the Blessed Virgin Mary, Easter Day, Ascension Day, Pentecost, and before the following saints' days: Matthias, John the Baptist, Peter, James, Bartholomew, Matthew, Simon and Jude, Andrew, Thomas, and All Saints. (If any of these days falls on Monday, the Vigil is to be kept on the previous Saturday.)

KEY TO LITURGICAL COLOURS

Common Worship suggests appropriate liturgical colours. They are not mandatory, and traditional or local use may be followed.

For a detailed discussion of when colours may be used, see *Common Worship: Services and Prayers for the Church of England* (Church House Publishing), *New Handbook of Pastoral Liturgy* (SPCK) or *A Companion to Common Worship: Volume I* (SPCK).

When a lower-case letter accompanies an upper-case letter, the lower-case letter indicates the liturgical colour appropriate to the Lesser Festival of that day, while the upper-case letter indicates the continuing seasonal colour.

W White
𝔚 Gold or white
R Red
P Purple (may vary from 'Roman purple' to violet, with blue as an alternative; a Lent array of sackcloth may be used in Lent, and rose pink on The Third Sunday of Advent and Fourth Sunday of Lent)
G Green

PRINCIPAL FEASTS, HOLY DAYS AND FESTIVALS

Principal Feasts and other Principal Holy Days (Ash Wednesday, Maundy Thursday, Good Friday) are printed in **LARGE BOLD CAPITALS** in the Lectionary.

There are no longer proper readings relating to the Holy Spirit on the six days after Pentecost. Instead they have been located on the nine days before Pentecost.

When Patronal and Dedication Festivals are kept as Principal Feasts, they may be transferred to the nearest Sunday, unless that day is already either a Principal Feast or The First Sunday of Advent, The Baptism of Christ, The First Sunday of Lent or Palm Sunday.

Festivals are printed in the Lectionary in **SMALL BOLD CAPITALS.**

For each day there is a full liturgical provision for the Holy Communion and for Morning and Evening Prayer. Most holy days that are in the category 'Festival' are provided with an optional First Evening Prayer. Its use is entirely at the discretion of the minister. Where it is used, the liturgical colour for the next day should be used at that First Evening Prayer, and this has been indicated in the provision on the following pages.

LESSER FESTIVALS AND COMMEMORATIONS

Lesser Festivals (printed in **medium-bold roman** typeface) are observed at the level appropriate to a particular church. The readings and psalms for The Common of the Saints are listed on page 10. In addition, there are special readings appropriate to the Festival listed in the first column. The daily psalms and readings at Morning and Evening Prayer are not usually superseded by those for Lesser Festivals, but the readings and psalms for Holy Communion may on occasion be used at Morning or Evening Prayer.

Commemorations are printed in the Lectionary in *italic* typeface. They do not have collect, psalm or readings, but may be observed by mention in prayers of intercession and thanksgiving. For local reasons, or where there is an established tradition in the wider Church, they may be kept as Lesser Festivals using the appropriate material from The Common of the Saints. Equally, it may be desirable to observe some Lesser Festivals as Commemorations.

If a Lesser Festival or a Commemoration falls on a Principal Feast, Principal Holy Day, Sunday or Festival, it is not normally observed that year, although it may be celebrated, where there is sufficient reason, on the nearest available day. Lesser Festivals and Commemorations which, for this reason, would not be celebrated in 2019 are listed on pages 9–10, so that, if desired, they may be mentioned in prayers of intercession and thanksgiving.

LESSER FESTIVALS AND COMMEMORATIONS NOT OBSERVED IN 2019

The Lesser Festivals and Commemorations (shown in italics) listed below fall on a Sunday or during Holy Week or Easter Week this year, and are thus not observed in this Lectionary.

COMMON WORSHIP 2019

January

13 Hilary, Bishop of Poitiers, Teacher, 367
Kentigern (Mungo), Missionary Bishop in Strathclyde and Cumbria, 603
George Fox, Founder of the Society of Friends (Quakers), 1691
20 *Richard Rolle of Hampole, Spiritual Writer, 1349*

February

3 Anskar, Archbishop of Hamburg, Missionary in Denmark and Sweden, 865
10 *Scholastica, sister of Benedict, Abbess of Plombariola, c. 543*
17 Janani Luwum, Archbishop of Uganda, Martyr, 1977

March

17 Patrick, Bishop, Missionary, Patron of Ireland, c. 460
24 *Walter Hilton of Thurgarton, Augustinian Canon, Mystic, 1396*
Paul Couturier, Priest, Ecumenist, 1953
Oscar Romero, Archbishop of San Salvador, Martyr, 1980
31 *John Donne, Priest, Poet, 1631*

April

16 *Isabella Gilmore, Deaconess, 1923*
19 Alphege, Archbishop of Canterbury, Martyr, 1012
21 Anselm, Abbot of Le Bec, Archbishop of Canterbury, Teacher, 1109
24 *Mellitus, Bishop of London, first Bishop at St Paul's, 624*
The Seven Martyrs of the Melanesian Brotherhood, Solomon Islands, 2003
27 *Christina Rossetti, Poet, 1894*
28 *Peter Chanel, Missionary in the South Pacific, Martyr, 1841*
29 Catherine of Siena, Teacher, 1380
30 *Pandita Mary Ramabai, Translator of the Scriptures, 1922*

May

12 *Gregory Dix, Priest, Monk, Scholar, 1952*
19 Dunstan, Archbishop of Canterbury, Restorer of Monastic Life, 988
26 Augustine, first Archbishop of Canterbury, 605
John Calvin, Reformer, 1564
Philip Neri, Founder of the Oratorians, Spiritual Guide, 1595
30 Josephine Butler, Social Reformer, 1906
Joan of Arc, Visionary, 1431
Apolo Kivebulaya, Priest, Evangelist in Central Africa, 1933

June

9 Columba, Abbot of Iona, Missionary, 597
Ephrem of Syria, Deacon, Hymn Writer, Teacher, 373
16 Richard, Bishop of Chichester, 1253
Joseph Butler, Bishop of Durham, Philosopher, 1752
23 Etheldreda, Abbess of Ely, c. 678

July

14 John Keble, Priest, Tractarian, Poet, 1866

August

4 *Jean-Baptiste Vianney, Curé d'Ars, Spiritual Guide, 1859*
11 Clare of Assisi, Founder of the Minoresses (Poor Clares), 1253

September

1 *Giles of Provence, Hermit, c. 710*
8 The Birth of the Blessed Virgin Mary
15 Cyprian, Bishop of Carthage, Martyr, 258

October

6 William Tyndale, Translator of the Scriptures, Reformation Martyr, 1536
13 Edward the Confessor, King of England, 1066

November

3 Richard Hooker, Priest, Anglican Apologist, Teacher, 1600
Martin of Porres, Friar, 1639
10 Leo the Great, Bishop of Rome, Teacher, 461
17 Hugh, Bishop of Lincoln, 1200

December

1 *Charles de Foucauld, Hermit in the Sahara, 1916*
8 The Conception of the Blessed Virgin Mary
29 Thomas Becket, Archbishop of Canterbury, Martyr, 1170

BOOK OF COMMON PRAYER 2019

January
13 Hilary, Bishop of Poitiers, Teacher, 367
20 Fabian, Bishop of Rome, Martyr, 250

February
3 Blasius, Bishop of Sebastopol, Martyr, c. 316

April
19 Alphege, Archbishop of Canterbury, Martyr, 1012

May
19 Dunstan, Archbishop of Canterbury, Restorer of Monastic Life, 988
26 Augustine, first Archbishop of Canterbury, 605

September
1 Giles of Provence, Hermit, c. 710
8 The Birth of the Blessed Virgin Mary

October
6 Faith of Aquitaine, Martyr, c. 304
13 Edward the Confessor, King of England, 1066

November
17 Hugh, Bishop of Lincoln, 1200

December
8 The Conception of the Blessed Virgin Mary

THE COMMON OF THE SAINTS

The Blessed Virgin Mary
Genesis 3. 8-15, 20; Isaiah 7. 10-14; Micah 5. 1-4
Psalms 45. 10-17; 113; 131
Acts 1. 12-14; Romans 8. 18-30; Galatians 4. 4-7
Luke 1. 26-38; Luke I. 39-47; John 19. 25-27

Martyrs
2 Chronicles 24. 17-21; Isaiah 43. 1-7; Jeremiah 11. 18-20; Wisdom 4. 10-15
Psalms 3; 11; 31. 1-5; 44. 18-24; 126
Romans 8. 35-end; 2 Corinthians 4. 7-15; 2 Timothy 2. 3-7 [8-13]; Hebrews 11. 32-end; 1 Peter 4. 12-end; Revelation 12. 10-12a
Matthew 10. 16-22; Matthew 10. 28-39; Matthew 16. 24-26; John 12. 24-26; John 15. 18-21

Teachers of the Faith and Spiritual Writers
I Kings 3. [6-10] 11-14; Proverbs 4. 1-9; Wisdom 7. 7-10, 15-16; Ecclesiasticus 39. 1-10
Psalms 19. 7-10; 34. 11-17; 37. 31-35; 119. 89-96; 119. 97-104
I Corinthians 1. 18-25; I Corinthians 2. 1-10; I Corinthians 2. 9-end; Ephesians 3. 8-12; 2 Timothy 4. 1-8; Titus 2. 1-8
Matthew 5. 13-19; Matthew 13. 52-end; Matthew 23. 8-12; Mark 4. 1-9; John 16. 12-15

Bishops and Other Pastors
I Samuel 16. I, 6-13; Isaiah 6. 1-8; Jeremiah 1. 4-10; Ezekiel 3. 16-21; Malachi 2. 5-7
Psalms 1; 15; 16. 5-end; 96; 110
Acts 20. 28-35; I Corinthians 4. 1-5; 2 Corinthians 4. 1-10 (*or* 1-2, 5-7); 2 Corinthians 5. 14-20; 1 Peter 5. 1-4
Matthew 11. 25-end; Matthew 24. 42-46; John 10. 11-16; John 15. 9-17; John 21. 15-17

Members of Religious Communities
I Kings 19. 9-18; Proverbs 10. 27-end; Song of Solomon 8. 6-7; Isaiah 61.10 - 62.5; Hosea 2. 14-15, 19-20
Psalms 34. 1-8; 112. 1-9; 119. 57-64; 123; 131
Acts 4. 32-35; 2 Corinthians 10.17 - 11.2; Philippians 3. 7-14; 1 John 2. 15-17; Revelation 19. 1, 5-9
Matthew 11. 25-end; Matthew 19. 3-12; Matthew 19. 23-end; Luke 9. 57-end; Luke 12. 32-37

Missionaries
Isaiah 52. 7-10; Isaiah 61. 1-3a; Ezekiel 34. 11-16; Jonah 3. 1-5
Psalms 67; 87; 97; 100; 117
Acts 2. 14, 22-36; Acts 13. 46-49; Acts 16. 6-10; Acts 26. 19-23; Romans 15. 17-21;
2 Corinthians 5.11 - 6.2
Matthew 9. 35-end; Matthew 28. 16-end; Mark 16. 15-20; Luke 5. 1-11; Luke 10. 1-9

Any Saint
Genesis 12. 1-4; Proverbs 8. 1-11; Micah 6. 6-8; Ecclesiasticus 2. 7-13 [14-end]
Psalms 32; 33. 1-5; 119. 1-8; 139. 1-4 [5-12]; 145. 8-14
Ephesians 3. 14-19; Ephesians 6. 11-18; Hebrews 13. 7-8, 15-16; James 2. 14-17; 1 John 4. 7-16; Revelation 21. [1-4] 5-7
Matthew 19. 16-21; Matthew 25. 1-13; Matthew 25. 14-30; John 15. 1-8; John 17. 20-end

SPECIAL OCCASIONS

The Guidance of the Holy Spirit
Proverbs 24. 3–7; Isaiah 30. 15–21; Wisdom 9. 13–17
Psalms 25. 1–9; 104. 26–33; 143. 8–10
Acts 15. 23–29; Romans 8. 22–27;
1 Corinthians 12. 4–13
Luke 14. 27–33; John 14. 23–26; John 16. 13–15

The Commemoration of the Faithful Departed
Lamentations 3. 17–26, 31–33 *or* Wisdom 3. 1–9
Psalm 23 *or* Psalm 27. 1–6, 16–end
Romans 5. 5–11 *or* I Peter 1. 3–9
John 5. 19–25 *or* John 6. 37–40

Rogation Days
Deuteronomy 8. 1–10; 1 Kings 8. 35–40; Job 28. 1–11
Psalms 104. 21–30; 107. 1–9; 121
Philippians 4. 4–7; 2 Thessalonians 3. 6–13;
1 John 5. 12–15
Matthew 6. 1–15; Mark 11. 22–24; Luke 11. 5–13

Harvest Thanksgiving

Year A
Deuteronomy 8. 7–18 *or* Deuteronomy 28. 1–14
Psalm 65
2 Corinthians 9. 6–end
Luke 12. 16–30 *or* Luke 17. 11–19

Year B
Joel 2. 21–27
Psalm 126
1 Timothy 2. 1–7 *or* 1 Timothy 6. 6–10
Matthew 6. 25–33

Year C
Deuteronomy 26. 1–11
Psalm 100
Philippians 4. 4–9 *or* Revelation 14. 14–18
John 6. 25–35

Mission and Evangelism
Isaiah 49. 1–6; Isaiah 52. 7–10; Micah 4. 1–5
Psalms 2; 46; 67
Acts 17. 12–end; 2 Corinthians 5.14 - 6.2;
Ephesians 2. 13–end
Matthew 5. 13–16; Matthew 28. 16–end;
John 17. 20–end

The Unity of the Church
Jeremiah 33. 6–9a; Ezekiel 36. 23–28;
Zephaniah 3. 16–end
Psalms 100; 122; 133
Ephesians 4. 1–6; Colossians 3. 9–17;
1 John 4. 9–15
Matthew 18. 19–22; John 11. 45–52;
John 17. 11b–23

The Peace of the World
Isaiah 9. 1–6; Isaiah 57. 15–19; Micah 4. 1–5
Psalms 40. 14–17; 72. 1–7; 85. 8–13
Philippians 4. 6–9; 1 Timothy 2. 1–6;
James 3. 13–18
Matthew 5. 43–end; John 14. 23–29; John 15. 9–17

Social Justice and Responsibility
Isaiah 32. 15–end; Amos 5. 21–24; Amos 8. 4–7;
Acts 5. 1–11
Psalms 31. 21–24; 85. 1–7; 146. 5–10
Colossians 3. 12–15; James 2. 1–4
Matthew 5. 1–12; Matthew 25. 31–end;
Luke 16. 19–end

Ministry (including Ember Days)
Numbers 11. 16–17, 24–29; Numbers 27. 15–end;
1 Samuel 16. 1–13a
Isaiah 6. 1–8; Isaiah 61. 1–3; Jeremiah 1. 4–10
Psalms 40. 8–13; 84. 8–12; 89. 19–25;
101. 1–5, 7; 122
Acts 20. 28–35; 1 Corinthians 3. 3–11;
Ephesians 4. 4–16; Philippians 3. 7–14
Luke 4. 16–21; Luke 12. 35–43; Luke 22. 24–27;
John 4. 31–38; John 15. 5–17

In Time of Trouble
Genesis 9. 8–17; Job 1. 13–end; Isaiah 38. 6–11
Psalms 86. 1–7; 107. 4–15; 142. 1–7
Romans 3. 21–26; Romans 8. 18–25;
2 Corinthians 8. 1–5, 9
Mark 4. 35–end; Luke 12. 1–7; John 16. 31–end

For the Sovereign
Joshua 1. 1–9; Proverbs 8. 1–16
Psalms 20; 101; 121
Romans 13. 1–10; Revelation 21.22 - 22.4
Matthew 22. 16–22; Luke 22. 24–30

		Sunday Principal Service Weekday Eucharist	Third Service Morning Prayer	Second Service Evening Prayer

December 2018

2 Sunday	**THE FIRST SUNDAY OF ADVENT** *CW* Year C begins			
P		Jer. 33. 14–16 Ps. 25. 1–9 1 Thess. 3. 9–end Luke 21. 25–36	Ps. 44 Isa. 51. 4–11 Rom. 13. 11–end	Ps. 9 (*or* 9. 1–8) Joel 3. 9–end Rev. 14.13 – 15.4 *Gospel*: John 3. 1–17
3 Monday	*Francis Xavier, Missionary, Apostle of the Indies, 1552* Daily Eucharistic Lectionary Year 1 begins			
P		Isa. 2. 1–5 Ps. 122 Matt. 8. 5–11	Ps. ***50***; 54 *alt.* Ps. ***1***; 2; 3 Isaiah 42. 18–end Rev. ch. 19	Ps. 70; ***71*** *alt.* Ps. ***4***; 7 Isa. 25. 1–9 Matt. 12. 1–21
4 Tuesday	*John of Damascus, Monk, Teacher, c. 749; Nicholas Ferrar, Deacon, Founder of the Little Gidding Community, 1637*			
P		Isa. 11. 1–10 Ps. 72. 1–4, 18–19 Luke 10. 21–24	Ps. ***80***; 82 *alt.* Ps. ***5***; 6; (8) Isa. 43. 1–13 Rev. ch. 20	Ps. ***74***; 75 *alt.* Ps. ***9***; 10† Isa. 26. 1–13 Matt. 12. 22–37
5 Wednesday				
P		Isa. 25. 6–10a Ps. 23 Matt. 15. 29–37	Ps. 5; ***7*** *alt.* Ps. 119. 1–32 Isa. 43. 14–end Rev. 21. 1–8	Ps. 76; ***77*** *alt.* Ps. ***11***; 12; 13 Isa. 28. 1–13 Matt. 12. 38–end
6 Thursday	**Nicholas, Bishop of Myra, c. 326**			
Pw	Com. Bishop *or* *also* Isa. 61. 1–3 1 Tim. 6. 6–11 Mark 10. 13–16	Isa. 26. 1–6 Ps. 118. 18–27a Matt. 7. 21, 24–27	Ps. ***42***; 43 *alt.* Ps. 14; ***15***; 16 Isa. 44. 1–8 Rev. 21. 9–21	Ps. ***40***; 46 *alt.* Ps. 18† Isa. 28. 14–end Matt. 13. 1–23
7 Friday	**Ambrose, Bishop of Milan, Teacher, 397**			
Pw	Com. Teacher *or* *also* Isa. 41. 9b–13 Luke 22. 24–30	Isa. 29. 17–end Ps. 27. 1–4, 16–17 Matt. 9. 27–31	Ps. ***25***; 26 *alt.* Ps. 17; ***19*** Isa. 44. 9–23 Rev. 21.22 – 22.5	Ps. 16; ***17*** *alt.* Ps. 22 Isa. 29. 1–14 Matt. 13. 24–43
8 Saturday	**The Conception of the Blessed Virgin Mary**			
Pw	Com. BVM *or*	Isa. 30. 19–21, 23–26 Ps. 146. 4–9 Matt. 9.35 – 10.1, 6–8	Ps. ***9***; (10) *alt.* Ps. 20; 21; ***23*** Isa. 44.24 – 45.13 Rev. 22. 6–end	Ps. ***27***; 28 *alt.* Ps. ***24***; 25 Isa. 29. 15–end Matt. 13. 44–end **ct**
9 Sunday	**THE SECOND SUNDAY OF ADVENT**			
P		Baruch ch. 5 *or* Mal. 3. 1–4 *Canticle*: Benedictus Phil. 1. 3–11 Luke 3. 1–6	Ps. 80 Isa. 64. 1–7 Matt. 11. 2–11	Ps. 75; [76] Isa. 40. 1–11 Luke 1. 1–25

	Calendar and Holy Communion	Morning Prayer	Evening Prayer	NOTES
	THE FIRST SUNDAY IN ADVENT			
P	Advent 1 Collect until Christmas Eve			
	Mic. 4. 1–4, 6–7 Ps. 25. 1–9 Rom. 13. 8–14 Matt. 21. 1–13	Ps. 44 Isa. 51. 4–11 Rom. 13. 11–end	Ps. 9 (*or* 9. 1–8) Joel 3. 9–end Rev. 14.13 - 15.4	
P		Isa. 42. 18–end Rev. ch. 19	Isa. 25. 1–9 Matt. 12. 1–21	
P		Isa. 43. 1–13 Rev. ch. 20	Isa. 26. 1–13 Matt. 12. 22–37	
P		Isa. 43. 14–end Rev. 21. 1–8	Isa. 28. 1–13 Matt. 12. 38–end	
	Nicholas, Bishop of Myra, c. 326			
Pw	Com. Bishop	Isa. 44. 1–8 Rev. 21. 9–21	Isa. 28. 14–end Matt. 13. 1–23	
P		Isa. 44. 9–23 Rev. 21.22 - 22.5	Isa. 29. 1–14 Matt. 13. 24–43	
	The Conception of the Blessed Virgin Mary			
Pw		Isa. 44.24 - 45.13 Rev. 22. 6–end	Isa. 29. 15–end Matt. 13. 44–end **ct**	
THE SECOND SUNDAY IN ADVENT				
P	2 Kings 22. 8–10; 23. 1–3 Ps. 50. 1–6 Rom. 15. 4–13 Luke 21. 25–33	Ps. 40 Isa. 64. 1–7 Luke 3. 1–6	Ps. 75 [76] Mal. 3. 1–4 Luke 1. 1–25	

		Sunday Principal Service Weekday Eucharist	Third Service Morning Prayer	Second Service Evening Prayer
10 Monday				
P		Isa. ch. 35 Ps. 85. 7–end Luke 5. 17–26	Ps. 44 *alt.* Ps. 27; ***30*** Isa. 45. 14–end 1 Thess. ch. 1	Ps. ***144***; 146 *alt.* Ps. 26; **28**; 29 Isa. 30. 1–18 Matt. 14. 1–12
11 Tuesday				
P		Isa. 40. 1–11 Ps. 96. 1, 10–end Matt. 18. 12–14	Ps. **56**; 57 *alt.* Ps. 32; ***36*** Isa. ch. 46 1 Thess. 2. 1–12	Ps. ***11***; 12; 13 *alt.* Ps. 33 Isa. 30. 19–end Matt. 14. 13–end
12 Wednesday	Ember Day*			
P		Isa. 40. 25–end Ps. 103. 8–13 Matt. 11. 28–end	Ps. ***62***; 63 *alt.* Ps. 34 Isa. ch. 47 1 Thess. 2. 13–end	Ps. ***10***; 14 *alt.* Ps. 119. 33–56 Isa. ch. 31 Matt. 15. 1–20
13 Thursday	**Lucy, Martyr at Syracuse, 304** *Samuel Johnson, Moralist, 1784*			
Pr	Com. Martyr *or* *also* Wisd. 3. 1–7 2 Cor. 4. 6–15	Isa. 41. 13–20 Ps. 145. 1, 8–13 Matt. 11. 11–15	Ps. 53; ***54***; 60 *alt.* Ps. 37† Isa. 48. 1–11 1 Thess. ch. 3	Ps. 73 *alt.* Ps. 39; ***40*** Isa. ch. 32 Matt. 15. 21–28
14 Friday	**John of the Cross, Poet, Teacher, 1591** Ember Day*			
Pw	Com. Teacher *or* *esp.* 1 Cor. 2. 1–10 *also* John 14. 18–23	Isa. 48. 17–19 Ps. 1 Matt. 11. 16–19	Ps. 85; ***86*** *alt.* Ps. 31 Isa. 48. 12–end 1 Thess. 4. 1–12	Ps. 82; ***90*** *alt.* Ps. 35 Isa. 33. 1–22 Matt. 15. 29–end
15 Saturday	Ember Day*			
P		Ecclus. 48. 1–4, 9–11 *or* 2 Kings 2. 9–12 Ps. 80. 1–4, 18–19 Matt. 17. 10–13	Ps. 145 *alt.* Ps. 41; ***42***; 43 Isa. 49. 1–13 1 Thess. 4. 13–end	Ps. 93; ***94*** *alt.* Ps. 45; ***46*** Isa. ch. 35 Matt. 16. 1–12 **ct**
16 Sunday	**THE THIRD SUNDAY OF ADVENT**			
P		Zeph. 3. 14–end *Canticle*: Isa. 12. 2–end *or* Ps. 146. 4–end Phil. 4. 4–7 Luke 3. 7–18	Ps. 12; 14 Isa. 25. 1–9 1 Cor. 4. 1–5	Ps. 50. 1–6; [62] Isa. ch. 35 Luke 1. 57–66 [67–end]
17 Monday	O Sapientia** *Eglantyne Jebb, Social Reformer, Founder of 'Save the Children', 1928*			
P		Gen. 49. 2, 8–10 Ps. 72. 1–5, 18–19 Matt. 1. 1–17	Ps. 40 *alt.* Ps. 44 Isa. 49. 14–25 1 Thess. 5. 1–11	Ps. 25; ***26*** *alt.* Ps. ***47***; 49 Isa. 38. 1–8, 21–22 Matt. 16. 13–end

*For Ember Day provision, see p. 11.
**The Evening Prayer readings from the Additional Weekday Lectionary (see p. 118) may be used from 17 to 23 December.

	Calendar and Holy Communion	Morning Prayer	Evening Prayer	NOTES
P		Isa. 45. 14–end 1 Thess. ch. 1	Isa. 30. 1–18 Matt. 14. 1–12	
P		Isa. ch. 46 1 Thess. 2. 1–12	Isa. 30. 19–end Matt. 14. 13–end	
P		Isa. ch. 47 1 Thess. 2. 13–end	Isa. ch. 31 Matt. 15. 1–20	
	Lucy, Martyr at Syracuse, 304			
Pr	Com. Virgin Martyr	Isa. 48. 1–11 1 Thess. ch. 3	Isa. ch. 32 Matt. 15. 21–28	
P		Isa. 48. 12–end 1 Thess. 4. 1–12	Isa. 33. 1–22 Matt. 15. 29–end	
P		Isa. 49. 1–13 1 Thess. 4. 13–end	Isa. ch. 35 Matt. 16. 1–12 **ct**	
	THE THIRD SUNDAY IN ADVENT O Sapientia			
P	Isa. ch. 35 Ps. 80. 1–7 1 Cor. 4. 1–5 Matt. 11. 2–10	Ps. 12; 14 Isa. 25. 1–9 Luke 3. 7–18	Ps. 62 Zeph. 3. 14–end Luke 1. 57–66 [67–end]	
P		Isa. 49. 14–25 1 Thess. 5. 1–11	Isa. 38. 1–8, 21–22 Matt. 16. 13–end	

		Sunday Principal Service Weekday Eucharist	Third Service Morning Prayer	Second Service Evening Prayer
18 Tuesday				
P		Jer. 23. 5–8 Ps. 72. 1–2, 12–13, 18–end Matt. 1. 18–24	Ps. ***70***; 74 *alt.* Ps. ***48***; 52 Isa. ch. 50 1 Thess. 5. 12–end	Ps. ***50***; 54 *alt.* Ps. 50 Isa. 38. 9–20 Matt. 17. 1–13
19 Wednesday				
P		Judg. 13. 2–7, 24–end Ps. 71. 3–8 Luke 1. 5–25	Ps. 144; ***146*** Isa. 51. 1–8 2 Thess. ch. 1	Ps. 10; ***57*** Isa. ch. 39 Matt. 17. 14–21
20 Thursday				
P		Isa. 7. 10–14 Ps. 24. 1–6 Luke 1. 26–38	Ps. ***46***; 95 Isa. 51. 9–16 2 Thess. ch. 2	Ps. ***4***; 9 Zeph. 1.1 – 2.3 Matt. 17. 22–end
21 Friday*				
P		Zeph. 3. 14–18 Ps. 33. 1–4, 11–12, 20–end Luke 1. 39–45	Ps. ***121***; 122; 123 Isa. 51. 17–end 2 Thess. ch. 3	Ps. 80; ***84*** Zeph. 3. 1–13 Matt. 18. 1–20
22 Saturday				
P		1 Sam. 1. 24–end Ps. 113 Luke 1. 46–56	Ps. ***124***; 125; 126; 127 Isa. 52. 1–12 Jude	Ps. 24; ***48*** Zeph. 3. 14–end Matt. 18. 21–end **ct**
23 Sunday	**THE FOURTH SUNDAY OF ADVENT**			
P		Mic. 5. 2–5a *Canticle*: Magnificat *or* Ps. 80. 1–8 Heb. 10. 5–10 Luke 1. 39–45 [46–55]	Ps. 144 Isa. 32. 1–8 Rev. 22. 6–end	Ps. 123; [131] Isa. 10.33 – 11.10 Matt. 1. 18–end
24 Monday	**CHRISTMAS EVE**			
P		*Morning Eucharist* 2 Sam. 7. 1–5, 8–11, 16 Ps. 89. 2, 19–27 Acts 13. 16–26 Luke 1. 67–79	Ps. ***45***; 113 Isa. 52.13 – 53.end 2 Pet. 1. 1–15	Ps. 85 Zech. ch. 2 Rev. 1. 1–8

*Thomas the Apostle may be celebrated on 21 December instead of 3 July.

	Calendar and Holy Communion	Morning Prayer	Evening Prayer
P		Isa. ch. 50 1 Thess. 5. 12–end	Isa. 38. 9–20 Matt. 17. 1–13
	Ember Day		
P	Ember CEG	Isa. 51. 1–8 2 Thess. ch. 1	Isa. ch. 39 Matt. 17. 14–21
P		Isa. 51. 9–16 2 Thess. ch. 2	Zeph. 1.1 – 2.3 Matt. 17. 22–end *or First EP of Thomas* (Ps. 27) Isa. ch. 35 Heb. 10.35 – 11.1 **R ct**
	THOMAS THE APOSTLE Ember Day		
R	Job 42. 1–6 Ps. 139. 1–11 Eph. 2. 19–end John 20. 24–end	(Ps. 92; 146) 2 Sam. 15. 17–21 *or* Ecclus. ch. 2 John 11. 1–16	(Ps. 139) Hab. 2. 1–4 1 Pet. 1. 3–12
	Ember Day		
P	Ember CEG	Isa. 52. 1–12 Jude	Zeph. 3. 14–end Matt. 18. 21–end **ct**
	THE FOURTH SUNDAY IN ADVENT		
P	Isa. 40. 1–9 Ps. 145. 17–end Phil. 4. 4–7 John 1. 19–28	Ps. 144 Isa. 32. 1–8 Rev. 22. 6–end	Ps. 123; [131] Isa. 10.33 – 11.10 Matt. 1. 18–end
	CHRISTMAS EVE		
P	Collect (1) Christmas Eve (2) Advent 1 Mic. 5. 2–5a Ps. 24 Titus 3. 3–7 Luke 2. 1–14	Isa. 52.13 – 53.end 2 Pet. 1. 1–15	Zech. ch. 2 Rev. 1. 1–8

NOTES

		Sunday Principal Service Weekday Eucharist	Third Service Morning Prayer	Second Service Evening Prayer
25 Tuesday	**CHRISTMAS DAY**			
𝔚	*Any of the following sets of readings may be used on the evening of Christmas Eve and on Christmas Day. Set III should be used at some service during the celebration.*	*I* Isa. 9. 2-7 Ps. 96 Titus 2. 11-14 Luke 2. 1-14 [15-20] *II* Isa. 62. 6-end Ps. 97 Titus 3. 4-7 Luke 2. [1-7] 8-20 *III* Isa. 52. 7-10 Ps. 98 Heb. 1. 1-4 [5-12] John 1. 1-14	*MP*: Ps. ***110***; 117 Isa. 62. 1-5 Matt. 1. 18-end	*EP*: Ps. 8 Isa. 65. 17-25 Phil. 2. 5-11 *or* Luke 2. 1-20 *if it has not been used at the principal service of the day*
26 Wednesday	**STEPHEN, DEACON, FIRST MARTYR**			
R		2 Chron. 24. 20-22 *or* Acts 7. 51-end Ps. 119. 161-168 Acts 7. 51-end *or* Gal. 2. 16b-20 Matt. 10. 17-22	*MP*: Ps. ***13***; 31. 1-8; 150 Jer. 26. 12-15 Acts ch. 6	*EP*: Ps. 57; ***86*** Gen. 4. 1-10 Matt. 23. 34-end
27 Thursday	**JOHN, APOSTLE AND EVANGELIST**			
W		Exod. 33. 7-11a Ps. 117 1 John ch. 1 John 21. 19b-end	*MP*: Ps. ***21***; 147. 13-end Exod. 33. 12-end 1 John 2. 1-11	*EP*: Ps. 97 Isa. 6. 1-8 1 John 5. 1-12
28 Friday	**THE HOLY INNOCENTS**			
R		Jer. 31. 15-17 Ps. 124 1 Cor. 1. 26-29 Matt. 2. 13-18	*MP*: Ps. ***36***; 146 Baruch 4. 21-27 *or* Gen. 37. 13-20 Matt. 18. 1-10	*EP*: Ps. 123; ***128*** Isa. 49. 14-25 Mark 10. 13-16
29 Saturday	**Thomas Becket, Archbishop of Canterbury, Martyr, 1170***			
Wr	Com. Martyr *or* *esp.* Matt. 10. 28-33 *also* Ecclus. 51. 1-8	1 John 2. 3-11 Ps. 96. 1-4 Luke 2. 22-35	Ps. ***19***; 20 Isa. 57. 15-end John 1. 1-18	Ps. 131; ***132*** Jonah ch. 1 Col. 1. 1-14 **ct**
30 Sunday	**THE FIRST SUNDAY OF CHRISTMAS**			
W		1 Sam. 2. 18-20, 26 Ps. 148 (*or* 148. 1-6) Col. 3. 12-17 Luke 2. 41-end	Ps. 105. 1-11 Isa. 41.21 - 42.1 1 John 1. 1-7	Ps. 132 Isa. ch. 61 Gal. 3.27 - 4.7 *Gospel*: Luke 2. 15-21

*Thomas Becket may be celebrated on 7 July instead of 29 December.

	Calendar and Holy Communion	Morning Prayer	Evening Prayer	NOTES
	CHRISTMAS DAY			
𝔚	Isa. 9. 2–7 Ps. 98 Heb. 1. 1–12 John 1. 1–14	Ps. 110; 117 Isa. 62. 1–5 Matt. 1. 18–end	Ps. 8 Isa. 65. 17–25 Phil. 2. 5–11 *or* Luke 2. 1–20	
	STEPHEN, DEACON, FIRST MARTYR			
R	Collect (1) Stephen (2) Christmas 2 Chron. 24. 20–22 Ps. 119. 161–168 Acts 7. 55–end Matt. 23. 34–end	(Ps. 13; 31. 1–8; 150) Jer. 26. 12–15 Acts ch. 6	(Ps. 57; 86) Gen. 4. 1–10 Matt. 10. 17–22	
	JOHN, APOSTLE AND EVANGELIST			
W	Collect (1) John (2) Christmas Exod. 33. 18–end Ps. 92. 11–end 1 John ch. 1 John 21. 19b–end	(Ps. 21; 147. 13–end) Exod. 33. 7–11a 1 John 2. 1–11	(Ps. 97) Isa. 6. 1–8 1 John 5. 1–12	
	THE HOLY INNOCENTS			
R	Collect (1) Innocents (2) Christmas Jer. 31. 10–17 Ps. 123 Rev. 14. 1–5 Matt. 2. 13–18	(Ps. 36; 146) Baruch 4. 21–27 *or* Gen. 37. 13–20 Matt. 18. 1–10	(Ps. 124; 128) Isa. 49. 14–25 Mark 10. 13–16	
W	CEG of Christmas	Isa. 57. 15–end John 1. 1–18	Jonah ch. 1 Col. 1. 1–14 **ct**	
	THE SUNDAY AFTER CHRISTMAS DAY			
W	Isa. 62. 10–12 Ps. 45. 1–7 Gal. 4. 1–7 Matt. 1. 18–end	Ps. 105. 1–11 Isa. 41.21 – 42.1 1 John 1. 1–7	Ps. 132 Isa. ch. 61 Luke 2. 15–21	

		Sunday Principal Service Weekday Eucharist	Third Service Morning Prayer	Second Service Evening Prayer
31 Monday	*John Wyclif, Reformer, 1384*			
W		1 John 2. 18–21 Ps. 96. 1, 11–end John 1. 1–18	Ps. 102 Isa. 59. 15b–end John 1. 29–34	Ps. ***90***; 148 Jonah chs 3 *&* 4 Col. 1.24 – 2.7 *or First EP of The Naming of Jesus* Ps. 148 Jer. 23. 1–6 Col. 2. 8–15 **ct**

January 2019

		Sunday Principal Service Weekday Eucharist	Third Service Morning Prayer	Second Service Evening Prayer
1 Tuesday	**THE NAMING AND CIRCUMCISION OF JESUS**			
W		Num. 6. 22–end Ps. 8 Gal. 4. 4–7 Luke 2. 15–21	*MP*: Ps. ***103***; 150 Gen. 17. 1–13 Rom. 2. 17–end	*EP*: Ps. 115 Deut. 30. [1–10] 11–end Acts 3. 1–16
2 Wednesday	**Basil the Great and Gregory of Nazianzus, Bishops, Teachers, 379 and 389** *Seraphim, Monk of Sarov, Spiritual Guide, 1833; Vedanayagam Samuel Azariah, Bishop in South India, Evangelist, 1945*			
W	Com. Teacher *or* *esp.* 2 Tim. 4. 1–8 Matt. 5. 13–19	1 John 2. 22–28 Ps. 98. 1–4 John 1. 19–28	Ps. 18. 1–30 Isa. 60. 1–12 John 1. 35–42	Ps. 45; ***46*** Ruth ch. 1 Col. 2. 8–end
3 Thursday				
W		1 John 2.29 – 3.6 Ps. 98. 2–7 John 1. 29–34	Ps. ***127***; 128; 131 Isa. 60. 13–end John 1. 43–end	Ps. ***2***; 110 Ruth ch. 2 Col. 3. 1–11
4 Friday				
W		1 John 3. 7–10 Ps. 98. I, 8–end John 1. 35–42	Ps. 89. 1–37 Isa. ch. 61 John 2. 1–12	Ps. 85; ***87*** Ruth ch. 3 Col. 3.12 – 4. 1
5 Saturday				
W		1 John 3. 11–21 Ps. 100 John 1. 43–end	Ps. 8; ***48*** Isa. ch. 62 John 2. 13–end	*First EP of The Epiphany* Ps. 96; ***97*** Isa. 49. 1–13 John 4. 7–26 **𝔚 ct**
6 Sunday	**THE EPIPHANY**			
𝔚		Isa. 60. 1–6 Ps. 72 (*or* 72. 10–15) Eph. 3. 1–12 Matt. 2. 1–12	*MP*: Ps. ***132***; 113 Jer. 31. 7–14 John 1. 29–34	*EP*: Ps. ***98***; 100 Baruch 4.36 – 5.end *or* Isa. 60. 1–9 John 2. 1–11
7 Monday				
W		1 John 3.22 – 4.6 Ps. 2. 7–end Matt. 4. 12–17, 23–end	Ps. ***99***; 147. 1–12 *alt.* Ps. 71 Isa. 63. 7–end 1 John ch. 3	Ps. 118 *alt.* Ps. ***72***; 75 Baruch 1.15 – 2.10 *or* Jer. 23. 1–8 Matt. 20. 1–16

	Calendar and Holy Communion	Morning Prayer	Evening Prayer	NOTES
	Silvester, Bishop of Rome, 335			
W	Com. Bishop	Isa. 59. 15b–end John 1. 29–34	Jonah chs 3 & 4 Col. 1.24 – 2.7 *or First EP of The Circumcision of Christ* (Ps. 148) Jer. 23. 1–6 Col. 2. 8–15 **ct**	
	THE CIRCUMCISION OF CHRIST			
W	Additional collect Gen. 17. 3b–10 Ps. 98 Rom. 4. 8–13 *or* Eph. 2. 11–18 Luke 2. 15–21	(Ps. 103; 150) Gen. 17. 1–13 Rom. 2. 17–end	(Ps. 115) Deut. 30. [1–10] 11–20 Acts 3. 1–16	
W		Isa. 60. 1–12 John 1. 35–42	Ruth ch. 1 Col. 2. 8–end	
W		Isa. 60. 13–end John 1. 43–end	Ruth ch. 2 Col. 3. 1–11	
W		Isa. ch. 61 John 2. 1–12	Ruth ch. 3 Col. 3.12 – 4. 1	
W		Isa. ch. 62 John 2. 13–end	*First EP of The Epiphany* Ps. 96; 97 Isa. 49. 1–13 John 4. 7–26 **𝔚 ct**	
	THE EPIPHANY			
𝔚	Isa. 60. 1–9 Ps. 100 Eph. 3. 1–12 Matt. 2. 1–12	Ps. 132; 113 Jer. 31. 7–14 John 1. 29–34	Ps. 72; 98 Baruch 4.36 – 5.end *or* Isa. 60. 1–9 John 2. 1–11	
W *or* **G**		Isa. 63. 7–end 1 John ch. 3	Baruch 1.15 – 2.10 *or* Jer. 23. 1–8 Matt. 20. 1–16	

		Sunday Principal Service Weekday Eucharist	Third Service Morning Prayer	Second Service Evening Prayer
8 Tuesday				
W		1 John 4. 7–10 Ps. 72. 1–8 Mark 6. 34–44	Ps. ***46***; 147. 13–end *alt.* Ps. 73 Isa. ch. 64 1 John 4. 7–end	Ps. 145 *alt.* Ps. 74 Baruch 2. 11–end *or* Jer. 30. 1–17 Matt. 20. 17–28
9 Wednesday				
W		1 John 4. 11–18 Ps. 72. 1, 10–13 Mark 6. 45–52	Ps. 2; ***148*** *alt.* Ps. 77 Isa. 65. 1–16 1 John 5. 1–12	Ps. ***67***; 72 *alt.* Ps. 119. 81–104 Baruch 3. 1–8 *or* Jer. 30.18 – 31.9 Matt. 20. 29–end
10 Thursday	*William Laud, Archbishop of Canterbury, 1645*			
W		1 John 4.19 – 5.4 Ps. 72. 1, 17–end Luke 4. 14–22	Ps. 97; ***149*** *alt.* Ps. 78. 1–39† Isa. 65. 17–end 1 John 5. 13–end	Ps. 27; ***29*** *alt.* Ps. 78. 40–end† Baruch 3.9 – 4.4 *or* Jer. 31. 10–17 Matt. 23. 1–12
11 Friday	*Mary Slessor, Missionary in West Africa, 1915*			
W		1 John 5. 5–13 Ps. 147. 13–end Luke 5. 12–16	Ps. 98; ***150*** *alt.* Ps. 55 Isa. 66. 1–11 2 John	Ps. ***93***; 132 *alt.* Ps. 69 Baruch 4. 21–30 *or* Jer. 33. 14–end Matt. 23. 13–28
12 Saturday	**Aelred of Hexham, Abbot of Rievaulx, 1167** *Benedict Biscop, Abbot of Wearmouth, Scholar, 689*			
W	Com. Religious *or* *also* Ecclus. 15. 1–6	1 John 5. 14–end Ps. 149. 1–5 John 3. 22–30	Ps. ***96***; 145 *alt.* Ps. ***76***; 79 Isa. 66. 12–23 3 John	*First EP of The Baptism* Ps. 36 Isa. ch. 61 Titus 2. 11–14; 3. 4–7 **𝔚 ct**
13 Sunday	**THE BAPTISM OF CHRIST (THE SECOND SUNDAY OF EPIPHANY)**			
𝔚		Isa. 43. 1–7 Ps. 29 Acts 8. 14–17 Luke 3. 15–17, 21–22	Ps. 89. 19–29 Isa. 42. 1–9 Acts 19. 1–7	Ps. 46; 47 Isa. 55. 1–11 Rom. 6. 1–11 *Gospel*: Mark 1. 4–11
14 Monday				
W **DEL 1**		Heb. 1. 1–6 Ps. 97. 1–2, 6–10 Mark 1. 14–20	Ps. ***2***; 110 *alt.* Ps. ***80***; 82 Amos ch. 1 1 Cor. 1. 1–17	Ps. ***34***; 36 *alt.* Ps. ***85***; 86 Gen. 1. 1–19 Matt. 21. 1–17

	Calendar and Holy Communion	Morning Prayer	Evening Prayer	NOTES
	Lucian, Priest and Martyr, 290			
Wr *or* **Gr**	Com. Martyr	Isa. ch. 64 1 John 4. 7–end	Baruch 2. 11–end *or* Jer. 30. 1–17 Matt. 20. 17–28	
W *or* **G**		Isa. 65. 1–16 1 John 5. 1–12	Baruch 3. 1–8 *or* Jer. 30.18 – 31.9 Matt. 20. 29–end	
W *or* **G**		Isa. 65. 17–end 1 John 5. 13–end	Baruch 3.9 – 4.4 *or* Jer. 31. 10–17 Matt. 23. 1–12	
W *or* **G**		Isa. 66. 1–11 2 John	Baruch 4. 21–30 *or* Jer. 33. 14–end Matt. 23. 13–28	
W *or* **G**		Isa. 66. 12–23 3 John	Baruch 4.36 – 5.end *or* Mic. 5. 2–end Matt. 23. 29–end **ct**	
	THE FIRST SUNDAY AFTER THE EPIPHANY To celebrate The Baptism of Christ, see *Common Worship* provision.			
W *or* **G**	Zech. 8. 1–8 Ps. 72. 1–8 Rom. 12. 1–5 Luke 2. 41–end	Ps. 89. 19–29 Isa. 42. 1–9 Acts 19. 1–7	Ps. 46; 47 Isa. 55. 1–11 Rom. 6. 1–11	
W *or* **G**		Amos ch. 1 1 Cor. 1. 1–17	Gen. 1. 1–19 Matt. 21. 1–17	

		Sunday Principal Service Weekday Eucharist	Third Service Morning Prayer	Second Service Evening Prayer
15 Tuesday				
W		Heb. 2. 5–12 Ps. 8 Mark 1. 21–28	Ps. 8; ***9*** *alt.* Ps. 87; ***89. 1–18*** Amos ch. 2 1 Cor. 1. 18–end	Ps. ***45***; 46 *alt.* Ps. 89. 19–end Gen. 1.20 - 2.3 Matt. 21. 18–32
16 Wednesday				
W		Heb. 2. 14–end Ps. 105. 1–9 Mark 1. 29–39	Ps. 19; ***20*** *alt.* Ps. 119. 105–128 Amos ch. 3 1 Cor. ch. 2	Ps. ***47***; 48 *alt.* Ps. ***91***; 93 Gen. 2. 4–end Matt. 21. 33–end
17 Thursday	**Antony of Egypt, Hermit, Abbot, 356** *Charles Gore, Bishop, Founder of the Community of the Resurrection, 1932*			
W	Com. Religious *or* *esp.* Phil. 3. 7–14 *also* Matt. 19. 16–26	Heb. 3. 7–14 Ps. 95. 1, 8–end Mark 1. 40–end	Ps. ***21***; 24 *alt.* Ps. 90; **92** Amos ch. 4 1 Cor. ch. 3	Ps. ***61***; 65 *alt.* Ps. 94 Gen. ch. 3 Matt. 22. 1–14
18 Friday	*Amy Carmichael, Founder of the Dohnavur Fellowship, Spiritual Writer, 1951* The Week of Prayer for Christian Unity until 25 January			
W		Heb. 4. 1–5, 11 Ps. 78. 3–8 Mark 2. 1–12	Ps. ***67***; 72 *alt.* Ps. ***88***; (95) Amos 5. 1–17 1 Cor. ch. 4	Ps. 68 *alt.* Ps. 102 Gen. 4. 1–16, 25–26 Matt. 22. 15–33
19 Saturday	**Wulfstan, Bishop of Worcester, 1095**			
W	Com. Bishop *or* *esp.* Matt. 24. 42–46	Heb. 4. 12–end Ps. 19. 7–end Mark 2. 13–17	Ps. 29; ***33*** *alt.* Ps. 96; ***97***; 100 Amos 5. 18–end 1 Cor. ch. 5	Ps. 84; ***85*** *alt.* Ps. 104 Gen. 6. 1–10 Matt. 22. 34–end **ct**
20 Sunday	**THE THIRD SUNDAY OF EPIPHANY**			
W		Isa. 62. 1–5 Ps. 36. 5–10 1 Cor. 12. 1–11 John 2. 1–11	Ps. 145. 1–13 Isa. 49. 1–7 Acts 16. 11–15	Ps. 96 1 Sam. 3. 1–20 Eph. 4. 1–16 *Gospel*: John 1. 29–42
21 Monday	**Agnes, Child Martyr at Rome, 304**			
Wr **DEL 2**	Com. Martyr *or* *also* Rev. 7. 13–end	Heb. 5. 1–10 Ps. 110. 1–4 Mark 2. 18–22	Ps. 145; ***146*** *alt.* Ps. ***98***; 99; 101 Amos ch. 6 1 Cor. 6. 1–11	Ps. 71 *alt.* Ps. 105† (*or* Ps. 103) Gen. 6.11 - 7.10 Matt. 24. 1–14
22 Tuesday	*Vincent of Saragossa, Deacon, first Martyr of Spain, 304*			
W		Heb. 6. 10–end Ps. 111 Mark 2. 23–end	Ps. ***132***; 147. 1–12 *alt.* Ps. 106† (*or* Ps. 103) Amos ch. 7 1 Cor. 6. 12–end	Ps. 89. 1–37 *alt.* Ps. 107† Gen. 7. 11–end Matt. 24. 15–28

	Calendar and Holy Communion	Morning Prayer	Evening Prayer	NOTES
W *or* **G**		Amos ch. 2 1 Cor. 1. 18–end	Gen. 1.20 – 2.3 Matt. 21. 18–32	
W *or* **G**		Amos ch. 3 1 Cor. ch. 2	Gen. 2. 4–end Matt. 21. 33–end	
W *or* **G**		Amos ch. 4 1 Cor. ch. 3	Gen. ch. 3 Matt. 22. 1–14	
	Prisca, Martyr at Rome, c. 265 For the Week of Prayer for Christian Unity, see *Common Worship* provision.			
Wr *or* **Gr**	Com. Virgin Martyr	Amos 5. 1–17 1 Cor. ch. 4	Gen. 4. 1–16, 25–26 Matt. 22. 15–33	
W *or* **G**		Amos 5. 18–end 1 Cor. ch. 5	Gen. 6. 1–10 Matt. 22. 34–end **ct**	
	THE SECOND SUNDAY AFTER THE EPIPHANY			
W *or* **G**	2 Kings 4. 1–17 Ps. 107. 13–22 Rom. 12. 6–16a John 2. 1–11	Ps. 145. 1–13 Isa. 49. 1–7 Acts 16. 11–15	Ps. 96 1 Sam. 3. 1–20 Eph. 4. 1–16	
	Agnes, Child Martyr at Rome, 304			
Wr *or* **Gr**	Com. Virgin Martyr	Amos ch. 6 1 Cor. 6. 1–11	Gen. 6.11 – 7.10 Matt. 24. 1–14	
	Vincent of Saragossa, Deacon, first Martyr of Spain, 304			
Wr *or* **Gr**	Com. Martyr	Amos ch. 7 1 Cor. 6. 12–end	Gen. 7. 11–end Matt. 24. 15–28	

		Sunday Principal Service Weekday Eucharist	Third Service Morning Prayer	Second Service Evening Prayer
23 Wednesday				
W		Heb. 7. 1–3, 15–17 Ps. 110. 1–4 Mark 3. 1–6	Ps. ***81***; 147. 13–end *alt.* Ps. 110; ***111***; 112 Amos ch. 8 1 Cor. 7. 1–24	Ps. ***97***; 98 *alt.* Ps. 119. 129–152 Gen. 8. 1–14 Matt. 24. 29–end
24 Thursday	**Francis de Sales, Bishop of Geneva, Teacher, 1622**			
W	Com. Teacher *or* *also* Prov. 3. 13–18 John 3. 17–21	Heb. 7.25 – 8.6 Ps. 40. 7–10, 17–end Mark 3. 7–12	Ps. ***76***; 148 *alt.* Ps. 113; ***115*** Amos ch. 9 1 Cor. 7. 25–end	Ps. 99; 100; ***111*** *alt.* Ps. 114; ***116***; 117 Gen. 8.15 – 9.7 Matt. 25. 1–13 *or First EP of The Conversion of Paul* Ps. 149 Isa. 49. 1–13 Acts 22. 3–16 **ct**
25 Friday	**THE CONVERSION OF PAUL**			
W		Jer. 1. 4–10 *or* Acts 9. 1–22 Ps. 67 Acts 9. 1–22 *or* Gal. 1. 11–16a Matt. 19. 27–end	*MP*: Ps. 66; 147. 13–end Ezek. 3. 22–end Phil. 3. 1–14	*EP*: Ps. 119. 41–56 Ecclus. 39. 1–10 *or* Isa. 56. 1–8 Col. 1.24 – 2.7
26 Saturday	**Timothy and Titus, Companions of Paul**			
W	Isa. 61. 1–3a *or* Ps. 100 2 Tim. 2. 1–8 *or* Titus 1. 1–5 Luke 10. 1–9	Heb. 9. 2–3, 11–14 Ps. 47. 1–8 Mark 3. 20–21	Ps. ***122***; 128; 150 *alt.* Ps. 120; ***121***; 122 Hos. 2. 2–17 1 Cor. 9. 1–14	Ps. ***61***; 66 *alt.* Ps. 118 Gen. 11. 1–9 Matt. 25. 31–end **ct**
27 Sunday	**THE FOURTH SUNDAY OF EPIPHANY**			
W		Neh. 8. 1–3, 5–6, 8–10 Ps. 19 (*or* 19. 1–6) 1 Cor. 12. 12–31a Luke 4. 14–21	Ps. 113 Deut. 30. 11–15 3 John 1. 5–8	Ps. 33 (*or* 33. 1–12) Num. 9. 15–end 1 Cor. 7. 17–24 *Gospel*: Mark 1. 21–28
28 Monday	**Thomas Aquinas, Priest, Philosopher, Teacher, 1274**			
W **DEL 3**	Com. Teacher *or* *esp.* Wisd. 7. 7–10, 15–16 1 Cor. 2. 9–end John 16. 12–15	Heb. 9. 15, 24–end Ps. 98. 1–7 Mark 3. 22–30	Ps. 40; ***108*** *alt.* Ps. 123; 124; 125; ***126*** Hos. 2.18 – 3.end 1 Cor. 9. 15–end	Ps. ***138***; 144 *alt.* Ps. ***127***; 128; 129 Gen. 11.27 – 12.9 Matt. 26. 1–16
29 Tuesday				
W		Heb. 10. 1–10 Ps. 40. 1–4, 7–10 Mark 3. 31–end	Ps. 34; ***36*** *alt.* Ps. ***132***; 133 Hos. 4. 1–16 1 Cor. 10. 1–13	Ps. 145 *alt.* Ps. (134); ***135*** Gen. 13. 2–end Matt. 26. 17–35

	Calendar and Holy Communion	Morning Prayer	Evening Prayer	NOTES
W *or* **G**		Amos ch. 8 1 Cor. 7. 1–24	Gen. 8. 1–14 Matt. 24. 29–end	
W *or* **G**		Amos ch. 9 1 Cor. 7. 25–end	Gen. 8.15 – 9.7 Matt. 25. 1–13 *or First EP of The Conversion of Paul* (Ps. 149) Isa. 49. 1–13 Acts 22. 3–16 **W ct**	
	THE CONVERSION OF PAUL			
W	Josh. 5. 13–end Ps. 67 Acts 9. 1–22 Matt. 19. 27–end	(Ps. 66; 147. 13–end) Ezek. 3. 22–end Phil. 3. 1–14	(Ps. 119. 41–56) Ecclus. 39. 1–10 *or* Isa. 56. 1–8 Col. 1.24 – 2.7	
W *or* **G**		Hos. 2. 2–17 1 Cor. 9. 1–14	Gen. 11. 1–9 Matt. 25. 31–end **ct**	
	THE THIRD SUNDAY AFTER THE EPIPHANY			
W *or* **G**	2 Kings 6. 14b–23 Ps. 102. 15–22 Rom. 12. 16b–end Matt. 8. 1–13	Ps. 113 Deut. 30. 11–15 3 John 1. 5–8	Ps. 33 (*or* 33. 1–12) Num. 9. 15–end 1 Cor. 7. 17–24	
W *or* **G**		Hos. 2.18 – 3.end 1 Cor. 9. 15–end	Gen. 11.27 – 12.9 Matt. 26. 1–16	
W *or* **G**		Hos. 4. 1–16 1 Cor. 10. 1–13	Gen. 13. 2–end Matt. 26. 17–35	

		Sunday Principal Service Weekday Eucharist	Third Service Morning Prayer	Second Service Evening Prayer
30 Wednesday	**Charles, King and Martyr, 1649**			
Wr	Com. Martyr *or* *also* Ecclus. 2. 12–17 1 Tim. 6. 12–16	Heb. 10. 11–18 Ps. 110. 1–4 Mark 4. 1–20	Ps. 45; ***46*** *alt.* Ps. 119. 153–end Hos. 5. 1–7 1 Cor. 10.14 – 11.1	Ps. 21; ***29*** *alt.* Ps. 136 Gen. ch. 14 Matt. 26. 36–46
31 Thursday	*John Bosco, Priest, Founder of the Salesian Teaching Order, 1888*			
W		Heb. 10. 19–25 Ps. 24. 1–6 Mark 4. 21–25	Ps. ***47***; 48 *alt.* Ps. ***143***; 146 Hos. 5.8 – 6.6 1 Cor. 11. 2–16	Ps. ***24***; 33 *alt.* Ps. ***138***; 140; 141 Gen. ch. 15 Matt. 26. 47–56

February 2019

		Sunday Principal Service Weekday Eucharist	Third Service Morning Prayer	Second Service Evening Prayer
1 Friday	*Brigid, Abbess of Kildare, c. 525*			
W		Heb. 10. 32–end Ps. 37. 3–6, 40–end Mark 4. 26–34	Ps. 61; ***65*** *alt.* Ps. 142; ***144*** Hos. 6.7 – 7.2 1 Cor. 11. 17–end	*First EP of The Presentation* Ps. 118 1 Sam. 1. 19b–end Heb. 4. 11–end **𝔚 ct** *or, if The Presentation is kept on 3 February*: Ps. ***67***; 77 *alt. Ps.* ***145*** Gen. ch. 16 Matt. 26, 57–end
2 Saturday	**THE PRESENTATION OF CHRIST IN THE TEMPLE (CANDLEMAS)**			
𝔚		Mal. 3. 1–5 Ps. 24 (*or* 24. 7–end) Heb. 2. 14–end Luke 2. 22–40	*MP*: Ps. ***48***; 146 Exod. 13. 1–16 Rom. 12. 1–5	*EP*: Ps. 122; ***132*** Hag. 2. 1–9 John 2. 18–22
	or, if The Presentation is observed on 3 February:			
W		Heb. 11. 1–2, 8–19 *Canticle*: Luke 1. 69–73 Mark 4. 35–end	Ps. 68 *alt.* Ps. 147 Hos. ch. 8 1 Cor. 12. 1–11	*First EP of The Presentation* Ps. 118 1 Sam. 1. 19b–end Heb. 4. 11–end **𝔚 ct**
3 Sunday	**THE FIFTH SUNDAY BEFORE LENT** *or The Presentation of Christ in the Temple (Candlemas)** Ordinary Time begins today (or on 4 February if The Presentation is celebrated today)			
G		Ezek. 43.27 – 44.4 Ps. 48 1 Cor. ch. 13 Luke 2. 22–40	Ps. 71. 1–6, 15–17 Mic. 6. 1–8 1 Cor. 6. 12–end	Ps. 34 1 Chron. 29. 6–19 Acts 7. 44–50 *Gospel*: John 4. 19–29a
4 Monday	*Gilbert of Sempringham, Founder of the Gilbertine Order, 1189*			
G **DEL 4**		Heb. 11. 32–end Ps. 31. 19–end Mark 5. 1–20	Ps. ***1***; 2; 3 1 Chron. 10.1 – 11.9 John 13. 1–11	Ps. ***4***; 7 Exod. 22. 21–27; 23. 1–17 Phil. 1. 1–11

*See provision for First EP on 1 February and throughout the day for The Presentation on 2 February.

	Calendar and Holy Communion	Morning Prayer	Evening Prayer	NOTES
	Charles, King and Martyr, 1649			
Wr *or* **Gr**	Com. Martyr	Hos. 5. 1-7 1 Cor. 10.14 - 11.1	Gen. ch. 14 Matt. 26. 36-46	
W *or* **G**		Hos. 5.8 - 6.6 1 Cor. 11. 2-16	Gen. ch. 15 Matt. 26. 47-56	
W *or* **G**		Hos. 6.7 - 7.2 1 Cor. 11. 17-end	*First EP of The Presentation* Ps. 118 1 Sam. 1. 19b-end Heb. 4. 11-end **𝔚 ct**	
	THE PRESENTATION OF CHRIST IN THE TEMPLE			
𝔚	Mal. 3. 1-5 Ps. 48. 1-7 Gal. 4. 1-7 Luke 2. 22-40	Ps. 48; 146 Exod. 13. 1-16 Rom. 12. 1-5	Ps. 122; 132 Hag. 2. 1-9 John 2. 18-22	
	THE FOURTH SUNDAY AFTER THE EPIPHANY			
G	1 Sam. 10. 17-24 Ps. 97 Rom. 13. 1-7 Matt. 8. 23-34	Ps. 71. 1-6, 15-17 Mic. 6. 1-8 1 Cor. 6. 12-end	Ps. 34 1 Chron. 29. 6-19 Acts 7. 44-50	
G		1 Chron. 10.1 - 11.9 John 13. 1-11	Exod. 22. 21-27; 23. 1-17 Phil. 1. 1-11	

		Sunday Principal Service Weekday Eucharist	Third Service Morning Prayer	Second Service Evening Prayer
5 Tuesday				
G		Heb. 12. 1–4 Ps. 22. 25b–end Mark 5. 21–43	Ps. ***5***; 6; (8) 1 Chron. ch. 13 John 13. 12–20	Ps. ***9***; 10† Exod. 29.38 – 30.16 Phil. 1. 12–end
6 Wednesday	*The Martyrs of Japan, 1597* (The Accession of Queen Elizabeth II may be observed on 6 February, and Collect, Readings and Post-Communion for the Sovereign used.)			
G		Heb. 12. 4–7, 11–15 Ps. 103. 1–2, 13–18 Mark 6. 1–6a	Ps. 119. 1–32 1 Chron. 15.1 – 16.3 John 13. 21–30	***11***; 12; 13 Lev. ch. 8 Phil. 2. 1–13
7 Thursday				
G		Heb. 12. 18–19, 21–24 Ps. 48. 1–3, 8–10 Mark 6. 7–13	Ps. 14; ***15***; 16 1 Chron. ch. 17 John 13. 31–end	Ps. 18 Lev. ch. 9 Phil. 2. 14–end
8 Friday				
G		Heb. 13. 1–8 Ps. 27. 1–6, 9–12 Mark 6. 14–29	Ps. 17; ***19*** 1 Chron. 21.1 – 22.1 John 14. 1–14	Ps. 22 Lev. 16. 2–24 Phil. 3.1 – 4.1
9 Saturday				
G		Heb. 13. 15–17, 20–21 Ps. 23 Mark 6. 30–34	Ps. 20; 21; ***23*** 1 Chron. 22. 2–end John 14. 15–end	Ps. ***24***; 25 Lev. ch. 17 Phil. 4. 2–end **ct**
10 Sunday	**THE FOURTH SUNDAY BEFORE LENT (Proper 1)**			
G		Isa. 6. 1–8 [9–end] Ps. 138 1 Cor. 15. 1–11 Luke 5. 1–11	Ps. 3; 4 Jer. 26. 1–16 Acts 3. 1–10	Ps. [1]; 2 Wisd. 6. 1–21 *or* Hos. ch. 1 Col. 3. 1–22 *Gospel*: Matt. 5. 13–20
11 Monday				
G **DEL 5**		Gen. 1. 1–19 Ps. 104. 1–2, 6–13, 26 Mark 6. 53–end	Ps. 27; ***30*** 1 Chron. 28. 1–10 John 15. 1–11	Ps. 26; ***28***; 29 Lev. 19. 1–18, 30–end 1 Tim. 1. 1–17
12 Tuesday				
G		Gen. 1.20 – 2.4a Ps. 8 Mark 7. 1–13	Ps. 32; ***36*** 1 Chron. 28. 11–end John 15. 12–17	Ps. 33 Lev. 23. 1–22 1 Tim. 1.18 – 2.end
13 Wednesday				
G		Gen. 2. 4b–9, 15–17 Ps. 104. 11–12, 29–32 Mark 7. 14–23	Ps. 34 1 Chron. 29. 1–9 John 15. 18–end	Ps. 119. 33–56 Lev. 23. 23–end 1 Tim. ch. 3

	Calendar and Holy Communion	Morning Prayer	Evening Prayer
	Agatha, Martyr in Sicily, 251		
Gr	Com. Martyr	1 Chron. ch. 13 John 13. 12–20	Exod. 29.38 – 30.16 Phil. 1. 12–end
	The Accession of Queen Elizabeth II, 1952		
G	*For Accession Service*: Ps. 20; 101; 121; Josh. 1. 1–9; Prov. 8. 1–16; Rom. 13. 1–10; Rev. 21.22 – 22.4		
	For The Accession: 1 Pet. 2. 11–17 Matt. 22. 16–22	1 Chron. 15.1 – 16.3 John 13. 21–30	Lev. ch. 8 Phil. 2. 1–13
G		1 Chron. ch. 17 John 13. 31–end	Lev. ch. 9 Phil. 2. 14–end
G		1 Chron. 21.1 – 22.1 John 14. 1–14	Lev. 16. 2–24 Phil. 3.1 – 4.1
G		1 Chron. 22. 2–end John 14. 15–end	Lev. ch. 17 Phil. 4. 2–end **ct**
	THE FIFTH SUNDAY AFTER THE EPIPHANY		
G	Hos. 6. 4–6 Ps. 118. 14–21 Col. 3. 12–17 Matt. 13. 24b–30	Ps. 3; 4 Jer. 26. 1–16 Acts 3. 1–10	Ps. [1]; 2 Wisd. 6. 1–21 *or* Hos. ch. 1 Col. 3. 1–22
G		1 Chron. 28. 1–10 John 15. 1–11	Lev. 19. 1–18, 30–end 1 Tim. 1. 1–17
G		1 Chron. 28. 11–end John 15. 12–17	Lev. 23. 1–22 1 Tim. 1.18 – 2.end
G		1 Chron. 29. 1–9 John 15. 18–end	Lev. 23. 23–end 1 Tim. ch. 3

NOTES

		Sunday Principal Service Weekday Eucharist	Third Service Morning Prayer	Second Service Evening Prayer
14 Thursday	**Cyril and Methodius, Missionaries to the Slavs, 869 and 885** *Valentine, Martyr at Rome, c. 269*			
Gw	Com. Missionaries *or* *esp.* Isa. 52. 7–10 *also* Rom. 10. 11–15	Gen. 2. 18–end Ps. 128 Mark 7. 24–30	Ps. 37† 1 Chron. 29. 10–20 John 16. 1–15	Ps. 39; ***40*** Lev. 24. 1–9 1 Tim. ch. 4
15 Friday	*Sigfrid, Bishop, Apostle of Sweden, 1045; Thomas Bray, Priest, Founder of the SPCK and SPG, 1730*			
G		Gen. 3. 1–8 Ps. 32. 1–8 Mark 7. 31–end	Ps. 31 1 Chron. 29. 21–end John 16. 16–22	Ps. 35 Lev. 25. 1–24 1 Tim. 5. 1–16
16 Saturday				
G		Gen. 3. 9–end Ps. 90. 1–12 Mark 8. 1–10	Ps. 41; ***42***; 43 2 Chron. 1. 1–13 John 16. 23–end	Ps. 45; ***46*** Num. 6. 1–5, 21–end 1 Tim. 5. 17–end **ct**
17 Sunday	**THE THIRD SUNDAY BEFORE LENT (Proper 2)**			
G		Jer. 17. 5–10 Ps. 1 1 Cor. 15. 12–20 Luke 6. 17–26	Ps. 7 Jer. 30. 1–3, 10–22 Acts ch. 6	Ps. [5]; 6 Wisd. 11.21 - 12.11 *or* Hos. 10. 1–8, 12 Gal. 4. 8–20 *Gospel*: Matt. 5. 21–37
18 Monday				
G **DEL 6**		Gen. 4. 1–15, 25 Ps. 50. 1, 8, 16–end Mark 8. 11–13	Ps. 44 2 Chron. 2. 1–16 John 17. 1–5	Ps. ***47***; 49 Gen. 24. 1–28 1 Tim. 6. 1–10
19 Tuesday				
G		Gen. 6. 5–8; 7. 1–5, 10 Ps. 29 Mark 8. 14–21	Ps. ***48***; 52 2 Chron. ch. 3 John 17. 6–19	Ps. 50 Gen. 24. 29–end 1 Tim. 6. 11–end
20 Wednesday				
G		Gen. 8. 6–13, 20–end Ps. 116. 10–end Mark 8. 22–26	Ps. 119. 57–80 2 Chron. ch. 5 John 17. 20–end	Ps. ***59***; 60; (67) Gen. 25. 7–11, 19–end 2 Tim. 1. 1–14
21 Thursday				
G		Gen. 9. 1–13 Ps. 102. 16–23 Mark 8. 27–33	Ps. 56; ***57***; (63†) 2 Chron. 6. 1–21 John 18. 1–11	61; ***62***; 64 Gen. 26.34 - 27.40 2 Tim. 1.15 - 2.13
22 Friday				
G		Gen. 11. 1–9 Ps. 33. 10–15 Mark 8.34 - 9.1	Ps. ***51***; 54 2 Chron. 6. 22–end John 18. 12–27	Ps. 38 Gen. 27.41 - 28.end 2 Tim. 2. 14–end
23 Saturday	**Polycarp, Bishop of Smyrna, Martyr, c. 155**			
Gr	Com. Martyr *or* *also* Rev. 2. 8–11	Heb. 11. 1–7 Ps. 145. 1–10 Mark 9. 2–13	Ps. 68 2 Chron. ch. 7 John 18. 28–end	Ps. 65; ***66*** Gen. 29. 1–30 2 Tim. ch. 3 **ct**

	Calendar and Holy Communion	Morning Prayer	Evening Prayer
	Valentine, Martyr at Rome, c. 269		
Gr	Com. Martyr	1 Chron. 29. 10–20 John 16. 1–15	Lev. 24. 1–9 1 Tim. ch. 4
G		1 Chron. 29. 21–end John 16. 16–22	Lev. 25. 1–24 1 Tim. 5. 1–16
G		2 Chron. 1. 1–13 John 16. 23–end	Num. 6. 1–5, 21–end 1 Tim. 5. 17–end **ct**
	SEPTUAGESIMA		
G	Gen. 1. 1–5 Ps. 9. 10–20 1 Cor. 9. 24–end Matt. 20. 1–16	Ps. 7 Jer. 30. 1–3, 10–22 Acts ch. 6	Ps. [5]; 6 Wisd. 11.21 - 12.11 *or* Hos. 10. 1–8, 12 Gal. 4. 8–20
G		2 Chron. 2. 1–16 John 17. 1–5	Gen. 24. 1–28 1 Tim. 6. 1–10
G		2 Chron. ch. 3 John 17. 6–19	Gen. 24. 29–end 1 Tim. 6. 11–end
G		2 Chron. ch. 5 John 17. 20–end	Gen. 25. 7–11, 19–end 2 Tim. 1. 1–14
G		2 Chron. 6. 1–21 John 18. 1–11	Gen. 26.34 - 27.40 2 Tim. 1.15 - 2.13
G		2 Chron. 6. 22–end John 18. 12–27	Gen. 27.41 - 28.end 2 Tim. 2. 14–end
G		2 Chron. ch. 7 John 18. 28–end	Gen. 29. 1–30 2 Tim. ch. 3 *or First EP of Matthias* (Ps. 147) Isa. 22. 15–22 Phil. 3.13b - 14.1 **R ct**

NOTES

			Sunday Principal Service Weekday Eucharist	Third Service Morning Prayer	Second Service Evening Prayer
24 Sunday*	**THE SECOND SUNDAY BEFORE LENT**				
G			Gen. 2. 4b–9, 15–end Ps. 65 Rev. ch. 4 Luke 8. 22–25	Ps. 104. 1–26 Job 28. 1–11 Acts 14. 8–17	Ps. 147 (*or* 147. 13–end) Gen. 1.1 – 2.3 Heb. 6. 25–end
25 Monday					
G **DEL 7**			Ecclus. 1. 1–10 *or* James 1. 1–11 Ps. 93 *or* Ps. 119. 65–72 Mark 9. 14–29	Ps. 71 2 Chron. 9. 1–12 John 19. 1–16	Ps. **72**; 75 Gen. 29.31 – 30.24 2 Tim. 4. 1–8
26 Tuesday					
G			Ecclus. 2. 1–11 *or* James 1. 12–18 Ps. 37. 3–6, 27–28 *or* Ps. 94. 12–18 Mark 9. 30–37	Ps. 73 2 Chron. 10.1 – 11.4 John 19. 17–30	Ps. 74 Gen. 31. 1–24 2 Tim. 4. 9–end
27 Wednesday	**George Herbert, Priest, Poet, 1633**				
Gw	Com. Pastor *esp.* Mal. 2. 5–7 Matt. 11. 25–end *also* Rev. 19. 5–9	*or*	Ecclus. 4. 11–19 *or* James 1. 19–end Ps. 119. 161–168 *or* Ps. 15 Mark 9. 38–40	Ps. 77 2 Chron. ch. 12 John 19. 31–end	Ps. 119. 81–104 Gen. 31.25 – 32.2 Titus ch. 1
28 Thursday					
G			Ecclus. 5. 1–8 *or* James 2. 1–9 Ps. 1 *or* Ps. 34. 1–7 Mark 9. 41–end	Ps. 78. 1–39† 2 Chron. 13.1 – 14.1 John 20. 1–10	Ps. 78. 40–end† Gen. 32. 3–30 Titus ch. 2

March 2019

1 Friday	**David, Bishop of Menevia, Patron of Wales, c. 601**				
Gw	Com. Bishop *also* 2 Sam. 23. 1–4 Ps. 89. 19–22, 24	*or*	Ecclus. 6. 5–17 *or* James 2. 14–24, 26 Ps. 119. 19–24 *or* Ps. 112 Mark 10. 1–12	Ps. 55 2 Chron. 14. 2–end John 20. 11–18	Ps. 69 Gen. 33. 1–17 Titus ch. 3

*Matthias may be celebrated on 24 February, displacing The Second Sunday before Lent, or be transferred to 25 February, instead of 14 May.

	Calendar and Holy Communion	Morning Prayer	Evening Prayer	NOTES
	MATTHIAS THE APOSTLE (or transferred to 25 February)			
R	1 Sam. 2. 27–35 Ps. 16. 1–7 Acts 1. 15–end Matt. 11. 25–end	Ps. 15 Jonah 1. 1–9 Acts 2. 37–end	Ps. 80 1 Sam. 16. 1–13a Matt. 7. 15–27	
G	*or for Sexagesima:* Gen. 3. 9–19 Ps. 83. 1–2, 13–end 2 Cor. 11. 19–31 Luke 8. 4–15	Ps. 104. 1–26 Job 28. 1–11 Acts 14. 8–17	Ps. 147 (*or* 147. 13–end) Gen. 1.1 - 2.3 Heb. 6. 25–end *or First EP of Matthias* Ps. 147 Isa. 22. 15–22 Phil. 3.13b - 14.1 **R ct**	
	For Matthias, see 24 February.			
G		2 Chron. 9. 1–12 John 19. 1–16	Gen. 29.31 - 30.24 2 Tim. 4. 1–8	
G		2 Chron. 10.1 - 11.4 John 19. 17–30	Gen. 31. 1–24 2 Tim. 4. 9–end	
G		2 Chron. ch. 12 John 19. 31–end	Gen. 31.25 - 32.2 Titus ch. 1	
G		2 Chron. 13.1 - 14.1 John 20. 1–10	Gen. 32. 3–30 Titus ch. 2	
	David, Bishop of Menevia, Patron of Wales, c. 601			
Gw	Com. Bishop	2 Chron. 14. 2–end John 20. 11–18	Gen. 33. 1–17 Titus ch. 3	

		Sunday Principal Service Weekday Eucharist	Third Service Morning Prayer	Second Service Evening Prayer
2 Saturday	**Chad, Bishop of Lichfield, Missionary, 672***			
Gw	Com. Missionary *or* *also* 1 Tim. 6. 11b–16	Ecclus. 17. 1–15 *or* James 3. 1–10 Ps. 103. 13–18 *or* Ps. 12. 1–7 Mark 10. 13–16	Ps. ***76***; 79 2 Chron. 15. 1–15 John 20. 19–end	Ps. 81; ***84*** Gen. ch. 35 Philemon **ct**
3 Sunday	**THE SUNDAY NEXT BEFORE LENT**			
G		Exod. 34. 29–end Ps. 99 2 Cor. 3.12 – 4.2 Luke 9. 28–36 [37–43a]	Ps. 2 Exod. 33. 17–end 1 John 3. 1–3	Ps. 89. 1–18 (*or* 89. 5–12) Exod. 3. 1–6 John 12. 27–36a
4 Monday				
G **DEL 8**		Ecclus. 17. 24–29 *or* James 3. 13–end Ps. 32. 1–8 *or* Ps. 19. 7–end Mark 10. 17–27	Ps. ***80***; 82 Jer. ch. 1 John 3. 1–21	Ps. ***85***; 86 Gen. 37. 1–11 Gal. ch. 1
5 Tuesday				
G		Ecclus. 35. 1–12 *or* James 4. 1–10 Ps. 50. 1–6 *or* Ps. 55. 7–9, 24 Mark 10. 28–31	Ps. 87; ***89. 1–18*** Jer. 2. 1–13 John 3. 22–end	Ps. 89. 19–end Gen. 37. 12–end Gal. 2. 1–10
6 Wednesday	**ASH WEDNESDAY**			
P		Joel 2. 1–2, 12–17 *or* Isa. 58. 1–12 Ps. 51. 1–18 2 Cor. 5.20b – 6.10 Matt. 6. 1–6, 16–21 *or* John 8. 1–11	*MP*: Ps. 38 Dan. 9. 3–6, 17–19 1 Tim. 6. 6–19	*EP*: Ps. ***51*** *or* Ps. 102 (*or* 102. 1–18) Isa. 1. 10–18 Luke 15. 11–end
7 Thursday	**Perpetua, Felicity and their Companions, Martyrs at Carthage, 203**			
Pr	Com. Martyr *or* *esp.* Rev. 12. 10–12a *also* Wisd. 3. 1–7	Deut. 30. 15–end Ps. 1 Luke 9. 22–25	Ps. 77 *alt.* Ps. 90; **92** Jer. 2. 14–32 John 4. 1–26	Ps. 74 *alt.* Ps. 94 Gen. ch. 39 Gal. 2. 11–end
8 Friday	**Edward King, Bishop of Lincoln, 1910** *Felix, Bishop, Apostle to the East Angles, 647; Geoffrey Studdert Kennedy, Priest, Poet, 1929*			
Pw	Com. Bishop *or* *also* Heb. 13. 1–8	Isa. 58. 1–9a Ps. 51. 1–5, 17–18 Matt. 9. 14–15	Ps. **3**; 7 *alt.* Ps. ***88***; (95) Jer. 3. 6–22 John 4. 27–42	Ps. 31 *alt.* Ps. 102 Gen. ch. 40 Gal. 3. 1–14
9 Saturday				
P		Isa. 58. 9b–end Ps. 86. 1–7 Luke 5. 27–32	Ps. 71 *alt.* Ps. 96; **97**; 100 Jer. 4. 1–18 John 4. 43–end	Ps. 73 *alt.* Ps. 104 Gen. 41. 1–24 Gal. 3. 15–22 **ct**

*Chad may be celebrated with Cedd on 26 October instead of 2 March.

	Calendar and Holy Communion	Morning Prayer	Evening Prayer
	Chad, Bishop of Lichfield, Missionary, 672		
Gw	Com. Bishop	2 Chron. 15. 1–15 John 20. 19–end	Gen. ch. 35 Philemon **ct**
	QUINQUAGESIMA		
G	Gen. 9. 8–17 Ps. 77. 11–end 1 Cor. ch. 13 Luke 18. 31–43	Ps. 2 Exod. 33. 17–end Luke 9. 28–43	Ps. 89. 1–18 (*or* 89. 5–12) Exod. 3. 1–6 John 12. 27–36a
G		Jer. ch. 1 John 3. 1–21	Gen. 37. 1–11 Gal. ch. 1
G		Jer. 2. 1–13 John 3. 22–end	Gen. 37. 12–end Gal. 2. 1–10
	ASH WEDNESDAY		
P	Ash Wed. Collect until 20 April Commination Joel 2. 12–17 Ps. 57 James 4. 1–10 Matt. 6. 16–21	Ps. 38 Dan. 9. 3–6, 17–19 1 Tim. 6. 6–19	Ps. 51 *or* Ps. 102 (*or* 102. 1–18) Isa. 1. 10–18 Luke 15. 11–end
	Perpetua, Martyr at Carthage, 203		
Pr	Com. Martyr *or* Exod. 24. 12–end Matt. 8. 5–13	Jer. 2. 14–32 John 4. 1–26	Gen. ch. 39 Gal. 2. 11–end
P	1 Kings 19. 3b–8 Matt. 5.43 - 6.6	Jer. 3. 6–22 John 4. 27–42	Gen. ch. 40 Gal. 3. 1–14
P	Isa. 38. 1–6a Mark 6. 45–end	Jer. 4. 1–18 John 4. 43–end	Gen. 41. 1–24 Gal. 3. 15–22 **ct**

NOTES

		Sunday Principal Service Weekday Eucharist	Third Service Morning Prayer	Second Service Evening Prayer
10 Sunday	**THE FIRST SUNDAY OF LENT**			
P		Deut. 26. 1–11 Ps. 91. 1–2, 9–end (*or* 91. 1–11) Rom. 10. 8b–13 Luke 4. 1–13	Ps. 50. 1–15 Mic. 6. 1–8 Luke 5. 27–end	Ps. 119. 73–88 Jonah ch. 3 Luke 18. 9–14
11 Monday				
P		Lev. 19. 1–2, 11–18 Ps. 19. 7–end Matt. 25. 31–end	Ps. 10; ***11*** *alt.* Ps. ***98***; 99; 101 Jer. 4. 19–end John 5. 1–18	Ps. 12; ***13***; 14 *alt.* Ps. ***105***† (*or* 103) Gen. 41. 25–45 Gal. 3.23 – 4.7
12 Tuesday				
P		Isa. 55. 10–11 Ps. 34. 4–6, 21–22 Matt. 6. 7–15	Ps. 44 *alt.* Ps. ***106***† (*or* 103) Jer. 5. 1–19 John 5. 19–29	Ps. 46; ***49*** *alt.* Ps. 107† Gen. 41.46 – 42.5 Gal. 4. 8–20
13 Wednesday	Ember Day*			
P		Jonah ch. 3 Ps. 51. 1–5, 17–18 Luke 11. 29–32	Ps. ***6***; 17 *alt.* Ps. 110; ***111***; 112 Jer. 5. 20–end John 5. 30–end	Ps. 9; ***28*** *alt.* Ps. 119. 129–152 Gen. 42. 6–17 Gal. 4.21 – 5.1
14 Thursday				
P		Esther 14. 1–5, 12–14 *or* Isa. 55. 6–9 Ps. 138 Matt. 7. 7–12	Ps. ***42***; 43 *alt.* Ps. 113; ***115*** Jer. 6. 9–21 John 6. 1–15	Ps. 137; 138; ***142*** *alt.* Ps. 114; ***116***; 117 Gen. 42. 18–28 Gal. 5. 2–15
15 Friday	Ember Day*			
P		Ezek. 18. 21–28 Ps. 130 Matt. 5. 20–26	Ps. 22 *alt.* Ps. 139 Jer. 6. 22–end John 6. 16–27	Ps. 54; ***55*** *alt.* Ps. ***130***; 131; 137 Gen. 42. 29–end Gal. 5. 16–end
16 Saturday	Ember Day*			
P		Deut. 26. 16–end Ps. 119. 1–8 Matt. 5. 43–end	Ps. 59; ***63*** *alt.* Ps. 120; ***121***; 122 Jer. 7. 1–20 John 6. 27–40	Ps. ***4***; 16 *alt.* Ps. 118 Gen. 43. 1–15 Gal. ch. 6 **ct**
17 Sunday	**THE SECOND SUNDAY OF LENT**			
P		Gen. 15. 1–12, 17–18 Ps. 27 Phil. 3.17 – 4.1 Luke 13. 31–end	Ps. 119. 161–end Gen. 17. 1–7, 15–16 Rom. 11. 13–24	Ps. 135 (*or* 135. 1–14) Jer. 22. 1–9, 13–17 Luke 14. 27–33

*For Ember Day provision, see p. 11.

	Calendar and Holy Communion	Morning Prayer	Evening Prayer	NOTES
	THE FIRST SUNDAY IN LENT			
P	Collect (1) Lent 1 (2) Ash Wednesday Ember until 16th Gen. 3. 1-6 Ps. 91. 1-12 2 Cor. 6. 1-10 Matt. 4. 1-11	Ps. 50. 1-15 Mic. 6. 1-8 Luke 5. 27-end	Ps. 119. 73-88 Jonah ch. 3 Luke 18. 9-14	
P	Ezek. 34. 11-16a Matt. 25. 31-end	Jer. 4. 19-end John 5. 1-18	Gen. 41. 25-45 Gal. 3.23 - 4.7	
	Gregory the Great, Bishop of Rome, 604			
Pw	Com. Doctor *or* Isa. 55. 6-11 Matt. 21. 10-16	Jer. 5. 1-19 John 5. 19-29	Gen. 41.46 - 42.5 Gal. 4. 8-20	
	Ember Day			
P	Ember CEG *or* Isa. 58. 1-9a Matt. 12. 38-end	Jer. 5. 20-end John 5. 30-end	Gen. 42. 6-17 Gal. 4.21 - 5.1	
P	Isa. 58. 9b-end John 8. 31-45	Jer. 6. 9-21 John 6. 1-15	Gen. 42. 18-28 Gal. 5. 2-15	
	Ember Day			
P	Ember CEG *or* Ezek. 18. 20-25 John 5. 2-15	Jer. 6. 22-end John 6. 16-27	Gen. 42. 29-end Gal. 5. 16-end	
	Ember Day			
P	Ember CEG *or* Ezek. 18. 26-end Matt. 17. 1-9 *or* Luke 4. 16-21 *or* John 10. 1-16	Jer. 7. 1-20 John 6. 27-40	Gen. 43. 1-15 Gal. ch. 6 **ct**	
	THE SECOND SUNDAY IN LENT			
P	Jer. 17. 5-10 Ps. 25. 13-end 1 Thess. 4. 1-8 Matt. 15. 21-28	Ps. 119. 161-end Gen. 17. 1-7, 15-16 Rom. 11. 13-24	Ps. 135 (*or* 135. 1-14) Jer. 22. 1-9, 13-17 Luke 14. 27-33	

		Sunday Principal Service Weekday Eucharist	Third Service Morning Prayer	Second Service Evening Prayer
18 Monday	*Cyril, Bishop of Jerusalem, Teacher, 386*			
P		Dan. 9. 4–10 Ps. 79. 8–9, 12, 14 Luke 6. 36–38	Ps. 26; ***32*** *alt.* Ps. 123; 124; 125; ***126*** Jer. 7. 21–end John 6. 41–51	Ps. 70; ***74*** *alt.* Ps. ***127***; 128; 129 Gen. 43. 16–end Heb. ch. 1 *or First EP of Joseph* Ps. 132 Hos. 11. 1–9 Luke 2. 41–end **W ct**
19 Tuesday	**JOSEPH OF NAZARETH**			
W		2 Sam. 7. 4–16 Ps. 89. 26–36 Rom. 4. 13–18 Matt. 1. 18–end	*MP*: Ps. 25; 147. 1–12 Isa. 11. 1–10 Matt. 13. 54–end	*EP*: Ps. 1; 112 Gen. 50. 22–end Matt. 2. 13–end
20 Wednesday	**Cuthbert, Bishop of Lindisfarne, Missionary, 687***			
Pw	Com. Missionary *or* *esp.* Ezek. 34. 11–16 *also* Matt. 18. 12–14	Jer. 18. 18–20 Ps. 31. 4–5, 14–18 Matt. 20. 17–28	Ps. 35 *alt.* Ps. 119. 153–end Jer. 8.18 - 9.11 John 6. 60–end	Ps. ***3***; 51 *alt.* Ps. 136 Gen. 44. 18–end Heb. 2. 10–end
21 Thursday	**Thomas Cranmer, Archbishop of Canterbury, Reformation Martyr, 1556**			
Pr	Com. Martyr *or*	Jer. 17. 5–10 Ps. 1 Luke 16. 19–end	Ps. 34 *alt.* Ps. ***143***; 146 Jer. 9. 12–24 John 7. 1–13	Ps. 71 *alt.* Ps. ***138***; 140; 141 Gen. 45. 1–15 Heb. 3. 1–6
22 Friday				
P		Gen. 37. 3–4, 12–13, 17–28 Ps. 105. 16–22 Matt. 21. 33–43, 45–46	Ps. 40; ***41*** *alt.* Ps. 142; ***144*** Jer. 10. 1–16 John 7. 14–24	Ps. ***6***; 38 *alt.* Ps. 145 Gen. 45. 16–end Heb. 3. 7–end
23 Saturday				
P		Mic. 7. 4–15, 18–20 Ps. 103. 1–4, 9–12 Luke 15. 1–3, 11–end	Ps. 3; ***25*** *alt.* Ps. 147 Jer. 10. 17–24 John 7. 25–36	Ps. ***23***; 27 *alt.* Ps. ***148***; 149; 150 Gen. 46. 1–7, 28–end Heb. 4. 1–13 **ct**
24 Sunday	**THE THIRD SUNDAY OF LENT**			
P		Isa. 55. 1–9 Ps. 63. 1–9 1 Cor. 10. 1–13 Luke 13. 1–9	Ps. 26; 28 Deut. 6. 4–9 John 17. 1a, 11b–19	Ps. 12; 13 Gen. 28. 10–19a John 1. 35–end *or First EP of The Annunciation* Ps. 85 Wisd. 9. 1–12 *or* Gen. 3. 8–15 Gal. 4. 1–5 **𝔚 ct**

*Cuthbert may be celebrated on 4 September instead of 20 March.

	Calendar and Holy Communion	Morning Prayer	Evening Prayer	NOTES
	Edward, King of the W. Saxons, 978			
Pr	Com. Martyr *or* Heb. 2. 1–10 John 8. 21–30	Jer. 7. 21–end John 6. 41–51	Gen. 43. 16–end Heb. ch. 1	
	To celebrate Joseph, see *Common Worship* provision.			
P	Heb. 2. 11–end Matt. 23. 1–12	Jer. 8. 1–15 John 6. 52–59	Gen. 44. 1–17 Heb. 2. 1–9	
P	Heb. 3. 1–6 Matt. 20. 17–28	Jer. 8.18 - 9.11 John 6. 60–end	Gen. 44. 18–end Heb. 2. 10–end	
	Benedict, Abbot of Monte Cassino, *c.* 550			
Pw	Com. Abbot *or* Heb. 3. 7–end John 5. 30–end	Jer. 9. 12–24 John 7. 1–13	Gen. 45. 1–15 Heb. 3. 1–6	
P	Heb. ch. 4 Matt. 21. 33–end	Jer. 10. 1–16 John 7. 14–24	Gen. 45. 16–end Heb. 3. 7–end	
P	Heb. ch. 5 Luke 15. 11–end	Jer. 10. 17–24 John 7. 25–36	Gen. 46. 1–7, 28–end Heb. 4. 1–13 **ct**	
	THE THIRD SUNDAY IN LENT			
P	Num. 22. 21–31 Ps. 9. 13–end Eph. 5. 1–14 Luke 11. 14–28	Ps. 26; 28 Deut. 6. 4–9 John 17. 1a, 11b–19	Ps. 12; 13 Gen. 28. 10–19a John 1. 35–end *or First EP of The Annunciation* Ps. 85 Wisd. 9. 1–12 *or* Gen. 3. 8–15 Gal. 4. 1–5 **W ct**	

		Sunday Principal Service Weekday Eucharist	Third Service Morning Prayer	Second Service Evening Prayer
25 Monday*	**THE ANNUNCIATION OF OUR LORD TO THE BLESSED VIRGIN MARY**			
𝔚		Isa. 7. 10–14 Ps. 40. 5–11 Heb. 10. 4–10 Luke 1. 26–38	*MP*: Ps. 111; 113 1 Sam. 2. 1–10 Rom. 5. 12–end	*EP*: Ps. 131; 146 Isa. 52. 1–12 Heb. 2. 5–end
26 Tuesday	*Harriet Monsell, Founder of the Community of St John the Baptist, Clewer, 1883*			
P		Song of the Three 2, 11–20 *or* Dan. 2. 20–23 Ps. 25. 3–10 Matt. 18. 21–end	Ps. 6; ***9*** *alt.* Ps. ***5***; 6; (8) Jer. 11.18 – 12.6 John 7.53 – 8.11	Ps. 61; 62; ***64*** *alt.* Ps. ***9***; 10† Gen. 47.28 – 48.end Heb. 5.11 – 6.12
27 Wednesday				
P		Deut. 4. 1, 5–9 Ps. 147. 13–end Matt. 5. 17–19	Ps. 38 *alt.* Ps. 119. 1–32 Jer. 13. 1–11 John 8. 12–30	Ps. 36; ***39*** *alt.* Ps. ***11***; 12; 13 Gen. 49. 1–32 Heb. 6. 13–end
28 Thursday				
P		Jer. 7. 23–28 Ps. 95. 1–2, 6–end Luke 11. 14–23	Ps. ***56***; 57 *alt.* Ps. 14; ***15***; 16 Jer. ch. 14 John 8. 31–47	Ps. ***59***; 60 *alt.* Ps. 18† Gen. 49.33 – 50.end Heb. 7. 1–10
29 Friday				
P		Hos. ch. 14 Ps. 81. 6–10, 13, 16 Mark 12. 28–34	Ps. 22 *alt.* Ps. 17; ***19*** Jer. 15. 10–end John 8. 48–end	Ps. 69 *alt.* Ps. 22 Exod. 1. 1–14 Heb. 7. 11–end
30 Saturday				
P		Hos. 5.15 – 6.6 Ps. 51. 1–2, 17–end Luke 18. 9–14	Ps. 31 *alt.* Ps. 20; 21; ***23*** Jer. 16.10 – 17.4 John 9. 1–17	Ps. ***116***; 130 *alt.* Ps. ***24***; 25 Exod. 1.22 – 2.10 Heb. ch. 8 **ct**
31 Sunday	**THE FOURTH SUNDAY OF LENT** (Mothering Sunday)			
P		Josh. 5. 9–12 Ps. 32 2 Cor. 5. 16–end Luke 15. 1–3, 11b–end	Ps. 84; 85 Gen. 37. 3–4, 12–end 1 Pet. 2. 16–end	Ps. 30 Prayer of Manasseh *or* Isa. 40.27 – 41.13 2 Tim. 4. 1–18 *Gospel*: John 11. 17–44 *If the Principal Service readings for The Fourth Sunday of Lent are displaced by Mothering Sunday provisions, they may be used at the Second Service.* *(continued overleaf)*

*The following readings may replace those provided for Holy Communion on any day (except The Annunciation) during the Third Week of Lent: Exod. 17. 1–7; Ps. 95. 1–2, 6–end; John 4. 5–42.

	Calendar and Holy Communion	Morning Prayer	Evening Prayer	NOTES
	THE ANNUNCIATION OF THE BLESSED VIRGIN MARY			
𝔚	Isa. 7. 10–14 [15] Ps. 113 Rom. 5. 12–19 Luke 1. 26–38	Ps. 111 1 Sam. 2. 1–10 Heb. 10. 4–10	Ps. 131; 146 Isa. 52. 1–12 Heb. 2. 5–end	
P	Heb. 6. 11–end Matt. 18. 15–22	Jer. 11.18 - 12.6 John 7.53 - 8.11	Gen. 47.28 - 48.end Heb. 5.11 - 6.12	
P	Heb. 7. 1–10 Matt. 15. 1–20	Jer. 13. 1–11 John 8. 12–30	Gen. 49. 1–32 Heb. 6. 13–end	
P	Heb. 7. 11–25 John 6. 26–35	Jer. ch. 14 John 8. 31–47	Gen. 49.33 - 50.end Heb. 7. 1–10	
P	Heb. 7. 26–end John 4. 5–26	Jer. 15. 10–end John 8. 48–end	Exod. 1. 1–14 Heb. 7. 11–end	
P	Heb. 8. 1–6 John 8. 1–11	Jer. 16.10 - 17.4 John 9. 1–17	Exod. 1.22 - 2.10 Heb. ch. 8 **ct**	
	THE FOURTH SUNDAY IN LENT To celebrate Mothering Sunday, see *Common Worship* provision.			
P	Exod. 16. 2–7a Ps. 122 Gal. 4. 21–end *or* Heb. 12. 22–24 John 6. 1–14	Ps. 84; 85 Gen. 37. 3–4, 12–end 1 Pet. 2. 16–end	Ps. 30 Prayer of Manasseh *or* Isa. 40.27 - 41.13 2 Tim. 4. 1–18	

		Sunday Principal Service Weekday Eucharist	Third Service Morning Prayer	Second Service Evening Prayer
31 Sunday	**THE FOURTH SUNDAY OF LENT** *(continued)* (Mothering Sunday)			
	or, for Mothering Sunday:	Exod. 2. 1–10 *or* 1 Sam. 1. 20–end Ps. 34. 11–20 *or* Ps. 127. 1–4 2 Cor. 1. 3–7 *or* Col. 3. 12–17 Luke 2. 33–35 *or* John 19. 25b–27		

April 2019

		Sunday Principal Service Weekday Eucharist	Third Service Morning Prayer	Second Service Evening Prayer
1 Monday*	*Frederick Denison Maurice, Priest, Teacher, 1872*			
P		Isa. 65. 17–21 Ps. 30. 1–5, 8, 11–end John 4. 43–end	Ps. 70; ***77*** *alt.* Ps. 27; ***30*** Jer. 17. 5–18 John 9. 18–end	Ps. ***25***; 28 *alt.* Ps. 26; ***28***; 29 Exod. 2. 11–22 Heb. 9. 1–14
2 Tuesday				
P		Ezek. 47. 1–9, 12 Ps. 46. 1–8 John 5. 1–3, 5–16	Ps. 54; ***79*** *alt.* Ps. 32; ***36*** Jer. 18. 1–12 John 10. 1–10	Ps. ***80***; 82 *alt.* Ps. 33 Exod. 2.23 - 3.20 Heb. 9. 15–end
3 Wednesday				
P		Isa. 49. 8–15 Ps. 145. 8–18 John 5. 17–30	Ps. **63**; *90* *alt.* Ps. 34 Jer. 18. 13–end John 10. 11–21	Ps. 52; ***91*** *alt.* Ps. 119. 33–56 Exod. 4. 1–23 Heb. 10. 1–18
4 Thursday				
P		Exod. 32. 7–14 Ps. 106. 19–23 John 5. 31–end	Ps. 53; ***86*** *alt.* Ps. 37† Jer. 19. 1–13 John 10. 22–end	Ps. 94 *alt.* Ps. 39; ***40*** Exod. 4.27 - 6.1 Heb. 10. 19–25
5 Friday				
P		Wisd. 2. 1, 12–22 *or* Jer. 26. 8–11 Ps. 34. 15–end John 7. 1–2, 10, 25–30	Ps. 102 *alt.* Ps. 31 Jer. 19.14 - 20.6 John 11. 1–16	Ps. 13; ***16*** *alt.* Ps. 35 Exod. 6. 2–13 Heb. 10. 26–end
6 Saturday				
P		Jer. 11. 18–20 Ps. 7. 1–2, 8–10 John 7. 40–52	Ps. 32 *alt.* Ps. 41; ***42***; 43 Jer. 20. 7–end John 11. 17–27	Ps. ***140***; 141; 142 *alt.* Ps. 45; ***46*** Exod. 7. 8–end Heb. 11. 1–16 **ct**
7 Sunday	**THE FIFTH SUNDAY OF LENT (Passiontide begins)**			
P		Isa. 43. 16–21 Ps. 126 Phil. 3. 4b–14 John 12. 1–8	Ps. 111; 112 Isa. ch. 35 Rom. 7.21 - 8.4	Ps. 35 (*or* 35. 1–9) 2 Chron. 35. 1–6, 10–16 Luke 22. 1–13

*The following readings may replace those provided for Holy Communion on any day during the Fourth Week of Lent: Mic. 7. 7–9; Ps. 27. 1, 9–10, 16–17; John ch. 9.

	Calendar and Holy Communion	Morning Prayer	Evening Prayer
P	Heb. 11. 1–6 John 2. 13–end	Jer. 17. 5–18 John 9. 18–end	Exod. 2. 11–22 Heb. 9. 1–14
P	Heb. 11. 13–16a John 7. 14–24	Jer. 18. 1–12 John 10. 1–10	Exod. 2.23 - 3.20 Heb. 9. 15–end
	Richard, Bishop of Chichester, 1253		
Pw	Com. Bishop *or* Heb. 12. 1–11 John 9. 1–17	Jer. 18. 13–end John 10. 11–21	Exod. 4. 1–23 Heb. 10. 1–18
	Ambrose, Bishop of Milan, 397		
Pw	Com. Doctor *or* Heb. 12. 12–17 John 5. 17–27	Jer. 19. 1–13 John 10. 22–end	Exod. 4.27 - 6.1 Heb. 10. 19–25
P	Heb. 12. 22–end John 11. 33–46	Jer. 19.14 - 20.6 John 11. 1–16	Exod. 6. 2–13 Heb. 10. 26–end
P	Heb. 13. 7–21 John 8. 12–20	Jer. 20. 7–end John 11. 17–27	Exod. 7. 8–end Heb. 11. 1–16 **ct**
	THE FIFTH SUNDAY IN LENT		
P	Exod. 24. 4–8 Ps. 143 Heb. 9. 11–15 John 8. 46–end	Ps. 111; 112 Isa. ch. 35 Rom. 7.21 - 8.4	Ps. 35 (*or* 35. 1–9) 2 Chron. 35. 1–6, 10–16 Luke 22. 1–13

NOTES

		Sunday Principal Service Weekday Eucharist	Third Service Morning Prayer	Second Service Evening Prayer
8 Monday*				
P		Susanna 1–9, 15–17, 19–30, 33–62 (*or* 41b–62) *or* Josh. 2. 1–14 Ps. 23 John 8. 1–11	Ps. ***73***; 121 *alt.* Ps. 44 Jer. 21. 1–10 John 11. 28–44	Ps. ***26***; 27 *alt.* Ps. ***47***; 49 Exod. 8. 1–19 Heb. 11. 17–31
9 Tuesday	*Dietrich Bonhoeffer, Lutheran Pastor, Martyr, 1945*			
P		Num. 21. 4–9 Ps. 102. 1–3, 16–23 John 8. 21–30	Ps. ***35***; 123 *alt.* Ps. ***48***; 52 Jer. 22. 1–5, 13–19 John 11. 45–end	Ps. ***61***; 64 *alt.* Ps. 50 Exod. 8. 20–end Heb. 11.32 – 12.2
10 Wednesday	**William Law, Priest, Spiritual Writer, 1761** *William of Ockham, Friar, Philosopher, Teacher, 1347*			
Pw	Com. Teacher *or* *esp.* 1 Cor. 2. 9–end *also* Matt. 17. 1–9	Dan. 3. 14–20, 24–25, 28 *Canticle*: Bless the Lord John 8. 31–42	Ps. ***55***; 124 *alt.* Ps. 119. 57–80 Jer. 22.20 – 23.8 John 12. 1–11	Ps. 56; ***62*** *alt.* Ps. ***59***; 60 (67) Exod. 9. 1–12 Heb. 12. 3–13
11 Thursday	*George Augustus Selwyn, first Bishop of New Zealand, 1878*			
P		Gen. 17. 3–9 Ps. 105. 4–9 John 8. 51–end	Ps. ***40***; 125 *alt.* Ps. 56; ***57***; (63†) Jer. 23. 9–32 John 12. 12–19	Ps. 42; ***43*** *alt.* Ps. 61; ***62***; 64 Exod. 9. 13–end Heb. 12. 14–end
12 Friday				
P		Jer. 20. 10–13 Ps. 18. 1–6 John 10. 31–end	Ps. ***22***; 126 *alt.* Ps. ***51***; 54 Jer. ch. 24 John 12. 20–36a	Ps. 31 *alt.* Ps. 38 Exod. ch. 10 Heb. 13. 1–16
13 Saturday				
P		Ezek. 37. 21–end *Canticle*: Jer. 31. 10–13 *or* Ps. 121 John 11. 45–end	Ps. ***23***; 127 *alt.* Ps. 68 Jer. 25. 1–14 John 12. 36b–end	Ps. 128; 129; ***130*** *alt.* Ps. 65; ***66*** Exod. ch. 11 Heb. 13. 17–end **ct**
14 Sunday	**PALM SUNDAY**			
R	*Liturgy of the Palms* Luke 19. 28–40 Ps. 118. 1–2, 19–end (*or* 118. 19–24)	*Liturgy of the Passion* Isa. 50. 4–9a Ps. 31. 9–16 (*or* 31. 9–18) Phil. 2. 5–11 Luke 22.14 – 23.end *or* Luke 23. 1–49	Ps. 61; 62 Zech. 9. 9–12 1 Cor. 2. 1–12	Ps. 69. 1–20 Isa. 5. 1–7 Luke 20. 9–19
15 Monday	**MONDAY OF HOLY WEEK**			
R		Isa. 42. 1–9 Ps. 36. 5–11 Heb. 9. 11–15 John 12. 1–11	*MP*: Ps. 41 Lam. 1. 1–12a Luke 22. 1–23	*EP*: Ps. 25 Lam. 2. 8–19 Col. 1. 18–23

*The following readings may replace those provided for Holy Communion on any day during the Fifth Week of Lent: 2 Kings 4. 18–21, 32–37; Ps. 17. 1–8, 16; John 11. 1–45.

	Calendar and Holy Communion	Morning Prayer	Evening Prayer	NOTES
P	Col. 1. 13–23a John 7. 1–13	Jer. 21. 1–10 John 11. 28–44	Exod. 8. 1–19 Heb. 11. 17–31	
P	Col. 2. 8–12 John 7. 32–39	Jer. 22. 1–5, 13–19 John 11. 45–end	Exod. 8. 20–end Heb. 11.32 - 12.2	
P	Col. 2. 13–19 John 7. 40–end	Jer. 22.20 - 23.8 John 12. 1–11	Exod. 9. 1–12 Heb. 12. 3–13	
P	Col. 3. 8–11 John 10. 22–38	Jer. 23. 9–32 John 12. 12–19	Exod. 9. 13–end Heb. 12. 14–end	
P	Col. 3. 12–17 John 11. 47–54	Jer. ch. 24 John 12. 20–36a	Exod. ch. 10 Heb. 13. 1–16	
P	Col. 4. 2–6 John 6. 53–end	Jer. 25. 1–14 John 12. 36b–end	Exod. ch. 11 Heb. 13. 17–end **ct**	
	THE SUNDAY NEXT BEFORE EASTER (PALM SUNDAY)			
R	Zech. 9. 9–12 Ps. 73. 22–end Phil. 2. 5–11 Passion acc. to Matthew Matt. 27. 1–54 *or* Matt. 26.1 - 27.61 *or* Matt. 21. 1–13	Ps. 61; 62 Isa. 42. 1–9 1 Cor. 2. 1–12	Ps. 69. 1–20 Isa. 5. 1–7 Luke 20. 9–19	
	MONDAY IN HOLY WEEK			
R	Isa. 63. 1–19 Ps. 55. 1–8 Gal. 6. 1–11 Mark ch. 14	Ps. 41 Lam. 1. 1–12a John 12. 1–11	Ps. 25 Lam. 2. 8–19 Col. 1. 18–23	

		Sunday Principal Service Weekday Eucharist	Third Service Morning Prayer	Second Service Evening Prayer
16 Tuesday	**TUESDAY OF HOLY WEEK**			
R		Isa. 49. 1–7 Ps. 71. 1–14 (*or* 71. 1–8) 1 Cor. 1. 18–31 John 12. 20–36	*MP*: Ps. 27 Lam. 3. 1–18 Luke 22. 24–53 (*or* 39–53)	*EP*: Ps. 55. 13–24 Lam. 3. 40–51 Gal. 6. 11–end
17 Wednesday	**WEDNESDAY OF HOLY WEEK**			
R		Isa. 50. 4–9a Ps. 70 Heb. 12. 1–3 John 13. 21–32	*MP*: Ps. 102 (*or* 102. 1–18) Wisd. 1.16 - 2.1, 12–22 *or* Jer. 11. 18–20 Luke 22. 54–end	*EP*: Ps. 88 Isa. 63. 1–9 Rev. 14.18 - 15.4
18 Thursday	**MAUNDY THURSDAY**			
W (HC) R		Exod. 12. 1–4 [5–10], 11–14 Ps. 116. 1, 10–end (*or* 116. 9–end) 1 Cor. 11. 23–26 John 13. 1–17, 31b–35	*MP*: Ps. 42; 43 Lev. 16. 2–24 Luke 23. 1–25	*EP*: Ps. 39 Exod. ch. 11 Eph. 2. 11–18
19 Friday	**GOOD FRIDAY**			
R		Isa. 52.13 - 53.end Ps. 22 (*or* 22. 1–11 *or* 22. 1–21) Heb. 10. 16–25 *or* Heb. 4. 14–16; 5. 7–9 John 18.1 - 19.end	*MP*: Ps. 69 Gen. 22. 1–18 *A part of* John 18 - 19 *if not read at the Principal Service* *or* Heb. 10. 1–10	*EP*: Ps. 130; 143 Lam. 5. 15–end *A part of* John 18 - 19 *if not read at the Principal Service, especially* John 19. 38–end *or* Col. 1. 18–23
20 Saturday	**EASTER EVE**			
	These readings are for use at services other than the Easter Vigil.	Job 14. 1–14 *or* Lam. 3. 1–9, 19–24 Ps. 31. 1–4, 15–16 (*or* 31. 1–5) 1 Pet. 4. 1–8 Matt. 27. 57–end *or* John 19. 38–end	Ps. 142 Hos. 6. 1–6 John 2. 18–22	Ps. 116 Job 19. 21–27 1 John 5. 5–12
21 Sunday	**EASTER DAY**			
𝔚	*The following readings and psalms (or canticles) are provided for use at the Easter Vigil. A minimum of three Old Testament readings should be chosen. The reading from* Exodus ch. 14 *should always be used.*	Gen. 1.1 - 2.4a & Ps. 136. 1–9, 23–end Gen. 7. 1–5, 11–18; 8. 6–18; 9. 8–13 & Ps. 46 Gen. 22. 1–18 & Ps. 16 Exod. 14. 10–end; 15. 20–21 & *Canticle*: Exod. 15. 1b–13, 17–18 Isa. 55. 1–11 & *Canticle*: Isa. 12. 2–end Baruch 3.9–15, 32 - 4.4 & Ps. 19 *or* Prov. 8. 1–8, 19–21; 9. 4b–6 & Ps. 19 Ezek. 36. 24–28 & Ps. 42; 43 Ezek. 37. 1–14 & Ps. 143 Zeph. 3. 14–end & Ps. 98 Rom. 6. 3–11 & Ps. 114 Luke 24. 1–12		

(continued overleaf)

	Calendar and Holy Communion	Morning Prayer	Evening Prayer	NOTES
	TUESDAY IN HOLY WEEK			
R	Isa. 50. 5–11 Ps. 13 Rom. 5. 6–19 Mark 15. 1–39	Ps. 27 Lam. 3. 1–18 John 12. 20–36	Ps. 55. 13–24 Lam. 3. 40–51 Gal. 6. 11–end	
	WEDNESDAY IN HOLY WEEK			
R	Isa. 49. 1–9a Ps. 54 Heb. 9. 16–end Luke ch. 22	Ps. 102 (*or* 102. 1–18) Wisd. 1.16 - 2.1, 12–22 *or* Jer. 11. 18–20 John 13. 21–32	Ps. 88 Isa. 63. 1–9 Rev. 14.18 - 15.4	
	MAUNDY THURSDAY			
W (HC) R	Exod. 12. 1–11 Ps. 43 1 Cor. 11. 17–end Luke 23. 1–49	Ps. 42; 43 Lev. 16. 2–24 John 13. 1–17, 31b–35	Ps. 39 Exod. ch. 11 Eph. 2. 11–18	
	GOOD FRIDAY			
R	Alt. Collect Passion acc. to John Alt. Gospel, if Passion is read Num. 21. 4–9 Ps. 140. 1–9 Heb. 10. 1–25 John 19. 1–37 *or* John 19. 38–end	Ps. 69 Gen. 22. 1–18 John ch. 18	Ps. 130; 143 Lam. 5. 15–end John 19. 38–end	
	EASTER EVE			
	Job 14. 1–14 1 Pet. 3. 17–22 Matt. 27. 57–end	Ps. 142 Hos. 6. 1–6 John 2. 18–22	Ps. 116 Job 19. 21–27 1 John 5. 5–12	
	EASTER DAY			
𝔚	Exod. 12. 21–28 Ps. 111 Col. 3. 1–7 John 20. 1–10	Ps. 114; 117 Ezek. 47. 1–12 John 2. 13–22	Ps. 105 *or* Ps. 66. 1–11 Isa. 43. 1–21 1 Cor. 15. 1–11 *or* John 20. 19–23	

		Sunday Principal Service Weekday Eucharist	Third Service Morning Prayer	Second Service Evening Prayer
21 Sunday	**EASTER DAY** *(continued)*			
𝔚	*Easter Day Services* *The reading from Acts must be used as either the first or second reading at the Principal Service.*	Acts 10. 34–43 *or* Isa. 65. 17–end Ps. 118. 1–2, 14–24 (*or* 118. 14–24) 1 Cor. 15. 19–26 *or* Acts 10. 34–43 John 20. 1–18 *or* Luke 24. 1–12	*MP*: Ps. 114; 117 Ezek. 47. 1–12 John 2. 13–22	*EP*: Ps. 105 *or* Ps. 66. 1–11 Isa. 43. 1–21 1 Cor. 15. 1–11 *or* John 20. 19–23
22 Monday	**MONDAY OF EASTER WEEK**			
W		Acts 2. 14, 22–32 Ps. 16. 1–2, 6–end Matt. 28. 8–15	Ps. ***111***; 117; 146 Song of Sol. 1.9 - 2.7 Mark 16. 1–8	Ps. 135 Exod. 12. 1–14 1 Cor. 15. 1–11
23 Tuesday	**TUESDAY OF EASTER WEEK** (George transferred to 29 April)			
W		Acts 2. 36–41 Ps. 33. 4–5, 18–end John 20. 11–18	Ps. ***112***; 147. 1–12 Song of Sol. 2. 8–end Luke 24. 1–12	Ps. 136 Exod. 12. 14–36 1 Cor. 15. 12–19
24 Wednesday	**WEDNESDAY OF EASTER WEEK**			
W		Acts 3. 1–10 Ps. 105. 1–9 Luke 24. 13–35	Ps. ***113***; 147. 13–end Song of Sol. ch. 3 Matt. 28. 16–end	Ps. 105 Exod. 12. 37–end 1 Cor. 15. 20–28
25 Thursday	**THURSDAY OF EASTER WEEK** (Mark transferred to 30 April)			
W		Acts 3. 11–end Ps. 8 Luke 24. 35–48	Ps. ***114***; 148 Song of Sol. 5.2 - 6.3 Luke 7. 11–17	Ps. 106 Exod. 13. 1–16 1 Cor. 15. 29–34
26 Friday	**FRIDAY OF EASTER WEEK**			
W		Acts 4. 1–12 Ps. 118. 1–4, 22–26 John 21. 1–14	Ps. ***115***; 149 Song of Sol. 7.10 - 8.4 Luke 8. 41–end	Ps. 107 Exod. 13.17 - 14.14 1 Cor. 15. 35–50
27 Saturday	**SATURDAY OF EASTER WEEK**			
W		Acts 4. 13–21 Ps. 118. 1–4, 14–21 Mark 16. 9–15	Ps. ***116***; 150 Song of Sol. 8. 5–7 John 11. 17–44	Ps. 145 Exod. 14. 15–end 1 Cor. 15. 51–end **ct**
28 Sunday	**THE SECOND SUNDAY OF EASTER**			
W	*The reading from Acts must be used as either the first or second reading at the Principal Service.*	Acts 5. 27–32 [*or* Exod. 14. 10–end; 15. 20–21] Ps. 118. 14–end *or* Ps. 150 Rev. 1. 4–8 John 20. 19–end	Ps. 136. 1–16 Exod. 12. 1–13 1 Pet. 1. 3–12	Ps. 16 Isa. 52.13 - 53.12 *or* 53. 1–6, 9–12 Luke 24. 13–35 *or First EP of George*: Ps. 111; 116 Jer. 15. 15–end Heb. 11.32 - 12.2 **R ct**

	Calendar and Holy Communion	Morning Prayer	Evening Prayer	NOTES
	EASTER DAY			
	MONDAY IN EASTER WEEK			
W	Hos. 6. 1–6 Easter Anthems Acts 10. 34–43 Luke 24. 13–35	Song of Sol. 1.9 – 2.7 Mark 16. 1–8	Exod. 12. 1–14 1 Cor. 15. 1–11	
	TUESDAY IN EASTER WEEK			
W	1 Kings 17. 17–end Ps. 16. 9–end Acts 13. 26–41 Luke 24. 36b–48	Song of Sol. 2. 8–end Luke 24. 1–12	Exod. 12. 14–36 1 Cor. 15. 12–19	
W	Isa. 42. 10–16 Ps. 111 Acts 3. 12–18 John 20. 11–18	Song of Sol. ch. 3 Matt. 28. 16–end	Exod. 12. 37–end 1 Cor. 15. 20–28	
	(Mark transferred to 30 April)			
W	Isa. 43. 16–21 Ps. 113 Acts 8. 26–end John 21. 1–14	Song of Sol. 5.2 – 6.3 Luke 7. 11–17	Exod. 13. 1–16 1 Cor. 15. 29–34	
W	Ezek. 37. 1–14 Ps. 116. 1–9 1 Pet. 3. 18–end Matt. 28. 16–end	Song of Sol. 7.10 – 8.4 Luke 8. 41–end	Exod. 13.17 – 14.14 1 Cor. 15. 35–50	
W	Zech. 8. 1–8 Ps. 118. 14–21 1 Pet. 2. 1–10 John 20. 24–end	Song of Sol. 8. 5–7 John 11. 17–44	Exod. 14. 15–end 1 Cor. 15. 51–end **ct**	
	THE FIRST SUNDAY AFTER EASTER			
W	Ezek. 37. 1–10 Ps. 81. 1–4 1 John 5. 4–12 John 20. 19–23	Ps. 136. 1–16 Exod. 12. 1–13 1 Pet. 1. 3–12	Ps. 16 Isa. 52.13 – 53.12 *or* 53. 1–6, 9–12 Luke 24. 13–35	

		Sunday Principal Service Weekday Eucharist	Third Service Morning Prayer	Second Service Evening Prayer
29 Monday	**GEORGE, MARTYR, PATRON OF ENGLAND, c. 304**			
R		1 Macc. 2. 59–64 *or* Rev. 12. 7–12 Ps. 126 2 Tim. 2. 3–13 John 15. 18–21	*MP*: Ps. 5; 146 Josh. 1. 1–9 Eph. 6. 10–20	*EP*: Ps. 3; 11 Isa. 43. 1–7 John 15. 1–8
30 Tuesday	**MARK THE EVANGELIST**			
R		Prov. 15. 28–end *or* Acts 15. 35–end Ps. 119. 9–16 Eph. 4. 7–16 Mark 13. 5–13	*MP*: Ps. 37. 23–end; 148 Isa. 62. 6–10 *or* Ecclus. 51. 13–end Acts 12.25 – 13.13	*EP*: Ps. 45 Ezek. 1. 4–14 2 Tim. 4. 1–11

May 2019

1 Wednesday	**PHILIP AND JAMES, APOSTLES**			
R		Isa. 30. 15–21 Ps. 119. 1–8 Eph. 1. 3–10 John 14. 1–14	*MP*: Ps. 139; 146 Prov. 4. 10–18 James 1. 1–12	*EP*: Ps. 149 Job 23. 1–12 John 1. 43–end
2 Thursday	**Athanasius, Bishop of Alexandria, Teacher, 373**			
W	Com. Teacher *or* *also* Ecclus. 4. 20–28 Matt. 10. 24–27	Acts 5. 27–33 Ps. 34. 1, 15–end John 3. 31–end	Ps. ***28***; 29 *alt.* Ps. 14; ***15***; 16 Deut. 4. 1–14 John 21. 1–14	Ps. 34 *alt.* Ps. 18† Exod. ch. 17 Col. 2.16 – 3.11
3 Friday				
W		Acts 5. 34–42 Ps. 27. 1–5, 16–17 John 6. 1–15	Ps. 57; ***61*** *alt.* Ps. 17; ***19*** Deut. 4. 15–31 John 21. 15–19	Ps. 118 *alt.* Ps. 22 Exod. 18. 1–12 Col. 3.12 – 4.1
4 Saturday	**English Saints and Martyrs of the Reformation Era**			
W	Isa. 43. 1–7 *or* *or* Ecclus. 2. 10–17 Ps. 87 2 Cor. 4. 5–12 John 12. 20–26	Acts 6. 1–7 Ps. 33. 1–5, 18–19 John 6. 16–21	Ps. 63; ***84*** *alt.* Ps. 20; 21; ***23*** Deut. 4. 32–40 John 21. 20–end	Ps. 66 *alt.* Ps. ***24***; 25 Exod. 18. 13–end Col. 4. 2–end **ct**
5 Sunday	**THE THIRD SUNDAY OF EASTER**			
W	*The reading from Acts must be used as either the first or second reading at the Principal Service.*	Acts 9. 1–6 [7–20] [*or* Zeph. 3. 14–end] Ps. 30 Rev. 5. 11–end John 21. 1–19	Ps. 80. 1–8 Exod. 15. 1–2, 9–18 John 10. 1–19	Ps. 86 Isa. 38. 9–20 John 11. [17–26] 27–44
6 Monday				
W		Acts 6. 8–15 Ps. 119. 17–24 John 6. 22–29	Ps. 96; ***97*** *alt.* Ps. 27; ***30*** Deut. 5. 1–22 Eph. 1. 1–14	Ps. ***61***; 65 *alt.* Ps. 26; ***28***; 29 Exod. ch. 19 Luke 1. 1–25

	Calendar and Holy Communion	Morning Prayer	Evening Prayer
	George, Martyr, Patron of England, c. 304 To celebrate George, see *Common Worship* provision.		
Wr	Com. Martyr	Deut. 1. 3–18 John 20. 1–10	Exod. 15. 1–21 Col. 1. 1–14 *or First EP of Mark*: (Ps. 19) Isa. 52. 7–10 Mark 1. 1–15 **R ct**
	MARK THE EVANGELIST		
R	Prov. 15. 28–end Ps. 119. 9–16 Eph. 4. 7–16 John 15. 1–11	(Ps. 37. 23–end; 148) Isa. 62. 6–10 *or* Ecclus. 51. 13–end Acts 12.25 – 13.13	(Ps. 45) Ezek. 1. 4–14 2 Tim. 4. 1–11
	PHILIP AND JAMES, APOSTLES		
R	Prov. 4. 10–18 Ps. 25. 1–9 James 1. [1] 2–12 John 14. 1–14	(Ps. 139; 146) Isa. 30. 1–5 John 12. 20–26	(Ps. 149) Job 23. 1–12 John 1. 43–end
W		Deut. 4. 1–14 John 21. 1–14	Exod. ch. 17 Col. 2.16 – 3.11
	The Invention of the Cross		
Wr		Deut. 4. 15–31 John 21. 15–19	Exod. 18. 1–12 Col. 3.12 – 4.1
W		Deut. 4. 32–40 John 21. 20–end	Exod. 18. 13–end Col. 4. 2–end **ct**
	THE SECOND SUNDAY AFTER EASTER		
W	Ezek. 34. 11–16a Ps. 23 1 Pet. 2. 19–end John 10. 11–16	Ps. 80. 1–8 Exod. 15. 1–2, 9–18 John 21. 1–19	Ps. 86 Isa. 38. 9–20 John 11. [17–26] 27–44
	John the Evangelist, ante Portam Latinam		
W	CEG of 27 December	Deut. 5. 1–22 Eph. 1. 1–14	Exod. ch. 19 Luke 1. 1–25

NOTES

		Sunday Principal Service Weekday Eucharist	Third Service Morning Prayer	Second Service Evening Prayer
7 Tuesday				
W		Acts 7.51 - 8.1a Ps. 31. 1–5, 16 John 6. 30–35	Ps. ***98***; 99; 100 *alt.* Ps. 32; ***36*** Deut. 5. 22–end Eph. 1. 15–end	Ps. 71 *alt.* Ps. 33 Exod. 20. 1–21 Luke 1. 26–38
8 Wednesday	**Julian of Norwich, Spiritual Writer, c. 1417**			
W	Com. Religious *or* *also* 1 Cor. 13. 8–end Matt. 5. 13–16	Acts 8. 1b–8 Ps. 66. 1–6 John 6. 35–40	Ps. 105 *alt.* Ps. 34 Deut. ch. 6 Eph. 2. 1–10	Ps. 67; ***72*** *alt.* Ps. 119. 33–56 Exod. ch. 24 Luke 1. 39–56
9 Thursday				
W		Acts 8. 26–end Ps. 66. 7–8, 14–end John 6. 44–51	Ps. 136 *alt.* Ps. 37† Deut. 7. 1–11 Eph. 2. 11–end	Ps. 73 *alt.* Ps. 39; ***40*** Exod. 25. 1–22 Luke 1. 57–end
10 Friday				
W		Acts 9. 1–20 Ps. 117 John 6. 52–59	Ps. 107 *alt.* Ps. 31 Deut. 7. 12–end Eph. 3. 1–13	Ps. 77 *alt.* Ps. 35 Exod. 28. 1–4a, 29–38 Luke 2. 1–20
11 Saturday				
W		Acts 9. 31–42 Ps. 116. 10–15 John 6. 60–69	Ps. 108; ***110***; 111 *alt.* Ps. 41; ***42***; 43 Deut. ch. 8 Eph. 3. 14–end	Ps. 23; ***27*** *alt.* Ps. 45; ***46*** Exod. 29. 1–9 Luke 2. 21–40 **ct**
12 Sunday	**THE FOURTH SUNDAY OF EASTER**			
W	*The reading from Acts must be used as either the first or second reading at the Principal Service.*	Acts 9. 36–end [*or* Gen. 7. 1–5, 11–18; 8. 6–18; 9. 8–13] Ps. 23 Rev. 7. 9–end John 10. 22–30	Ps. 146 1 Kings 17. 17–end Luke 7. 11–23	Ps. 113; 114 Isa. 63. 7–14 Luke 24. 36–49
13 Monday				
W		Acts 11. 1–18 Ps. 42. 1–2; 43. 1–4 John 10. 1–10 (*or* 11–18)	Ps. 103 *alt.* Ps. 44 Deut. 9. 1–21 Eph. 4. 1–16	Ps. 112; 113; ***114*** *alt.* Ps. ***47***; 49 Exod. 32. 1–14 Luke 2. 41–end *or First EP of Matthias* Ps. 147 Isa. 22. 15–22 Phil. 3.13b - 4.1 **R ct**
14 Tuesday	**MATTHIAS THE APOSTLE***			
R		Isa. 22. 15–end *or* Acts 1. 15–end Ps. 15 Acts 1. 15–end *or* 1 Cor. 4. 1–7 John 15. 9–17	*MP*: Ps. 16; 147. 1–12 1 Sam. 2. 27–35 Acts 2. 37–end	*EP*: Ps. 80 1 Sam. 16. 1–13a Matt. 7. 15–27

(*continued overleaf*)

* Matthias may be celebrated on 24 February instead of 14 May.

	Calendar and Holy Communion	Morning Prayer	Evening Prayer	NOTES
W		Deut. 5. 22-end Eph. 1. 15-end	Exod. 20. 1-21 Luke 1. 26-38	
W		Deut. ch. 6 Eph. 2. 1-10	Exod. ch. 24 Luke 1. 39-56	
W		Deut. 7. 1-11 Eph. 2. 11-end	Exod. 25. 1-22 Luke 1. 57-end	
W		Deut. 7. 12-end Eph. 3. 1-13	Exod. 28. 1-4a, 29-38 Luke 2. 1-20	
W		Deut. ch. 8 Eph. 3. 14-end	Exod. 29. 1-9 Luke 2. 21-40 **ct**	
	THE THIRD SUNDAY AFTER EASTER			
W	Gen. 45. 3-10 Ps. 57 1 Pet. 2. 11-17 John 16. 16-22	1 Kings 17. 17-end Luke 7. 11-23	Ps. 113; 114 Isa. 63. 7-14 Luke 24. 36-49	
W		Deut. 9. 1-21 Eph. 4. 1-16	Exod. 32. 1-14 Luke 2. 41-end	
W		Deut. 9.23 - 10.5 Eph. 4. 17-end	Exod. 32. 15-34 Luke 3. 1-14	

		Sunday Principal Service Weekday Eucharist	Third Service Morning Prayer	Second Service Evening Prayer
14 Tuesday	**MATTHIAS THE APOSTLE** *(continued)*			
	or, if Matthias is celebrated on 24 February:			
W		Acts 11. 19–26 Ps. 87 John 10. 22–30	Ps. 139 *alt.* ***48***; 52 Deut. 9.23 - 10.5 Eph. 4. 17–end	Ps. 115; ***116*** *alt.* Ps. 50 Exod. 32. 15–34 Luke 3. 1–14
15 Wednesday				
W		Acts 12.24 - 13.5 Ps. 67 John 12. 44–end	Ps. 135 *alt.* Ps. 119. 57–80 Deut. 10. 12–end Eph. 5. 1–14	Ps. ***47***; 48 *alt.* Ps. ***59***; 60 (67) Exod. ch. 33 Luke 3. 15–22
16 Thursday	*Caroline Chisholm, Social Reformer, 1877*			
W		Acts 13. 13–25 Ps. 89. 1–2, 20–26 John 13. 16–20	Ps. 118 *alt.* 56; ***57***; (63†) Deut. 11. 8–end Eph. 5. 15–end	Ps. 81; ***85*** *alt.* Ps. 61; ***62***; 64 Exod. 34. 1–10, 27–end Luke 4. 1–13
17 Friday				
W		Acts 13. 26–33 Ps. 2 John 14. 1–6	Ps. 33 *alt.* Ps. ***51***; 54 Deut. 12. 1–14 Eph. 6. 1–9	Ps. ***36***; 40 *alt.* Ps. 38 Exod. 35.20 - 36.7 Luke 4. 14–30
18 Saturday				
W		Acts 13. 44–end Ps. 98. 1–5 John 14. 7–14	Ps. 34 *alt.* Ps. 68 Deut. 15. 1–18 Eph. 6. 10–end	Ps. ***84***; 86 *alt.* Ps. 65; ***66*** Exod. 40. 17–end Luke 4. 31–37 **ct**
19 Sunday	**THE FIFTH SUNDAY OF EASTER**			
W	*The reading from Acts must be used as either the first or second reading at the Principal Service.*	Acts 11. 1–18 [*or* Baruch 3.9–15, 32 - 4.4 *or* Gen. 22. 1–18] Ps. 148 (*or* 148. 1–6) Rev. 21. 1–6 John 13. 31–35	Ps. 16 2 Sam. 7. 4–13 Acts 2. 14a, 22–32 [33–36]	Ps. 98 Dan. 6. [1–5] 6–23 Mark 15.46 - 16.8
20 Monday	**Alcuin of York, Deacon, Abbot of Tours, 804**			
W	Com. Religious *or* *also* Col. 3. 12–16 John 4. 19–24	Acts 14. 5–18 Ps. 118. 1–3, 14–15 John 14. 21–26	Ps. 145 *alt.* Ps. 71 Deut. 16. 1–20 1 Pet. 1. 1–12	Ps. 105 *alt.* Ps. ***72***; 75 Num. 9. 15–end; 10. 33–end Luke 4. 38–end
21 Tuesday	*Helena, Protector of the Holy Places, 330*			
W		Acts 14. 19–end Ps. 145. 10–end John 14. 27–end	Ps. ***19***; 147. 1–12 *alt.* Ps. 73 Deut. 17. 8–end 1 Pet. 1. 13–end	Ps. 96; ***97*** *alt.* Ps. 74 Num. 11. 1–33 Luke 5. 1–11

	Calendar and Holy Communion	Morning Prayer	Evening Prayer	NOTES
W		Deut. 10. 12–end Eph. 5. 1–14	Exod. ch. 33 Luke 3. 15–22	
W		Deut. 11. 8–end Eph. 5. 15–end	Exod. 34. 1–10, 27–end Luke 4. 1–13	
W		Deut. 12. 1–14 Eph. 6. 1–9	Exod. 35.20 - 36.7 Luke 4. 14–30	
W		Deut. 15. 1–18 Eph. 6. 10–end	Exod. 40. 17–end Luke 4. 31–37 **ct**	
	THE FOURTH SUNDAY AFTER EASTER			
W	Job 19. 21–27a Ps. 66. 14–end James 1. 17–21 John 16. 5–15	Ps. 16 2 Sam. 7. 4–13 Acts 2. 14a, 22–32 [33–36]	Ps. 98 Dan. 6. [1–5] 6–23 Mark 15.46 - 16.8	
W		Deut. 16. 1–20 1 Pet. 1. 1–12	Num. 9. 15–end; 10. 33–end Luke 4. 38–end	
W		Deut. 17. 8–end 1 Pet. 1. 13–end	Num. 11. 1–33 Luke 5. 1–11	

		Sunday Principal Service Weekday Eucharist	Third Service Morning Prayer	Second Service Evening Prayer
22 Wednesday				
W		Acts 15. 1–6 Ps. 122. 1–5 John 15. 1–8	Ps. ***30***; 147. 13–end *alt.* Ps. 77 Deut. 18. 9–end 1 Pet. 2. 1–10	Ps. 98; ***99***; 100 *alt.* Ps. 119. 81–104 Num. ch. 12 Luke 5. 12–26
23 Thursday				
W		Acts 15. 7–21 Ps. 96. 1–3, 7–10 John 15. 9–11	Ps. ***57***; 148 *alt.* Ps. 78. 1–39† Deut. ch. 19 1 Pet. 2. 11–end	Ps. 104 *alt.* Ps. 78. 40–end† Num. 13. 1–3, 17–end Luke 5. 27–end
24 Friday	**John and Charles Wesley, Evangelists, Hymn Writers, 1791 and 1788**			
W	Com. Pastor *or* *also* Eph. 5. 15–20	Acts 15. 22–31 Ps. 57. 8–end John 15. 12–17	Ps. ***138***; 149 *alt.* Ps. 55 Deut. 21.22 - 22.8 1 Pet. 3. 1–12	Ps. 66 *alt.* Ps. 69 Num. 14. 1–25 Luke 6. 1–11
25 Saturday	**The Venerable Bede, Monk at Jarrow, Scholar, Historian, 735** *Aldhelm, Bishop of Sherborne, 709*			
W	Com. Religious *or* *also* Ecclus. 39. 1–10	Acts 16. 1–10 Ps. 100 John 15. 18–21	Ps. ***146***; 150 *alt.* Ps. ***76***; 79 Deut. 24. 5–end 1 Pet. 3. 13–end	Ps. 118 *alt.* Ps. 81; ***84*** Num. 14. 26–end Luke 6. 12–26 **ct**
26 Sunday	**THE SIXTH SUNDAY OF EASTER**			
W	*The reading from Acts must be used as either the first or second reading at the Principal Service.*	Acts 16. 9–15 [*or* Ezek. 37. 1–14] Ps. 67 Rev. 21.10, 22 - 22.5 John 14. 23–29 *or* John 5. 1–9	Ps. 40. 1–9 Gen. 1. 26–28 [29–end] Col. 3. 1–11	Ps. 126; 127 Zeph. 3. 14–end Matt. 28. 1–10, 16–end
27 Monday	Rogation Day*			
W		Acts 16. 11–15 Ps. 149. 1–5 John 15.26 - 16.4	Ps. ***65***; 67 *alt.* Ps. ***80***; 82 Deut. ch. 26 1 Pet. 4. 1–11	Ps. ***121***; 122; 123 *alt.* Ps. ***85***; 86 Num. 16. 1–35 Luke 6. 27–38
28 Tuesday	**Lanfranc, Prior of Le Bec, Archbishop of Canterbury, Scholar, 1089** Rogation Day*			
W		Acts 16. 22–34 Ps. 138 John 16. 5–11	Ps. 124; 125; ***126***; 127 *alt.* Ps. 87; ***89. 1–18*** Deut. 28. 1–14 1 Pet. 4. 12–end	Ps. ***128***; 129; 130; 131 *alt.* Ps. 89. 19–end Num. 16. 36–end Luke 6. 39–end
29 Wednesday	Rogation Day*			
W		Acts 17.15, 22 - 18.1 Ps. 148. 1–2, 11–end John 16. 12–15	Ps. ***132***; 133 *alt.* Ps. 119. 105–128 Deut. 28. 58–end 1 Pet. ch. 5	*First EP of Ascension Day* Ps. 15; 24 2 Sam. 23. 1–5 Col. 2.20 - 3.4 **𝔚 ct**

*For Rogation Day provision, see p. 11.

	Calendar and Holy Communion	Morning Prayer	Evening Prayer	NOTES
W		Deut. 18. 9–end 1 Pet. 2. 1–10	Num. ch. 12 Luke 5. 12–26	
W		Deut. ch. 19 1 Pet. 2. 11–end	Num. 13. 1–3, 17–end Luke 5. 27–end	
W		Deut. 21.22 – 22.8 1 Pet. 3. 1–12	Num. 14. 1–25 Luke 6. 1–11	
W		Deut. 24. 5–end 1 Pet. 3. 13–end	Num. 14. 26–end Luke 6. 12–26 **ct**	
	THE FIFTH SUNDAY AFTER EASTER Rogation Sunday			
W	Joel 2. 21–26 Ps. 66. 1–8 James 1. 22–end John 16. 23b–end	Ps. 40. 1–9 Gen. 1. 26–28 [29–end] John 5. 1–9	Ps. 126; 127 Zeph. 3. 14–end Matt. 28. 1–10, 16–end	
	The Venerable Bede, Monk at Jarrow, Scholar, Historian, 735 Rogation Day			
W	Com. Religious *or* Job 28. 1–11 Ps. 107. 1–9 James 5. 7–11 Luke 6. 36–42	Deut. ch. 26 1 Pet. 4. 1–11	Num. 16. 1–35 Luke 6. 27–38	
	Rogation Day			
W	Deut. 8. 1–10 Ps. 121 James 5. 16–end Luke 11. 5–13	Deut. 28. 1–14 1 Pet. 4. 12–end	Num. 16. 36–end Luke 6. 39–end	
	Rogation Day			
W	Deut. 34. 1–7 Ps. 108. 1–6 Eph. 4. 7–13 John 17. 1–11	Deut. 28. 58–end 1 Pet. ch. 5	*First EP of Ascension Day* Ps. 15; 24 2 Sam. 23. 1–5 Col. 2.20 – 3.4 **𝔚 ct**	

		Sunday Principal Service Weekday Eucharist	Third Service Morning Prayer	Second Service Evening Prayer
30 Thursday	**ASCENSION DAY**			
𝔚	*The reading from Acts must be used as either the first or second reading at the Eucharist.*	Acts 1. 1–11 *or* Dan. 7. 9–14 Ps. 47 *or* Ps. 93 Eph. 1. 15–end *or* Acts 1. 1–11 Luke 24. 44–end	*MP*: Ps. 110; 150 Isa. 52. 7–end Heb. 7. [11–25] 26–end	*EP*: Ps. 8 Song of the Three 29–37 *or* 2 Kings 2. 1–15 Rev. ch. 5 *Gospel*: Matt. 28. 16–end
31 Friday	**THE VISIT OF THE BLESSED VIRGIN MARY TO ELIZABETH***			
W		Zeph. 3. 14–18 Ps. 113 Rom. 12. 9–16 Luke 1. 39–49 [50–56]	*MP*: Ps. 85; 150 1 Sam. 2. 1–10 Mark 3. 31–end	*EP*: Ps. 122; 127; 128 Zech. 2. 10–end John 3. 25–30
	or, if The Visitation is celebrated on 2, 3 or 4 July:	Acts 18. 9–18 Ps. 47. 1–6 John 16. 20–23	Ps. 20; ***81*** *alt.* Ps. ***88***; (95) Deut. 29. 2–15 1 John 1.1 – 2.6 [Exod. 35.30 – 36.1 Gal. 5. 13–end]**	Ps. 145 *alt.* Ps. 102 Num. 20. 1–13 Luke 7. 11–17

June 2019

		Sunday Principal Service Weekday Eucharist	Third Service Morning Prayer	Second Service Evening Prayer
1 Saturday	**Justin, Martyr at Rome, c. 165**			
Wr	Com. Martyr *or* *esp.* John 15. 18–21 *also* 1 Macc. 2. 15–22 1 Cor. 1. 18–25	Acts 18. 22–end Ps. 47. 1–2, 7–end John 16. 23–28	Ps. 21; ***47*** *alt.* Ps. 96; **97**; 100 Deut. ch. 30 1 John 2. 7–17 [Num. 11. 16–17, 24–29 1 Cor. ch. 2]**	Ps. 84; ***85*** *alt.* Ps. 104 Num. 21. 4–9 Luke 7. 18–35 **ct**
2 Sunday	**THE SEVENTH SUNDAY OF EASTER**			
W	*The reading from Acts must be used as either the first or second reading at the Principal Service.*	Acts 16. 16–34 [*or* Ezek. 36. 24–28] Ps. 97 Rev. 22. 12–14, 16–17, 20–end John 17. 20–end	Ps. 99 Deut. ch. 34 Luke 24. 44–end *or* Acts 1. 1–8	Ps. 68 (*or* 68. 1–13, 18–19) Isa. 44. 1–8 Eph. 4. 7–16 *Gospel*: Luke 24. 44–end
3 Monday	*The Martyrs of Uganda, 1885–87 and 1977*			
W		Acts 19. 1–8 Ps. 68. 1–6 John 16. 29–end	Ps. ***93***; 96; 97 *alt.* Ps. ***98***; 99; 101 Deut. 31. 1–13 1 John 2. 18–end [Num. 27. 15–end 1 Cor. ch. 3]**	Ps. 18 *alt.* Ps. ***105***† (*or* 103) Num. 22. 1–35 Luke 7. 36–end
4 Tuesday	*Petroc, Abbot of Padstow, 6th century*			
G		Acts 20. 17–27 Ps. 68. 9–10, 18–19 John 17. 1–11	Ps. 98; ***99***; 100 *alt.* Ps. ***106***† (*or* 103) Deut. 31. 14–29 1 John 3. 1–10 [1 Sam. 10. 1–10 1 Cor. 12. 1–13]**	Ps. 68 *alt.* Ps. 107† Num. 22.36 – 23.12 Luke 8. 1–15

*The Visit of the Blessed Virgin Mary to Elizabeth may be celebrated on 2 July instead of 31 May.
**The alternative readings in square brackets may be used at one of the offices, in preparation for the Day of Pentecost.

	Calendar and Holy Communion	Morning Prayer	Evening Prayer
	ASCENSION DAY		
𝔚	Dan. 7. 13–14 Ps. 68. 1–6 Acts 1. 1–11 Mark 16. 14–end *or* Luke 24. 44–end	Ps. 110; 150 Isa. 52. 7–end Heb. 7. [11–25] 26–end	Ps. 8 Song of the Three 29–37 *or* 2 Kings 2. 1–15 Rev. ch. 5
W	Ascension CEG	Deut. 29. 2–15 1 John 1.1 - 2.6 [Exod. 35.30 - 36.1 Gal. 5. 13–end]**	Num. 20. 1–13 Luke 7. 11–17
	Nicomede, Priest and Martyr at Rome (date unknown)		
Wr	Com. Martyr *or* Ascension CEG	Deut. ch. 30 1 John 2. 7–17 [Num. 11. 16–17, 24–29 1 Cor. ch. 2]**	Num. 21. 4–9 Luke 7. 18–35 **ct**
	THE SUNDAY AFTER ASCENSION DAY		
W	2 Kings 2. 9–15 Ps. 68. 32–end 1 Pet. 4. 7–11 John 15.26 - 16.4a	Ps. 99 Deut. ch. 34 Luke 24. 44–end *or* Acts 1. 1–8	Ps. 68 (*or* 68. 1–13, 18–19) Isa. 44. 1–8 Eph. 4. 7–16
W		Deut. 31. 1–13 1 John 2. 18–end [Num. 27. 15–end 1 Cor. ch. 3]**	Num. 22. 1–35 Luke 7. 36–end
W		Deut. 31. 14–29 1 John 3. 1–10 [1 Sam. 10. 1–10 1 Cor. 12. 1–13]**	Num. 22.36 - 23.12 Luke 8. 1–15

NOTES

		Sunday Principal Service Weekday Eucharist	Third Service Morning Prayer	Second Service Evening Prayer
5 Wednesday	**Boniface (Wynfrith) of Crediton, Bishop, Apostle of Germany, Martyr, 754**			
Wr	Com. Martyr *or* *also* Acts 20. 24–28	Acts 20. 28–end Ps. 68. 27–28, 32–end John 17. 11–19	Ps. 2; ***29*** *alt.* Ps. 110; ***111***; 112 Deut. 31.30 – 32.14 1 John 3. 11–end [1 Kings 19. 1–18 Matt. 3. 13–end]*	Ps. 36; ***46*** *alt.* Ps. 119. 129–152 Num. 23. 13–end Luke 8. 16–25
6 Thursday	*Ini Kopuria, Founder of the Melanesian Brotherhood, 1945*			
W		Acts 22. 30; 23. 6–11 Ps. 16. 1, 5–end John 17. 20–end	Ps. ***24***; 72 *alt.* Ps. 113; ***115*** Deut. 32. 15–47 1 John 4. 1–6 [Ezek. 11. 14–20 Matt. 9.35 – 10.20]*	Ps. 139 *alt.* Ps. 114; ***116***; 117 Num. ch. 24 Luke 8. 26–39
7 Friday				
W		Acts 25. 13–21 Ps. 103. 1–2, 11–12, 19–20 John 21. 15–19	Ps. ***28***; 30 *alt.* Ps. 139 Deut. ch. 33 1 John 4. 7–end [Ezek. 36. 22–28 Matt. 12. 22–32]*	Ps. 147 *alt.* Ps. ***130***; 131; 137 Num. 27. 12–end Luke 8. 40–end
8 Saturday	**Thomas Ken, Bishop of Bath and Wells, Nonjuror, Hymn Writer, 1711**			
W	Com. Bishop *or* *esp.* 2 Cor. 4. 1–10 Matt. 24. 42–46	Acts 28. 16–20, 30–end Ps. 11. 4–end John 21. 20–end	Ps. 42; ***43*** *alt.* Ps. 120; ***121***; 122 Deut. 32. 48–end; ch. 34 1 John ch. 5 [Mic. 3. 1–8 Eph. 6. 10–20]*	*First EP of Pentecost* Ps. 48 Deut. 16. 9–15 John 7. 37–39 **R ct**
9 Sunday	**DAY OF PENTECOST (Whit Sunday)**			
R	*The reading from Acts must be used as either the first or second reading at the Principal Service.*	Acts 2. 1–21 *or* Gen. 11. 1–9 Ps. 104. 26–36, 37b (*or* 104. 26–end) Rom. 8. 14–17 *or* Acts 2. 1–21 John 14. 8–17 [25–27]	*MP*: Ps. 36. 5–10; 150 Isa. 40. 12–23 *or* Wisd. 9. 9–17 1 Cor. 2. 6–end	*EP*: Ps. 33. 1–12 Exod. 33. 7–20 2 Cor. 3. 4–end *Gospel*: John 16. 4b–15
10 Monday	Ordinary Time resumes today			
G **DEL 10**		2 Cor. 1. 1–7 Ps. 34. 1–8 Matt. 5. 1–12	Ps. 123; 124; 125; ***126*** 2 Chron. 17. 1–12 Rom. 1. 1–17	Ps. ***127***; 128; 129 Josh. ch. 1 Luke 9. 18–27 *or First EP of Barnabas* Ps. 1; 15 Isa. 42. 5–12 Acts 14. 8–end **R ct**
11 Tuesday	**BARNABAS THE APOSTLE**			
R		Job 29. 11–16 *or* Acts 11. 19–end Ps. 112 Acts 11. 19–end *or* Gal. 2. 1–10 John 15. 12–17	*MP*: Ps. 100; 101; 117 Jer. 9. 23–24 Acts 4. 32–end	*EP*: Ps. 147 Eccles. 12. 9–end *or* Tobit 4. 5–11 Acts 9. 26–31

*The alternative readings in square brackets may be used at one of the offices, in preparation for the Day of Pentecost.

	Calendar and Holy Communion	Morning Prayer	Evening Prayer	NOTES
	Boniface (Wynfrith) of Crediton, Bishop, Apostle of Germany, Martyr, 754			
Wr	Com. Martyr	Deut. 31.30 - 32.14 1 John 3. 11–end [1 Kings 19. 1–18 Matt. 3. 13–end]*	Num. 23. 13–end Luke 8. 16–25	
W		Deut. 32. 15–47 1 John 4. 1–6 [Ezek. 11. 14–20 Matt. 9.35 - 10.20]*	Num. ch. 24 Luke 8. 26–39	
W		Deut. ch. 33 1 John 4. 7–end [Ezek. 36. 22–28 Matt. 12. 22–32]*	Num. 27. 12–end Luke 8. 40–end	
W		Deut. 32. 48–end; ch. 34 1 John ch. 5 [Mic. 3. 1–8 Eph. 6. 10–20]*	*First EP of Whit Sunday* Ps. 48 Deut. 16. 9–15 John 7. 37–39 **R ct**	
	WHIT SUNDAY			
R	Deut. 16. 9–12 Ps. 122 Acts 2. 1–11 John 14. 15–31a	Ps. 36. 5–10; 150 Isa. 40. 12–23 *or* Wisd. 9. 9–17 1 Cor. 2. 6–end	Ps. 33. 1–12 Exod. 33. 7–20 2 Cor. 3. 4–end	
	Monday in Whitsun Week			
R	Acts 10. 34–end John 3. 16–21	Ezek. 11. 14–20 Acts 2. 12–36	Exod. 35.30 - 36.1 Acts 2. 37–end *or First EP of Barnabas* (Ps. 1; 15) Isa. 42. 5–12 Acts 14. 8–end **R ct**	
	BARNABAS THE APOSTLE			
R	Job 29. 11–16 Ps. 112 Acts 11. 22–end John 15. 12–16	(Ps. 100; 101; 117) Jer. 9. 23–24 Acts 4. 32–end	(Ps. 147) Eccles. 12. 9–end *or* Tobit 4. 5–11 Acts 9. 26–31	

		Sunday Principal Service Weekday Eucharist	Third Service Morning Prayer	Second Service Evening Prayer
12 Wednesday				
G		2 Cor. 3. 4–11 Ps. 78. 1–4 Matt. 5. 17-19	Ps. 119. 153–end 2 Chron. 18.28 – 19.end Rom. 2. 1–16	Ps. 136 Josh. ch. 3 Luke 9. 37–50
13 Thursday				
G		2 Cor. 3.15 – 4.1, 3–6 Ps. 78. 36–40 Matt. 5. 20–26	Ps. ***143***; 146 2 Chron. 20. 1–23 Rom. 2. 17–end	Ps. ***138***; 140; 141 Josh. 4.1 – 5.1 Luke 9. 51–end
14 Friday	*Richard Baxter, Puritan Divine, 1691*			
G		2 Cor. 4. 7–15 Ps. 99 Matt. 5. 27–32	Ps. ***142***; 144 2 Chron. 22.10 – 23.end Rom. 3. 1–20	Ps. 145 Josh. 5. 2–end Luke 10. 1–16
15 Saturday	*Evelyn Underhill, Spiritual Writer, 1941*			
G		2 Cor. 5. 14–end Ps. 103. 1–12 Matt. 5. 33–37	Ps. 147 2 Chron. 24. 1–22 Rom. 3. 21–end	*First EP of Trinity Sunday* Ps. 97; 98 Isa. 40. 12–end Mark 1. 1–13 **𝔚 ct**
16 Sunday	**TRINITY SUNDAY**			
𝔚		Prov. 8. 1–4, 22–31 Ps. 8 Rom. 5. 1–5 John 16. 12–15	*MP*: Ps. 29 Isa. 6. 1–8 Rev. ch. 4	*EP*: Ps. 73. 1–3, 16–end Exod. 3. 1–15 John 3. 1–17
17 Monday	*Samuel and Henrietta Barnett, Social Reformers, 1913 and 1936*			
G		2 Cor. 6. 1–10 Ps. 98 Matt. 5. 38–42	Ps. ***1***; 2; 3 2 Chron. 26. 1–21 Rom. 4. 1–12	Ps. ***4***; 7 Josh. 7. 1–15 Luke 10. 25–37
18 Tuesday	*Bernard Mizeki, Apostle of the MaShona, Martyr, 1896*			
G		2 Cor. 8. 1–9 Ps. 146 Matt. 5. 43–end	Ps. ***5***; 6; (8) 2 Chron. ch. 28 Rom. 4. 13–end	Ps. ***9***; 10† Josh. 7. 16–end Luke 10. 38–end
19 Wednesday	*Sundar Singh of India, Sadhu (holy man), Evangelist, Teacher, 1929*			
G		2 Cor. 9. 6–11 Ps. 112 Matt. 6. 1–6, 16–18	Ps. 119. 1–32 2 Chron. 29. 1–19 Rom. 5. 1–11	Ps. ***11***; 12; 13 Josh. 8. 1–29 Luke 11. 1–13 *or First EP of Corpus Christi* Ps. 110; 111 Exod. 16. 2–15 John 6. 22–35 **W ct**
20 Thursday	**DAY OF THANKSGIVING FOR HOLY COMMUNION (CORPUS CHRISTI)**			
W		Gen. 14. 18–20 Ps. 116. 10–end 1 Cor. 11. 23–26 John 6. 51–58	*MP*: Ps. 147 Deut. 8. 2–16 1 Cor. 10. 1–17	*EP*: Ps. 23; 42; 43 Prov. 9. 1–5 Luke 9. 11–17 *(continued overleaf)*

	Calendar and Holy Communion	Morning Prayer	Evening Prayer	NOTES
	Ember Day			
R	Ember CEG *or* Acts 2. 14–21 John 6. 44–51	2 Chron. 18.28 - 19.end Rom. 2. 1–16	Josh. ch. 3 Luke 9. 37–50	
R	Acts 2. 22–28 Luke 9. 1–6	2 Chron. 20. 1–23 Rom. 2. 17–end	Josh. 4.1 - 5.1 Luke 9. 51–end	
	Ember Day			
R	Ember CEG *or* Acts 8. 5–8 Luke 5. 17–26	2 Chron. 22.10 - 23.end Rom. 3. 1–20	Josh. 5. 2–end Luke 10. 1–16	
	Ember Day			
R	Ember CEG *or* Acts 13. 44–end Matt. 20. 29–end	2 Chron. 24. 1–22 Rom. 3. 21–end	*First EP of Trinity Sunday* Ps. 97; 98 Isa. 40. 12–end Mark 1. 1–13 **𝔚 ct**	
	TRINITY SUNDAY			
𝔚	Isa. 6. 1–8 Ps. 8 Rev. 4. 1–11 John 3. 1–15	Ps. 29 Prov. 8. 1–4, 22–31 Rom. 5. 1–5	Ps. 73. 1–3, 16–end Exod. 3. 1–15 Matt. 28. 16–end	
	Alban, first Martyr of Britain, *c.* 250			
Gr	Com. Martyr	2 Chron. 26. 1–21 Rom. 4. 1–12	Josh. 7. 1–15 Luke 10. 25–37	
G		2 Chron. ch. 28 Rom. 4. 13–end	Josh. 7. 16–end Luke 10. 38–end	
G		2 Chron. 29. 1–19 Rom. 5. 1–11	Josh. 8. 1–29 Luke 11. 1–13	
	Translation of Edward, King of the West Saxons, 979 To celebrate Corpus Christi, see *Common Worship* provision.			
Gr	Com. Martyr	2 Chron. 29. 20–end Rom. 5. 12–end	Josh. 8. 30–end Luke 11. 14–28	

		Sunday Principal Service Weekday Eucharist	Third Service Morning Prayer	Second Service Evening Prayer
20 Thursday	**DAY OF THANKSGIVING FOR HOLY COMMUNION (CORPUS CHRISTI)** *(continued)*			
	or the ferial readings for the day:			
G		2 Cor. 11. 1–11 Ps. 111 Matt. 6. 7–15	Ps. 14; ***15***; 16 2 Chron. 29. 20–end Rom. 5. 12–end	Ps. 18† Josh. 8. 30–end Luke 11. 14–28
21 Friday				
G		Cor. 11. 18, 21b–30 Ps. 34. 1–6 Matt. 6. 19–23	Ps. 17; ***19*** 2 Chron. ch. 30 Rom. 6. 1–14	Ps. 22 Josh. 9. 3–26 Luke 11. 29–36
22 Saturday	**Alban, first Martyr of Britain, c. 250**			
Gr	Com. Martyr *or* *esp.* 2 Tim. 2. 3–13 John 12. 24–26	2 Cor. 12. 1–10 Ps. 89. 20–33 Matt. 6. 24–end	Ps. 20; 21; ***23*** 2 Chron. 32. 1–22 Rom. 6. 15–end	Ps. ***24***; 25 Josh. 10. 1–15 Luke 11. 37–end **ct**
23 Sunday	**THE FIRST SUNDAY AFTER TRINITY (Proper 7)**			
G	*Track 1* 1 Kings 19. 1–4 [5–7] 8–15a Ps. 42; 43 (*or* Ps. 42 *or* 43) Gal. 3. 23–end Luke 8. 26–39	*Track 2* Isa. 65. 1–9 Ps. 22. 19–28 Gal. 3. 23–end Luke 8. 26–39	Ps. 55. 1–16, 18–21 Deut. 11. 1–15 Acts 27. 1–12	Ps. [50]; 57 Gen. 24. 1–27 Mark 5. 21–end *or First EP of The Birth of John the Baptist* Ps. 71 Judges 13. 2–7, 24–end Luke 1. 5–25 **W ct**
24 Monday	**THE BIRTH OF JOHN THE BAPTIST**			
W **DEL 12**		Isa. 40. 1–11 Ps. 85. 7–end Acts 13. 14b–26 *or* Gal. 3. 23–end Luke 1. 57–66, 80	*MP*: Ps. 50; 149 Ecclus. 48. 1–10 *or* Mal. 3. 1–6 Luke 3. 1–17	*EP*: Ps. 80; 82 Mal. ch. 4 Matt. 11. 2–19
25 Tuesday				
G		Gen. 13. 2, 5–end Ps. 15 Matt. 7. 6, 12–14	Ps. 32; ***36*** 2 Chron. 34. 1–18 Rom. 7. 7–end	Ps. 33 Josh. 21.43 - 22.8 Luke 12. 13–21
26 Wednesday	Ember Day*			
G *or* **R**		Gen. 15. 1–12, 17–18 Ps. 105. 1–9 Matt. 7. 15–20	Ps. 34 2 Chron. 34. 19–end Rom. 8. 1–11	Ps. 119. 33–56 Josh. 22. 9–end Luke 12. 22–31
27 Thursday	*Cyril, Bishop of Alexandria, Teacher, 444*			
G		Gen. 16. 1–12, 15–16 Ps. 106. 1–5 Matt. 7. 21–end	Ps. 37† 2 Chron. 35. 1–19 Rom. 8. 12–17	Ps. 39; ***40*** Josh. ch. 23 Luke 12. 32–40

*For Ember Day provision, see p. 11.

	Calendar and Holy Communion	Morning Prayer	Evening Prayer	NOTES
G		2 Chron. ch. 30 Rom. 6. 1–14	Josh. 9. 3–26 Luke 11. 29–36	
G		2 Chron. 32. 1–22 Rom. 6. 15–end	Josh. 10. 1–15 Luke 11. 37–end **ct**	
	THE FIRST SUNDAY AFTER TRINITY			
G	2 Sam. 9. 6–end Ps. 41. 1–4 1 John 4. 7–end Luke 16. 19–31	Ps. 52; 53 Deut. 11. 1–15 Acts 27. 1–12	Ps. [50]; 57 Gen. 24. 1–27 Mark 5. 21–end *or First EP of The Nativity of John the Baptist* Ps. 71 Judges 13. 2–7, 24–end Luke 1. 5–25 **W ct**	
	THE NATIVITY OF JOHN THE BAPTIST			
W	Isa. 40. 1–11 Ps. 80. 1–7 Acts 13. 22–26 Luke 1. 57–80	(Ps. 50; 149) Ecclus. 48. 1–10 *or* Mal. 3. 1–6 Luke 3. 1–17	(Ps. 82) Mal. ch. 4 Matt. 11. 2–19	
G		2 Chron. 34. 1–18 Rom. 7. 7–end	Josh. 21.43 – 22.8 Luke 12. 13–21	
G		2 Chron. 34. 19–end Rom. 8. 1–11	Josh. 22. 9–end Luke 12. 22–31	
G		2 Chron. 35. 1–19 Rom. 8. 12–17	Josh. ch. 23 Luke 12. 32–40	

		Sunday Principal Service Weekday Eucharist	Third Service Morning Prayer	Second Service Evening Prayer
28 Friday	**Irenaeus, Bishop of Lyons, Teacher, c. 200** Ember Day*			
Gw *or* **Rw**	Com. Teacher *or* *also* 2 Pet. 1. 16-end	Gen. 17. 1, 9-10, 15-22 Ps. 128 Matt. 8. 1-4	Ps. 31 2 Chron. 35.20 - 36.10 Rom. 8. 18-30	Ps. 35 Josh. 24. 1-28 Luke 12. 41-48 *or First EP of Peter and Paul* Ps. 66; 67 Ezek. 3. 4-11 Gal. 1.13 - 2.8 *or, for Peter alone*: Acts 9. 32-end **R ct**
29 Saturday	**PETER AND PAUL, APOSTLES** Ember Day*			
R		Zech. 4. 1-6a, 10b-end *or* Acts 12. 1-11 Ps. 125 Acts 12. 1-11 *or* 2 Tim. 4. 6-8, 17-18 Matt. 16. 13-19	*MP*: Ps. 71; 113 Isa. 49. 1-6 Acts 11. 1-18	*EP*: Ps. 124; 138 Ezek. 34. 11-16 John 21. 15-22
	or, if Peter is commemorated alone:			
R		Ezek. 3. 22-end *or* Acts 12. 1-11 Ps. 125 Acts 12. 1-11 *or* 1 Pet. 2. 19-end Matt. 16. 13-19	*MP*: Ps. 71; 113 Isa. 49. 1-6 Acts 11. 1-18	*EP*: Ps. 124; 138 Ezek. 34. 11-16 John 21. 15-22
30 Sunday	**THE SECOND SUNDAY AFTER TRINITY (Proper 8)**			
G	*Track 1* 2 Kings 2. 1-2, 6-14 Ps. 77. 1-2, 11-end (*or* 77. 11-end) Gal. 5. 1, 13-25 Luke 9. 51-end	*Track 2* 1 Kings 19. 15-16, 19-end Ps. 16 Gal. 5. 1, 13-25 Luke 9. 51-end	Ps. 64 Deut. 15. 1-11 Acts 27. [13-32] 33-end	Ps. [59. 1-6, 18-end]; 60 Gen. 27. 1-40 Mark 6. 1-6

July 2019

1 Monday	*Henry, John and Henry Venn the Younger, Priests, Evangelical Divines, 1797, 1813 and 1873*			
G **DEL 13**		Gen. 18. 16-end Ps. 103. 6-17 Matt. 8. 18-22	Ps. 44 Ezra ch. 1 Rom. 9. 1-18	Ps. ***47***; 49 Judg. ch. 2 Luke 13. 1-9
2 Tuesday				
G		Gen. 19. 15-29 Ps. 26 Matt. 8. 23-27	Ps. ***48***; 52 Ezra ch. 3 Rom. 9. 19-end	Ps. 50 Judg. 4. 1-23 Luke 13. 10-21 *or First EP of Thomas* Ps. 27 Isa. ch. 35 Heb. 10.35 - 11.1 **R ct**

*For Ember Day provision, see p. 11.
*******Common Worship* Morning and Evening Prayer provision for 31 May may be used.

	Calendar and Holy Communion	Morning Prayer	Evening Prayer	NOTES
G		2 Chron. 35.20 - 36.10 Rom. 8. 18–30	Josh. 24. 1–28 Luke 12. 41–48 *or First EP of Peter* (Ps. 66; 67) Ezek. 3. 4–11 Acts 9. 32–end	
			R ct	
	PETER THE APOSTLE			
R	Ezek. 3. 4–11 Ps. 125 Acts 12. 1–11 Matt. 16. 13–19	(Ps. 71; 113) Isa. 49. 1–6 Acts 11. 1–18	(Ps. 124; 138) Ezek. 34. 11–16 John 21. 15–22	
	THE SECOND SUNDAY AFTER TRINITY			
G	Gen. 12. 1–4 Ps. 120 1 John 3. 13–end Luke 14. 16–24	Ps. 64 Deut. 15. 1–11 Acts 27. [13–32] 33–end	Ps. [59. 1–6, 18–end]; 60 Gen. 27. 1–40 Mark 6. 1–6	
G		Ezra ch. 1 Rom. 9. 1–18	Judg. ch. 2 Luke 13. 1–9	
	The Visitation of the Blessed Virgin Mary**			
Gw	1 Sam. 2. 1–3 Ps. 113 Gal. 4. 1–5 Luke 1. 39–45	Ezra ch. 3 Rom. 9. 19–end	Judg. 4. 1–23 Luke 13. 10–21	

		Sunday Principal Service Weekday Eucharist	Third Service Morning Prayer	Second Service Evening Prayer
3 Wednesday	**THOMAS THE APOSTLE***			
R		Hab. 2. 1–4 Ps. 31. 1–6 Eph. 2. 19–end John 20. 24–29	*MP*: Ps. 92; 146 2 Sam. 15. 17–21 *or* Ecclus. ch. 2 John 11. 1–16	*EP*: Ps. 139 Job 42. 1–6 1 Pet. 1. 3–12
	or, if Thomas is not celebrated:			
G		Gen. 21. 5, 8–20 Ps. 34. 1–12 Matt. 8. 28–end	Ps. 119. 57–80 Ezra 4. 1–5 Rom. 10. 1–10	Ps. ***59***; 60; (67) Judg. ch. 5 Luke 13. 22–end
4 Thursday				
G		Gen. 22. 1–19 Ps. 116. 1–7 Matt. 9. 1–8	Ps. 56; ***57***; (63†) Ezra 4. 7–end Rom. 10. 11–end	Ps. 61; ***62***; 64 Judg. 6. 1–24 Luke 14. 1–11
5 Friday				
G		Gen. 23. 1–4, 19; 24. 1–8, 62–end Ps. 106. 1–5 Matt. 9. 9–13	Ps. ***51***; 54 Ezra ch. 5 Rom. 11. 1–12	Ps. 38 Judg. 6. 25–end Luke 14. 12–24
6 Saturday	*Thomas More, Scholar, and John Fisher, Bishop of Rochester, Reformation Martyrs, 1535*			
G		Gen. 27. 1–5a, 15–29 Ps. 135. 1–6 Matt. 9. 14–17	Ps. 68 Ezra ch. 6 Rom. 11. 13–24	Ps. 65; ***66*** Judg. ch. 7 Luke 14. 25–end **ct**
7 Sunday	**THE THIRD SUNDAY AFTER TRINITY (Proper 9)**			
G	*Track 1* 2 Kings 5. 1–14 Ps. 30 Gal. 6. [1–6] 7–16 Luke 10. 1–11, 16–20	*Track 2* Isa. 66. 10–14 Ps. 66. 1–8 Gal. 6. [1–6] 7–16 Luke 10. 1–11, 16–20	Ps. 74 Deut. 24. 10–end Acts 28. 1–16	Ps. 65; [70] Gen. 29. 1–20 Mark 6. 7–29
8 Monday				
G **DEL 14**		Gen. 28. 10–end Ps. 91. 1–10 Matt. 9. 18–26	Ps. 71 Ezra ch. 7 Rom. 11. 25–end	Ps. ***72***; 75 Judg. 8. 22–end Luke 15. 1–10
9 Tuesday				
G		Gen. 32. 22–end Ps. 17. 1–8 Matt. 9. 32–end	Ps. 73 Ezra 8. 15–end Rom. 12. 1–8	Ps. 74 Judg. 9. 1–21 Luke 15. 11–end
10 Wednesday				
G		Gen. 41. 55–end; 42. 5–7, 17–end Ps. 33. 1–4, 18–end Matt. 10. 1–7	Ps. 77 Ezra ch. 9 Rom. 12. 9–end	Ps. 119. 81–104 Judg. 9. 22–end Luke 16. 1–18
11 Thursday	**Benedict of Nursia, Abbot of Monte Cassino, Father of Western Monasticism, c. 550**			
Gw	Com. Religious *or* *also* 1 Cor. 3. 10–11 Luke 18. 18–22	Gen. 44. 18–21, 23–29; 45. 1–5 Ps. 105. 11–17 Matt. 10. 7–15	Ps. 78. 1–39† Ezra 10. 1–7 Rom. 13. 1–7	Ps. 78. 40–end† Judg. 11. 1–11 Luke 16. 19–end

*Thomas the Apostle may be celebrated on 21 December instead of 3 July.

	Calendar and Holy Communion	Morning Prayer	Evening Prayer
G		Ezra 4. 1–5 Rom. 10. 1–10	Judg. ch. 5 Luke 13. 22–end
	Translation of Martin, Bishop of Tours, c. 397		
Gw	Com. Bishop	Ezra 4. 7–end Rom. 10. 11–end	Judg. 6. 1–24 Luke 14. 1–11
G		Ezra ch. 5 Rom. 11. 1–12	Judg. 6. 25–end Luke 14. 12–24
G		Ezra ch. 6 Rom. 11. 13–24	Judg. ch. 7 Luke 14. 25–end **ct**
	THE THIRD SUNDAY AFTER TRINITY		
G	2 Chron. 33. 9–13 Ps. 55. 17–23 1 Pet. 5. 5b–11 Luke 15. 1–10	Ps. 73 Deut. 24. 10–end Acts 28. 1–16	Ps. 65; [70] Gen. 29. 1–20 Mark 6. 7–29
G		Ezra ch. 7 Rom. 11. 25–end	Judg. 8. 22–end Luke 15. 1–10
G		Ezra 8. 15–end Rom. 12. 1–8	Judg. 9. 1–21 Luke 15. 11–end
G		Ezra ch. 9 Rom. 12. 9–end	Judg. 9. 22–end Luke 16. 1–18
G		Ezra 10. 1–7 Rom. 13. 1–7	Judg. 11. 1–11 Luke 16. 19–end

NOTES

		Sunday Principal Service Weekday Eucharist	Third Service Morning Prayer	Second Service Evening Prayer
12 Friday				
G		Gen. 46. 1-7, 28-30 Ps. 37. 3-6, 27-28 Matt. 10. 16-23	Ps. 55 Neh. ch. 1 Rom. 13. 8-end	Ps. 69 Judg. 11. 29-end Luke 17. 1-10
13 Saturday				
G		Gen. 49. 29-end; 50. 15-25 Ps. 105. 1-7 Matt. 10. 24-33	Ps. ***76***; 79 Neh. ch. 2 Rom. 14. 1-12	Ps. 81; ***84*** Judg. 12. 1-7 Luke 17. 11-19 **ct**
14 Sunday	**THE FOURTH SUNDAY AFTER TRINITY (Proper 10)**			
G	*Track 1* Amos 7. 7-end Ps. 82 Col. 1. 1-14 Luke 10. 25-37	*Track 2* Deut. 30. 9-14 Ps. 25. 1-10 Col. 1. 1-14 Luke 10. 25-37	Ps. 76 Deut. 28. 1-14 Acts 28. 17-end	Ps. 77 (*or* 77. 1-12) Gen. 32. 9-30 Mark 7. 1-23
15 Monday	**Swithun, Bishop of Winchester, c. 862** *Bonaventure, Friar, Bishop, Teacher, 1274*			
Gw **DEL 15**	Com. Bishop *or* *also* James 5. 7-11, 13-18	Exod. 1. 8-14, 22 Ps. 124 Matt. 10.34 - 11.1	Ps. ***80***; 82 Neh. ch. 4 Rom. 14. 13-end	Ps. ***85***; 86 Judg. 13. 1-24 Luke 17. 20-end
16 Tuesday	*Osmund, Bishop of Salisbury, 1099*			
G		Exod. 2. 1-15 Ps. 69. 1-2, 31-end Matt. 11. 20-24	Ps. 87; ***89. 1-18*** Neh. ch. 5 Rom. 15. 1-13	Ps. 89. 19-end Judg. ch. 14 Luke 18. 1-14
17 Wednesday				
G		Exod. 3. 1-6, 9-12 Ps. 103. 1-7 Matt. 11. 25-27	Ps. 119. 105-128 Neh. 6.1 - 7.4 Rom. 15. 14-21	Ps. ***91***; 93 Judg. 15.1 - 16.3 Luke 18. 15-30
18 Thursday	*Elizabeth Ferard, first Deaconess of the Church of England, Founder of the Community of St Andrew, 1883*			
G		Exod. 3. 13-20 Ps. 105. 1, 5, 8-9, 24-27 Matt. 11. 28-end	Ps. 90; **92** Neh. 7.73b - 8.end Rom. 15. 22-end	Ps. 94 Judg. 16. 4-end Luke 18. 31-end
19 Friday	**Gregory, Bishop of Nyssa, and his sister Macrina, Deaconess, Teachers, c. 394 and c. 379**			
Gw	Com. Teacher *or* *esp.* 1 Cor. 2. 9-13 *also* Wisd. 9. 13-17	Exod. 11.10 - 12.14 Ps. 116. 10-end Matt. 12. 1-8	Ps. ***88***; (95) Neh. 9. 1-23 Rom. 16. 1-16	Ps. 102 Judg. ch. 17 Luke 19. 1-10
20 Saturday	*Margaret of Antioch, Martyr, 4th century; Bartolomé de las Casas, Apostle to the Indies, 1566*			
G		Exod. 12. 37-42 Ps. 136. 1-4, 10-15 Matt. 12. 14-21	Ps. 96; **97**; 100 Neh. 9. 24-end Rom. 16. 17-end	Ps. 104 Judg. 18. 1-20, 27-end Luke 19. 11-27 **ct**

	Calendar and Holy Communion	Morning Prayer	Evening Prayer
G		Neh. ch. 1 Rom. 13. 8–end	Judg. 11. 29–end Luke 17. 1–10
G		Neh. ch. 2 Rom. 14. 1–12	Judg. 12. 1–7 Luke 17. 11–19 **ct**
	THE FOURTH SUNDAY AFTER TRINITY		
G	Gen. 3. 17–19 Ps. 79. 8–10 Rom. 8. 18–23 Luke 6. 36–42	Ps. 76 Deut. 28. 1–14 Acts 28. 17–end	Ps. 77 (*or* 77. 1–12) Gen. 32. 9–30 Mark 7. 1–23
	Swithun, Bishop of Winchester, *c.* 862		
Gw	Com. Bishop	Neh. ch. 4 Rom. 14. 13–end	Judg. 13. 1–24 Luke 17. 20–end
G		Neh. ch. 5 Rom. 15. 1–13	Judg. ch. 14 Luke 18. 1–14
G		Neh. 6.1 – 7.4 Rom. 15. 14–21	Judg. 15.1 – 16.3 Luke 18. 15–30
G		Neh. 7.73b – 8.end Rom. 15. 22–end	Judg. 16. 4–end Luke 18. 31–end
G		Neh. 9. 1–23 Rom. 16. 1–16	Judg. ch. 17 Luke 19. 1–10
	Margaret of Antioch, Martyr, 4th century		
Gr	Com. Virgin Martyr	Neh. 9. 24–end Rom. 16. 17–end	Judg. 18. 1–20, 27–end Luke 19. 11–27 **ct**

NOTES

		Sunday Principal Service Weekday Eucharist	Third Service Morning Prayer	Second Service Evening Prayer
21 Sunday	**THE FIFTH SUNDAY AFTER TRINITY (Proper 11)**			
G	*Track 1* Amos 8. 1–12 Ps. 52 Col. 1. 15–28 Luke 10. 38–end	*Track 2* Gen. 18. 1–10a Ps. 15 Col. 1. 15–28 Luke 10. 38–end	Ps. 82; 100 Deut. 30. 1–10 1 Pet. 3. 8–18	Ps. 81 Gen. 41. 1–16, 25–37 1 Cor. 4. 8–13 *Gospel*: John 4. 31–35 *or First EP of Mary Magdalene* Ps. 139 Isa. 25. 1–9 2 Cor. 1. 3–7 **W ct**
22 Monday	**MARY MAGDALENE**			
W **DEL 16**		Song of Sol. 3. 1–4 Ps. 42. 1–10 2 Cor. 5. 14–17 John 20. 1–2, 11–18	*MP*: Ps. 30; 32; 150 1 Sam. 16. 14–end Luke 8. 1–3	*EP*: Ps. 63 Zeph. 3. 14–end Mark 15.40 - 16.7
23 Tuesday	*Bridget of Sweden, Abbess of Vadstena, 1373*			
G		Exod. 14.21 - 15.1 Ps. 105. 37–44 *or Canticle*: Exod. 15. 8–10, 12, 17 Matt. 12. 46–end	Ps. ***106***†; (*or* 103) Neh. 13. 1–14 2 Cor. 1.15 - 2.4	Ps. 107† 1 Sam. 1.21 - 2.11 Luke 19. 41–end
24 Wednesday				
G		Exod. 16. 1–5, 9–15 Ps. 78. 17–31 Matt. 13. 1–9	Ps. 110; ***111***; 112 Neh. 13. 15–end 2 Cor. 2. 5–end	Ps. 119. 129–152 1 Sam. 2. 12–26 Luke 20. 1–8 *or First EP of James* Ps. 144 Deut. 30. 11–end Mark 5. 21–end **R ct**
25 Thursday	**JAMES THE APOSTLE**			
R		Jer. 45. 1–5 *or* Acts 11.27 - 12.2 Ps. 126 Acts 11.27 - 12.2 *or* 2 Cor. 4. 7–15 Matt. 20. 20–28	*MP*: Ps. 7; 29; 117 2 Kings 1. 9–15 Luke 9. 46–56	*EP*: Ps. 94 Jer. 26. 1–15 Mark 1. 14–20
26 Friday	**Anne and Joachim, Parents of the Blessed Virgin Mary**			
Gw	Zeph. 3. 14–18a Ps. 127 Rom. 8. 28–30 Matt. 13. 16–17	*or* Exod. 20. 1–17 Ps. 19. 7–11 Matt. 13. 18–23	Ps. 139 Esther ch. 2 2 Cor. ch. 4	Ps. ***130***; 131; 137 1 Sam. 3.1 - 4.1a Luke 20. 20–26
27 Saturday	*Brooke Foss Westcott, Bishop of Durham, Teacher, 1901*			
G		Exod. 24. 3–8 Ps. 50. 1–6, 14–15 Matt. 13. 24–30	Ps. 120; ***121***; 122 Esther ch. 3 2 Cor. ch. 5	Ps. 118 1 Sam. 4. 1b–end Luke 20. 27–40 **ct**

	Calendar and Holy Communion	Morning Prayer	Evening Prayer	NOTES
	THE FIFTH SUNDAY AFTER TRINITY			
G	1 Kings 19. 19–21 Ps. 84. 8–end 1. Pet. 3. 8–15a Luke 5. 1–11	Ps. 82; 100 Deut. 30. 1–10 1 Pet. 3. 8–18	Ps. 81 Gen. 41. 1–16, 25–37 1 Cor. 4. 8–13 *or First EP of Mary Magdalene* Ps. 139 Isa. 25. 1–9 2 Cor. 1. 3–7 **W ct**	
	MARY MAGDALENE			
W	Zeph. 3. 14–end Ps. 30. 1–5 2 Cor. 5. 14–17 John 20. 11–18	(Ps. 30; 32; 150) 1 Sam. 16. 14–end Luke 8. 1–3	(Ps. 63) Song of Sol. 3. 1–4 Mark 15.40 - 16.7	
G		Neh. 13. 1–14 2 Cor. 1.15 - 2.4	1 Sam. 1.21 - 2.11 Luke 19. 41–end	
G		Neh. 13. 15–end 2 Cor. 2. 5–end	1 Sam. 2. 12–26 Luke 20. 1–8 *or First EP of James* (Ps. 144) Deut. 30. 11–end Mark 5. 21–end **R ct**	
	JAMES THE APOSTLE			
R	2 Kings 1. 9–15 Ps. 15 Acts 11.27 - 12.3a Matt. 20. 20–28	(Ps. 7; 29; 117) Jer. 45. 1–5 Luke 9. 46–56	(Ps. 94) Jer. 26. 1–15 Mark 1. 14–20	
	Anne, Mother of the Blessed Virgin Mary			
Gw	Com. Saint	Esther ch. 2 2 Cor. ch. 4	1 Sam. 3.1 - 4.1a Luke 20. 20–26	
G		Esther ch. 3 2 Cor. ch. 5	1 Sam. 4. 1b–end Luke 20. 27–40 **ct**	

		Sunday Principal Service Weekday Eucharist		Third Service Morning Prayer	Second Service Evening Prayer
28 Sunday	**THE SIXTH SUNDAY AFTER TRINITY (Proper 12)**				
	G	*Track 1* Hos. 1. 2-10 Ps. 85 (*or* 85. 1-7) Col. 2. 6-15 [16-19] Luke 11. 1-13	*Track 2* Gen. 18. 20-32 Ps. 138 Col. 2. 6-15 [16-19] Luke 11. 1-13	Ps. 95 Song of Sol. ch. 2 *or* 1 Macc. 2. [1-14] 15-22 1 Pet. 4. 7-14	Ps. 88 (*or* 88. 1-10) Gen. 42. 1-25 1 Cor. 10. 1-24 *Gospel*: Matt. 13. 24-30 [31-43]
29 Monday	**Mary, Martha and Lazarus, Companions of Our Lord**				
	Gw **DEL 17**	Isa. 25. 6-9 Ps. 49. 5-10, 16 Heb. 2. 10-15 John 12. 1-8 *or*	Exod. 32. 15-24, 30-34 Ps. 106. 19-23 Matt. 13. 31-35	Ps. 123; 124; 125; ***126*** Esther ch. 4 2 Cor. 6.1 - 7.1	Ps. ***127***; 128; 129 1 Sam. ch. 5 Luke 20.41 - 21.4
30 Tuesday	**William Wilberforce, Social Reformer, Olaudah Equiano and Thomas Clarkson, Anti-Slavery Campaigners, 1833, 1797 and 1846**				
	Gw	Com. Saint *or* *also* Job 31. 16-23 Gal. 3. 26-end; 4. 6-7 Luke 4. 16-21	Exod. 33. 7-11; 34. 5-9, 28 Ps. 103. 8-12 Matt. 13. 36-43	Ps. ***132***; 133 Esther ch. 5 2 Cor. 7. 2-end	Ps. (134); ***135*** 1 Sam. 6. 1-16 Luke 21. 5-19
31 Wednesday	*Ignatius of Loyola, Founder of the Society of Jesus, 1556*				
	G		Exod. 34. 29-end Ps. 99 Matt. 13. 44-46	Ps. 119. 153-end Esther 6. 1-13 2 Cor. 8. 1-15	Ps. 136 1 Sam. ch. 7 Luke 21. 20-28

August 2019

		Sunday Principal Service Weekday Eucharist		Third Service Morning Prayer	Second Service Evening Prayer
1 Thursday					
	G		Exod. 40. 16-21, 34-end Ps. 84. 1-6 Matt. 13. 47-53	Ps. ***143***; 146 Esther 6.14 - 7.end 2 Cor. 8.16 - 9.5	Ps. ***138***; 140; 141 1 Sam. ch. 8 Luke 21. 29-end
2 Friday					
	G		Lev. 23. 1, 4-11, 15-16, 27, 34-37 Ps. 81. 1-8 Matt. 13. 54-end	Ps. 142; ***144*** Esther ch. 8 2 Cor. 9. 6-end	Ps. 145 1 Sam. 9. 1-14 Luke 22. 1-13
3 Saturday					
	G		Lev. 25. 1, 8-17 Ps. 67 Matt. 14. 1-12	Ps. 147 Esther 9. 20-28 2 Cor. ch. 10	Ps. ***148***; 149; 150 1 Sam. 9.15 - 10.1 Luke 22. 14-23 **ct**
4 Sunday	**THE SEVENTH SUNDAY AFTER TRINITY (Proper 13)**				
	G	*Track 1* Hos. 11. 1-11 Ps. 107. 1-9, 43 (*or* 107. 1-9) Col. 3. 1-11 Luke 12. 13-21	*Track 2* Eccles. 1. 2, 12-14; 2. 18-23 Ps. 49. 1-12 (*or* 49. 1-9) Col. 3. 1-11 Luke 12. 13-21	Ps. 106. 1-10 Song of Sol. 5. 2-end *or* 1 Macc. 3. 1-12 2 Pet. 1. 1-15	Ps. 107. 1-32 (*or* 107. 1-16) Gen. 50. 4-end 1 Cor. 14. 1-19 *Gospel*: Mark 6. 45-52

	Calendar and Holy Communion	Morning Prayer	Evening Prayer	NOTES
	THE SIXTH SUNDAY AFTER TRINITY			
G	Gen. 4. 2b–15 Ps. 90. 12–end Rom. 6. 3–11 Matt. 5. 20–26	Ps. 96 Song of Sol. ch. 2 *or* 1 Macc. 2. [1–14] 15–22 1 Pet. 4. 7–14	Ps. 88 (*or* 88. 1–10) Gen. 42. 1–25 1 Cor. 9. 16–end	
G		Esther ch. 4 2 Cor. 6.1 - 7.1	1 Sam. ch. 5 Luke 20.41 - 21.4	
G		Esther ch. 5 2 Cor. 7. 2–end	1 Sam. 6. 1–16 Luke 21. 5–19	
G		Esther 6. 1–13 2 Cor. 8. 1–15	1 Sam. ch. 7 Luke 21. 20–28	
	Lammas Day			
G		Esther 6.14 - 7.end 2 Cor. 8.16 - 9.5	1 Sam. ch. 8 Luke 21. 29–end	
G		Esther ch. 8 2 Cor. 9. 6–end	1 Sam. 9. 1–14 Luke 22. 1–13	
G		Esther 9. 20–28 2 Cor. ch. 10	1 Sam. 9.15 - 10.1 Luke 22. 14–23 **ct**	
	THE SEVENTH SUNDAY AFTER TRINITY			
G	1 Kings. 17. 8–16 Ps. 34. 11–end Rom. 6. 19–end Mark 8. 1–10a	Ps. 106. 1–10 Song of Sol. 5. 2–end *or* 1 Macc. 3. 1–12 2 Pet. 1. 1–15	Ps. 107. 1–32 (*or* 107. 1–16) Gen. 50. 4–end 1 Cor. 14. 1–19	

		Sunday Principal Service Weekday Eucharist	Third Service Morning Prayer	Second Service Evening Prayer
5 Monday	**Oswald, King of Northumbria, Martyr, 642**			
Gr **DEL 18**	Com. Martyr *or* *esp.* 1 Pet. 4. 12–end John 16. 29–end	Num. 11. 4–15 Ps. 81. 11–end Matt. 14. 13–21 (*or* 14. 22–end)	Ps. ***1***; 2; 3 Jer. ch. 26 2 Cor. 11. 1–15	Ps. ***4***; 7 1 Sam. 10. 1–16 Luke 22. 24–30 *or First EP of The Transfiguration* Ps. 99; 110 Exod. 24. 12–end John 12. 27–36a **𝔚 ct**
6 Tuesday	**THE TRANSFIGURATION OF OUR LORD**			
𝔚		Dan. 7. 9–10, 13–14 Ps. 97 2 Pet. 1. 16–19 Luke 9. 28–36	*MP*: Ps. 27; 150 Ecclus. 48. 1–10 *or* 1 Kings 19. 1–16 1 John 3. 1–3	*EP*: Ps. 72 Exod. 34. 29–end 2 Cor. ch. 3
7 Wednesday	*John Mason Neale, Priest, Hymn Writer, 1866*			
G		Num. 13.1–2, 25 – 14.1, 26–35 Ps. 106. 14–24 Matt. 15. 21–28	Ps. 119. 1–32 Jer. 29. 1–14 2 Cor. ch. 12	Ps. ***11***; 12; 13 1 Sam. ch. 11 Luke 22. 39–46
8 Thursday	**Dominic, Priest, Founder of the Order of Preachers, 1221**			
Gw	Com. Religious *or* *also* Ecclus. 39. 1–10	Num. 20. 1–13 Ps. 95. 1, 8–end Matt. 16. 13–23	Ps. 14; ***15***; 16 Jer. 30. 1–11 2 Cor. ch. 13	Ps. 18† 1 Sam. ch. 12 Luke 22. 47–62
9 Friday	**Mary Sumner, Founder of the Mothers' Union, 1921**			
Gw	Com. Saint *or* *also* Heb. 13. 1–5	Deut. 4. 32–40 Ps. 77. 11–end Matt. 16. 24–end	Ps. 17; ***19*** Jer. 30. 12–22 James 1. 1–11	Ps. 22 1 Sam. 13. 5–18 Luke 22. 63–end
10 Saturday	**Laurence, Deacon at Rome, Martyr, 258**			
Gr	Com. Martyr *or* *also* 2 Cor. 9. 6–10	Deut. 6. 4–13 Ps. 18. 1–2, 48–end Matt. 17. 14–20	Ps. 20; 21; ***23*** Jer. 31. 1–22 James 1. 12–end	Ps. ***24***; 25 1 Sam. 13.19 – 14.15 Luke 23. 1–12 **ct**
11 Sunday	**THE EIGHTH SUNDAY AFTER TRINITY (Proper 14)**			
G	*Track 1* Isa. 1. 1, 10–20 Ps. 50. 1–8, 23–end (*or* 50. 1–7) Heb. 11. 1–3, 8–16 Luke 12. 32–40	*Track 2* Gen. 15. 1–6 Ps. 33. 12–end (*or* 33. 12–21) Heb. 11. 1–3, 8–16 Luke 12. 32–40	Ps. 115 Song of Sol. 8. 5–7 *or* 1 Macc. 14. 4–15 2 Pet. 3. 8–13	Ps. 108; [116] Isa. 11.10 – 12.end 2 Cor. 1. 1–22 *Gospel*: Mark 7. 24–30
12 Monday				
G **DEL 19**		Deut. 10. 12–end Ps. 147. 13–end Matt. 17. 22–end	Ps. 27; ***30*** Jer. 31. 23–25, 27–37 James 2. 1–13	Ps. 26; ***28***; 29 1 Sam. 14. 24–46 Luke 23. 13–25

	Calendar and Holy Communion	Morning Prayer	Evening Prayer	NOTES
G		Jer. ch. 26 2 Cor. 11. 1–15	1 Sam. 10. 1–16 Luke 22. 24–30 *or First EP of The Transfiguration* (Ps. 99; 110) Exod. 24. 12–end John 12. 27–36a **W ct**	
	THE TRANSFIGURATION OF OUR LORD			
W	Exod. 24. 12–end Ps. 84. 1–7 1 John 3. 1–3 Mark 9. 2–7	(Ps. 27; 150) Ecclus. 48. 1–10 *or* 1 Kings 19. 1–16 2 Pet. 1. 16–19	(Ps. 72) Exod. 34. 29–end 2 Cor. ch. 3	
	The Name of Jesus			
Gw	Jer. 14. 7–9 Ps. 8 Acts 4. 8–12 Matt. 1. 20–23	Jer. 29. 1–14 2 Cor. ch. 12	1 Sam. ch. 11 Luke 22. 39–46	
G		Jer. 30. 1–11 2 Cor. ch. 13	1 Sam. ch. 12 Luke 22. 47–62	
G		Jer. 30. 12–22 James 1. 1–11	1 Sam. 13. 5–18 Luke 22. 63–end	
	Laurence, Deacon at Rome, Martyr, 258			
Gr	Com. Martyr	Jer. 31. 1–22 James 1. 12–end	1 Sam. 13.19 - 14.15 Luke 23. 1–12 **ct**	
	THE EIGHTH SUNDAY AFTER TRINITY			
G	Jer. 23. 16–24 Ps. 31. 1–6 Rom. 8. 12–17 Matt. 7. 15–21	Ps. 115 Song of Sol. 8. 5–7 *or* 1 Macc. 14. 4–15 2 Pet. 3. 8–13	Ps. 108; [116] Isa. 11.10 - 12.end 2 Cor. 1. 1–22	
G		Jer. 31. 23–25, 27–37 James 2. 1–13	1 Sam. 14. 24–46 Luke 23. 13–25	

		Sunday Principal Service Weekday Eucharist	Third Service Morning Prayer	Second Service Evening Prayer
13 Tuesday	**Jeremy Taylor, Bishop of Down and Connor, Teacher, 1667** *Florence Nightingale, Nurse, Social Reformer, 1910; Octavia Hill, Social Reformer, 1912*			
Gw	Com. Teacher *or* *also* Titus 2. 7–8, 11–14	Deut. 31. 1–8 Ps. 107. 1–3, 42–end *or Canticle*: Deut. 32. 3–4, 7–9 Matt. 18. 1–5, 10, 12–14	Ps. 32; ***36*** Jer. 32. 1–15 James 2. 14–end	Ps. 33 1 Sam. 15. 1–23 Luke 23. 26–43
14 Wednesday	*Maximilian Kolbe, Friar, Martyr, 1941*			
G		Deut. ch. 34 Ps. 66. 14–end Matt. 18. 15–20	Ps. 34 Jer. 33. 1–13 James ch. 3	Ps. 119. 33–56 1 Sam. ch. 16 Luke 23. 44–56a *or First EP of The Blessed Virgin Mary* Ps. 72 Prov. 8. 22–31 John 19. 23–27 **W ct**
15 Thursday	**THE BLESSED VIRGIN MARY***			
W		Isa. 61. 10–end *or* Rev. 11.19 - 12.6, 10 Ps. 45. 10–end Gal. 4. 4–7 Luke 1. 46–55	*MP*: Ps. 98; 138; 147. 1–12 Isa. 7. 10–15 Luke 11. 27–28	*EP*: Ps. 132 Song of Sol. 2. 1–7 Acts 1. 6–14
	or, if The Blessed Virgin Mary is celebrated on 8 September:			
G		Josh. 3. 7–11, 13–17 Ps. 114 Matt. 18.21 - 19.1	Ps. 37† Jer. 33. 14–end James 4. 1–12	Ps. 39; ***40*** 1 Sam. 17. 1–30 Luke 23.56b - 24.12
16 Friday				
G		Josh. 24. 1–13 Ps. 136. 1–3, 16–22 Matt. 19. 3–12	Ps. 31 Jer. ch. 35 James 4.13 - 5.6	Ps. 35 1 Sam. 17. 31–54 Luke 24. 13–35
17 Saturday				
G		Josh. 24. 14–29 Ps. 16. 1, 5–end Matt. 19. 13–15	Ps. 41; ***42***; 43 Jer. 36. 1–18 James 5. 7–end	Ps. 45; ***46*** 1 Sam. 17.55 - 18.16 Luke 24. 36–end **ct**
18 Sunday	**THE NINTH SUNDAY AFTER TRINITY (PROPER 15)**			
G	*Track 1* Isa. 5. 1–7 Ps. 80. 1–2, 9–end (*or* 80. 9–end) Heb. 11.29 - 12.2 Luke 12. 49–56	*Track 2* Jer. 23. 23–29 Ps. 82 Heb. 11.29 - 12.2 Luke 12. 49–56	Ps. 119. 33–48 Jonah ch. 1 *or* Ecclus. 3. 1–15 2 Pet. 3. 14–end	Ps. 119. 17–32 (*or* 119. 17–24) Isa. 28. 9–22 2 Cor. 8. 1–9 *Gospel*: Matt. 20. 1–16
19 Monday				
G **DEL 20**		Judg. 2. 11–19 Ps. 106. 34–42 Matt. 19. 16–22	Ps. 44 Jer. 36. 19–end Mark 1. 1–13	Ps. ***47***; 49 1 Sam. 19. 1–18 Acts 1. 1–14

*The Blessed Virgin Mary may be celebrated on 8 September instead of 15 August.

	Calendar and Holy Communion	Morning Prayer	Evening Prayer	NOTES
G		Jer. 32. 1–15 James 2. 14–end	1 Sam. 15. 1–23 Luke 23. 26–43	
G		Jer. 33. 1–13 James ch. 3	1 Sam. ch. 16 Luke 23. 44–56a	
	To celebrate The Blessed Virgin Mary, see *Common Worship* provision.			
G		Jer. 33. 14–end James 4. 1–12	1 Sam. 17. 1–30 Luke 23.56b - 24.12	
G		Jer. ch. 35 James 4.13 - 5.6	1 Sam. 17. 31–54 Luke 24. 13–35	
G		Jer. 36. 1–18 James 5. 7–end	1 Sam. 17.55 - 18.16 Luke 24. 36–end **ct**	
	THE NINTH SUNDAY AFTER TRINITY			
G	Num. 10.35 - 11.3 Ps. 95 1 Cor. 10. 1–13 Luke 16. 1–9 *or* Luke 15. 11–end	Ps. 119. 33–48 Jonah ch. 1 *or* Ecclus. 3. 1–15 2 Pet. 3. 14–end	Ps. 119. 17–32 (*or* 119. 17–24) Isa. 28. 9–22 2 Cor. 8. 1–9	
G		Jer. 36. 19–end Mark 1. 1–13	1 Sam. 19. 1–18 Acts 1. 1–14	

		Sunday Principal Service Weekday Eucharist	Third Service Morning Prayer	Second Service Evening Prayer
20 Tuesday	**Bernard, Abbot of Clairvaux, Teacher, 1153** *William and Catherine Booth, Founders of the Salvation Army, 1912 and 1890*			
Gw	Com. Teacher *or* *esp.* Rev. 19. 5–9	Judg. 6. 11–24 Ps. 85. 8–end Matt. 19. 23–end	Ps. ***48***; 52 Jer. ch. 37 Mark 1. 14–20	Ps. 50 1 Sam. 20. 1–17 Acts 1. 15–end
21 Wednesday				
G		Judg. 9. 6–15 Ps. 21. 1–6 Matt. 20. 1–16	Ps. 119. 57–80 Jer. 38. 1–13 Mark 1. 21–28	Ps. ***59***; 60; (67) 1 Sam. 20. 18–end Acts 2. 1–21
22 Thursday				
G		Judg. 11. 29–end Ps. 40. 4–11 Matt. 22. 1–14	Ps. 56; ***57***; (63†) Jer. 38. 14–end Mark 1. 29–end	Ps. 61; ***62***; 64 1 Sam. 21.1 – 22.5 Acts 2. 22–36
23 Friday				
G		Ruth 1. 1, 3–6, 14–16, 22 Ps. 146 Matt. 22. 34–40	Ps. ***51***; 54 Jer. ch. 39 Mark 2. 1–12	Ps. 38 1 Sam. 22. 6–end Acts 2. 37–end *or First EP of Bartholomew* Ps. 97 Isa. 61. 1–9 2 Cor. 6. 1–10 **R ct**
24 Saturday	**BARTHOLOMEW THE APOSTLE**			
R		Isa. 43. 8–13 *or* Acts 5. 12–16 Ps. 145. 1–7 Acts 5. 12–16 *or* 1 Cor. 4. 9–15 Luke 22. 24–30	*MP*: Ps. 86; 117 Gen. 28. 10–17 John 1. 43–end	*EP*: Ps. 91; 116 Ecclus. 39. 1–10 *or* Deut. 18. 15–19 Matt. 10. 1–22
25 Sunday	**THE TENTH SUNDAY AFTER TRINITY (Proper 16)**			
G	*Track 1* Jer. 1. 4–10 Ps. 71. 1–6 Heb. 12. 18–end Luke 13. 10–17	*Track 2* Isa. 58. 9b–end Ps. 103. 1–8 Heb. 12. 18–end Luke 13. 10–17	Ps. 119. 73–88 Jonah ch. 2 *or* Ecclus. 3. 17–29 Rev. ch. 1	Ps. 119. 49–72 (*or* 119. 49–56) Isa. 30. 8–21 2 Cor. ch. 9 *Gospel*: Matt. 21. 28–32
26 Monday				
G **DEL 21**		1 Thess. 1. 1–5, 8–end Ps. 149. 1–5 Matt. 23. 13–22	Ps. 71 Jer. ch. 41 Mark 2.23 – 3.6	Ps. ***72***; 75 1 Sam. ch. 24 Acts 3. 11–end
27 Tuesday	**Monica, Mother of Augustine of Hippo, 387**			
Gw	Com. Saint *or* *also* Ecclus. 26. 1–3, 13–16	1 Thess. 2. 1–8 Ps. 139. 1–9 Matt. 23. 23–26	Ps. 73 Jer. ch. 42 Mark 3. 7–19a	Ps. 74 1 Sam. ch. 26 Acts 4. 1–12
28 Wednesday	**Augustine, Bishop of Hippo, Teacher, 430**			
Gw	Com. Teacher *or* *esp.* Ecclus. 39. 1–10 *also* Rom. 13. 11–13	1 Thess. 2. 9–13 Ps. 126 Matt. 23. 27–32	Ps. 77 Jer. ch. 43 Mark 3. 19b–end	Ps. 119. 81–104 1 Sam. 28. 3–end Acts 4. 13–31

	Calendar and Holy Communion	Morning Prayer	Evening Prayer	NOTES
G		Jer. ch. 37 Mark 1. 14–20	1 Sam. 20. 1–17 Acts 1. 15–end	
G		Jer. 38. 1–13 Mark 1. 21–28	1 Sam. 20. 18–end Acts 2. 1–21	
G		Jer. 38. 14–end Mark 1. 29–end	1 Sam. 21.1 - 22.5 Acts 2. 22–36	
G		Jer. ch. 39 Mark 2. 1–12	1 Sam. 22. 6–end Acts 2. 37–end *or First EP of Bartholomew* (Ps. 97) Isa. 61. 1–9 2 Cor. 6. 1–10 **R ct**	
	BARTHOLOMEW THE APOSTLE			
R	Gen. 28. 10–17 Ps. 15 Acts 5. 12–16 Luke 22. 24–30	(Ps. 86; 117) Isa. 43. 8–13 John 1. 43–end	(Ps. 91; 116) Ecclus. 39. 1–10 *or* Deut. 18. 15–19 Matt. 10. 1–22	
	THE TENTH SUNDAY AFTER TRINITY			
G	Jer. 7. 9–15 Ps. 17. 1–8 1 Cor. 12. 1–11 Luke 19. 41–47a	Ps. 119. 73–88 Jonah ch. 2 *or* Ecclus. 3. 17–29 Rev. ch. 1	Ps. 119. 49–72 (*or* 119. 49–56) Isa. 30. 8–21 2 Cor. ch. 9	
G		Jer. ch. 41 Mark 2.23 - 3.6	1 Sam. ch. 24 Acts 3. 11–end	
G		Jer. ch. 42 Mark 3. 7–19a	1 Sam. ch. 26 Acts 4. 1–12	
	Augustine, Bishop of Hippo, Teacher, 430			
Gw	Com. Doctor	Jer. ch. 43 Mark 3. 19b–end	1 Sam. 28. 3–end Acts 4. 13–31	

			Sunday Principal Service Weekday Eucharist	Third Service Morning Prayer	Second Service Evening Prayer
29 Thursday		**The Beheading of John the Baptist**			
	Gr	Jer. 1. 4–10 *or* Ps. 11 Heb. 11.32 - 12.2 Matt. 14. 1-12	1 Thess. 3. 7–end Ps. 90. 13–end Matt. 24. 42–end	Ps. 78. 1–39† Jer. 44. 1–14 Mark 4. 1–20	Ps. 78. 40–end† 1 Sam. ch. 31 Acts 4.32 - 5.11
30 Friday		**John Bunyan, Spiritual Writer, 1688**			
	Gw	Com. Teacher *or* *also* Heb. 12. 1–2 Luke 21. 21, 34–36	1 Thess. 4. 1–8 Ps. 97 Matt. 25. 1–13	Ps. 55 Jer. 44. 15–end Mark 4. 21–34	Ps. 69 2 Sam. ch. 1 Acts 5. 12–26
31 Saturday		**Aidan, Bishop of Lindisfarne, Missionary, 651**			
	Gw	Com. Missionary *or* *also* 1 Cor. 9. 16–19	1 Thess. 4. 9–12 Ps. 98. 1–2, 8–end Matt. 25. 14–30	Ps. ***76***; 79 Jer. ch. 45 Mark 4. 35–end	Ps. 81; ***84*** 2 Sam. 2. 1–11 Acts 5. 27–end **ct**

September 2019

			Sunday Principal Service Weekday Eucharist	Third Service Morning Prayer	Second Service Evening Prayer
1 Sunday		**THE ELEVENTH SUNDAY AFTER TRINITY (Proper 17)**			
	G	*Track 1* Jer. 2. 4–13 Ps. 81. 1, 10–end (*or* 81. 1–11) Heb. 13. 1–8, 15–16 Luke 14. 1, 7–14	*Track 2* Ecclus. 10. 12–18 *or* Prov. 25. 6–7 Ps. 112 Heb. 13. 1–8, 15–16 Luke 14. 1, 7–14	Ps. 119. 161–end Jonah 3. 1–9 *or* Ecclus. 11. [7–17] 18–28 Rev. 3. 14–22	Ps. 119. 81–96 (*or* 119. 81–88) Isa. 33. 13–22 John 3. 22–36
2 Monday		*The Martyrs of Papua New Guinea, 1901 and 1942*			
	G **DEL 22**		1 Thess. 4. 13–end Ps. 96 Luke 4. 16–30	Ps. ***80***; 82 Mic. 1. 1–9 Mark 5. 1–20	Ps. ***85***; 86 2 Sam. 3. 12–end Acts ch. 6
3 Tuesday		**Gregory the Great, Bishop of Rome, Teacher, 604**			
	Gw	Com. Teacher *or* *also* 1 Thess. 2. 3–8	1 Thess. 5. 1–6, 9–11 Ps. 27. 1–8 Luke 4. 31–37	Ps. 87; ***89. 1–18*** Mic. ch. 2 Mark 5. 21–34	Ps. 89. 19–end 2 Sam. 5. 1–12 Acts 7. 1–16
4 Wednesday		*Birinus, Bishop of Dorchester (Oxon), Apostle of Wessex, 650**			
	G		Col. 1. 1–8 Ps. 34. 11–18 Luke 4. 38–end	Ps. 119. 105–128 Mic. ch. 3 Mark 5. 35–end	Ps. ***91***; 93 2 Sam. 6. 1–19 Acts 7. 17–43
5 Thursday					
	G		Col. 1. 9–14 Ps. 98. 1–5 Luke 5. 1–11	Ps. 90; **92** Mic. 4.1 - 5.1 Mark 6. 1–13	Ps. 94 2 Sam. 7. 1–17 Acts 7. 44–53
6 Friday		*Allen Gardiner, Founder of the South American Mission Society, 1851*			
	G		Col. 1. 15–20 Ps. 89. 19b–28 Luke 5. 33–end	Ps. ***88***; (95) Mic. 5. 2–end Mark 6. 14–29	Ps. 102 2 Sam. 7. 18–end Acts 7.54 - 8.3

*Cuthbert may be celebrated on 4 September instead of 20 March.

	Calendar and Holy Communion	Morning Prayer	Evening Prayer
	The Beheading of John the Baptist		
Gr	2 Chron. 24. 17–21 Ps. 92. 11–end Heb. 11.32 - 12.2 Matt. 14. 1–12	Jer. 44. 1–14 Mark 4. 1–20	1 Sam. ch. 31 Acts 4.32 - 5.11
G		Jer. 44. 15–end Mark 4. 21–34	2 Sam. ch. 1 Acts 5. 12–26
G		Jer. ch. 45 Mark 4. 35–end	2 Sam. 2. 1–11 Acts 5. 27–end **ct**
	THE ELEVENTH SUNDAY AFTER TRINITY		
G	1 Kings 3. 5–15 Ps. 28 1 Cor. 15. 1–11 Luke 18. 9–14	Ps. 119. 161–end Jonah 3. 1–9 *or* Ecclus. 11. [7–17] 18–28 Rev. 3. 14–22	Ps. 119. 81–96 (*or* 119. 81–88) Isa. 33. 13–22 John 3. 22–36
G		Mic. 1. 1–9 Mark 5. 1–20	2 Sam. 3. 12–end Acts ch. 6
G		Mic. ch. 2 Mark 5. 21–34	2 Sam. 5. 1–12 Acts 7. 1–16
G		Mic. ch. 3 Mark 5. 35–end	2 Sam. 6. 1–19 Acts 7. 17–43
G		Mic. 4.1 - 5.1 Mark 6. 1–13	2 Sam. 7. 1–17 Acts 7. 44–53
G		Mic. 5. 2–end Mark 6. 14–29	2 Sam. 7. 18–end Acts 7.54 - 8.3

NOTES

		Sunday Principal Service Weekday Eucharist	Third Service Morning Prayer	Second Service Evening Prayer
7 Saturday				
G		Col. 1. 21–23 Ps. 117 Luke 6. 1–5	Ps. 96; ***97***; 100 Mic. ch. 6 Mark 6. 30–44	Ps. 104 2 Sam. ch. 9 Acts 8. 4–25 **ct**
8 Sunday	**THE TWELFTH SUNDAY AFTER TRINITY (Proper 18)***			
G	*Track 1* Jer. 18. 1–11 Ps. 139. 1–5, 12–18 (*or* 139. 1–7) Philemon 1–21 Luke 14. 25–33	*Track 2* Deut. 30. 15–end Ps. 1 Philemon 1–21 Luke 14. 25–33	Ps. 122; 123 Jonah 3.10 – 4.end *or* Ecclus. 27.30 – 28.9 Rev. 8. 1–5	Ps. [120]; 121 Isa. 43.14 – 44.5 John 5. 30–end
9 Monday	*Charles Fuge Lowder, Priest, 1880*			
G **DEL 23**		Col. 1.24 – 2.3 Ps. 62. 1–7 Luke 6. 6–11	Ps. ***98***; 99; 101 Mic. 7. 1–7 Mark 6. 45–end	Ps. ***105***† (*or* 103) 2 Sam. ch. 11 Acts 8. 26–end
10 Tuesday				
G		Col. 2. 6–15 Ps. 8 Luke 6. 12–19	Ps. ***106***† (*or* 103) Mic. 7. 8–end Mark 7. 1–13	Ps. 107† 2 Sam. 12. 1–25 Acts 9. 1–19a
11 Wednesday				
G		Col. 3. 1–11 Ps. 15 Luke 6. 20–26	Ps. 110; ***111***; 112 Hab. 1. 1–11 Mark 7. 14–23	Ps. 119. 129–152 2 Sam. 15. 1–12 Acts 9. 19b–31
12 Thursday				
G		Col. 3. 12–17 Ps. 149. 1–5 Luke 6. 27–38	Ps. 113; ***115*** Hab. 1.12 – 2.5 Mark 7. 24–30	Ps. 114; ***116***; 117 2 Sam. 15. 13–end Acts 9. 32–end
13 Friday	**John Chrysostom, Bishop of Constantinople, Teacher, 407**			
Gw	Com. Teacher *or* *esp.* Matt. 5. 13–19 *also* Jer. 1. 4–10	1 Tim. 1. 1–2, 12–14 Ps. 16 Luke 6. 39–42	Ps. 139 Hab. 2. 6–end Mark 7. 31–end	Ps. ***130***; 131; 137 2 Sam. 16. 1–14 Acts 10. 1–16 *or First EP of Holy Cross Day* Ps. 66 Isa. 52.13 – 53.end Eph. 2. 11–end **R ct**
14 Saturday	**HOLY CROSS DAY**			
R		Num. 21. 4–9 Ps. 22. 23–28 Phil. 2. 6–11 John 3. 13–17	*MP*: Ps. 2; 8; 146 Gen. 3. 1–15 John 12. 27–36a	*EP*: Ps. 110; 150 Isa. 63. 1–16 1 Cor. 1. 18–25

*The Blessed Virgin Mary may be celebrated on 8 September instead of 15 August.

	Calendar and Holy Communion	Morning Prayer	Evening Prayer
	Evurtius, Bishop of Orleans, 4th century		
Gw	Com. Bishop	Mic. ch. 6 Mark 6. 30–44	2 Sam. ch. 9 Acts 8. 4–25 **ct**
	THE TWELFTH SUNDAY AFTER TRINITY		
G	Exod. 34. 29–end Ps. 34. 1–10 2 Cor. 3. 4–9 Mark 7. 31–37	Ps. 123; 133 Jonah 3.10 - 4.end *or* Ecclus. 27.30 - 28.9 Rev. 8. 1–5	Ps. [120]; 121 Isa. 43.14 - 44.5 John 5. 30–end
G		Mic. 7. 1–7 Mark 6. 45–end	2 Sam. ch. 11 Acts 8. 26–end
G		Mic. 7. 8–end Mark 7. 1–13	2 Sam. 12. 1–25 Acts 9. 1–19a
G		Hab. 1. 1–11 Mark 7. 14–23	2 Sam. 15. 1–12 Acts 9. 19b–31
G		Hab. 1.12 - 2.5 Mark 7. 24–30	2 Sam. 15. 13–end Acts 9. 32–end
G		Hab. 2. 6–end Mark 7. 31–end	2 Sam. 16. 1–14 Acts 10. 1–16
	Holy Cross Day To celebrate Holy Cross as a festival, see *Common Worship* provision.		
Gr	Num. 21. 4–9 Ps. 67 1 Cor. 1. 17–25 John 12. 27–33	Hab. 3. 2–19a Mark 8. 1–10	2 Sam. 17. 1–23 Acts 10. 17–33 **ct**

NOTES

		Sunday Principal Service Weekday Eucharist	Third Service Morning Prayer	Second Service Evening Prayer
15 Sunday	**THE THIRTEENTH SUNDAY AFTER TRINITY (Proper 19)**			
G	*Track 1* Jer. 4. 11–12, 22–28 Ps. 14 1 Tim. 1. 12–17 Luke 15. 1–10	*Track 2* Exod. 32. 7–14 Ps. 51. 1–11 1 Tim. 1. 12–17 Luke 15. 1–10	Ps. 126; 127 Isa. 44.24 - 45.8 Rev. 12. 1–12	Ps. 124; 125 Isa. ch. 60 John 6. 51–69
16 Monday	**Ninian, Bishop of Galloway, Apostle of the Picts, c. 432** *Edward Bouverie Pusey, Priest, Tractarian, 1882*			
Gw **DEL 24**	Com. Missionary *or* *esp.* Acts 13. 46–49 Mark 16. 15–end	1 Tim. 2. 1–8 Ps. 28 Luke 7. 1–10	Ps. 123; 124; 125; ***126*** Hag. 1. 1–11 Mark 8. 11–21	Ps. ***127***; 128; 129 2 Sam. 18. 1–18 Acts 10. 34–end
17 Tuesday	**Hildegard, Abbess of Bingen, Visionary, 1179**			
Gw	Com. Religious *or* *also* 1 Cor. 2. 9–13 Luke 10. 21–24	1 Tim. 3. 1–13 Ps. 101 Luke 7. 11–17	Ps. ***132***; 133 Hag. 1.12 - 2.9 Mark 8. 22–26	Ps. (134); ***135*** 2 Sam. 18.19 - 19.8a Acts 11. 1–18
18 Wednesday				
G		1 Tim. 3. 14–end Ps. 111. 1–5 Luke 7. 31–35	Ps. 119. 153–end Hag. 2. 10–end Mark 8.27 - 9.1	Ps. 136 2 Sam. 19. 8b–23 Acts 11. 19–end
19 Thursday	*Theodore of Tarsus, Archbishop of Canterbury, 690*			
G		1 Tim. 4. 12–end Ps. 111. 6–end Luke 7. 36–end	Ps. ***143***; 146 Zech. 1. 1–17 Mark 9. 2–13	Ps. ***138***; 140; 141 2 Sam. 19. 24–end Acts 12. 1–17
20 Friday	**John Coleridge Patteson, first Bishop of Melanesia, and his Companions, Martyrs, 1871**			
Gr	Com. Martyr *or* *esp.* 2 Chron. 24. 17–21 *also* Acts 7. 55–end	1 Tim. 6. 2b–12 Ps. 49. 1–9 Luke 8. 1–3	Ps. 142; ***144*** Zech. 1.18 - 2.end Mark 9. 14–29	Ps. 145 2 Sam. 23. 1–7 Acts 12. 18–end *or First EP of Matthew* Ps. 34 Isa. 33. 13–17 Matt. 6. 19–end **R ct**
21 Saturday	**MATTHEW, APOSTLE AND EVANGELIST**			
R		Prov. 3. 13–18 Ps. 119. 65–72 2 Cor. 4. 1–6 Matt. 9. 9–13	*MP*: Ps. 49; 117 1 Kings 19. 15–end 2 Tim. 3. 14–end	*EP*: Ps. 119. 33–40, 89–96 Eccles. 5. 4–12 Matt. 19. 16–end
22 Sunday	**THE FOURTEENTH SUNDAY AFTER TRINITY (Proper 20)**			
G	*Track 1* Jer. 8.18 - 9.1 Ps. 79. 1–9 1 Tim. 2. 1–7 Luke 16. 1–13	*Track 2* Amos 8. 4–7 Ps. 113 1 Tim. 2. 1–7 Luke 16. 1–13	Ps. 130; 131 Isa. 45. 9–22 Rev. 14. 1–5	Ps. [128]; 129 Ezra ch. 1 John 7. 14–36
23 Monday				
G **DEL 25**		Ezra 1. 1–6 Ps. 126 Luke 8. 16–18	Ps. **1**; 2; 3 Zech. ch. 4 Mark 9. 38–end	Ps. **4**; 7 1 Kings 1. 5–31 Acts 13. 13–43

	Calendar and Holy Communion	Morning Prayer	Evening Prayer	NOTES
	THE THIRTEENTH SUNDAY AFTER TRINITY			
G	Lev. 19. 13–18 Ps. 74. 20–end Gal. 3. 16–22 *or* Heb. 13. 1–6 Luke 10. 23b–37	Ps. 126; 127 Isa. 44.24 – 45.8 Rev. 12. 1–12	Ps. 124; 125 Isa. ch. 60 John 6. 51–69	
G		Hag. 1. 1–11 Mark 8. 11–21	2 Sam. 18. 1–18 Acts 10. 34–end	
	Lambert, Bishop of Maastricht, Martyr, 709			
Gr	Com. Martyr	Hag. 1.12 – 2.9 Mark 8. 22–26	2 Sam. 18.19 – 19.8a Acts 11. 1–18	
	Ember Day			
G	Ember CEG	Hag. 2. 10–end Mark 8.27 – 9.1	2 Sam. 19. 8b–23 Acts 11. 19–end	
G		Zech. 1. 1–17 Mark 9. 2–13	2 Sam. 19. 24–end Acts 12. 1–17	
	Ember Day			
G	Ember CEG	Zech. 1.18 – 2.end Mark 9. 14–29	2 Sam. 23. 1–7 Acts 12. 18–end *or First EP of Matthew* (Ps. 34) Prov. 3. 3–18 Matt. 6. 19–end **R ct**	
	MATTHEW, APOSTLE AND EVANGELIST Ember Day			
R	Isa. 33. 13–17 Ps. 119. 65–72 2 Cor. 4. 1–6 Matt. 9. 9–13	(Ps. 49; 117) 1 Kings 19. 15–end 2 Tim. 3. 14–end	(Ps. 119. 33–40, 89–96) Eccles. 5. 4–12 Matt. 19. 16–end	
	THE FOURTEENTH SUNDAY AFTER TRINITY			
G	2 Kings 5. 9–16 Ps. 118. 1–9 Gal. 5. 16–24 Luke 17. 11–19	Ps. 130; 131 Isa. 45. 9–22 Rev. 14. 1–5	Ps. [128]; 129 Ezra ch. 1 John 7. 14–36	
G		Zech. ch. 4 Mark 9. 38–end	1 Kings 1. 5–31 Acts 13. 13–43	

		Sunday Principal Service Weekday Eucharist	Third Service Morning Prayer	Second Service Evening Prayer
24 Tuesday				
G		Ezra 6. 7–8, 12, 14–20 Ps. 124 Luke 8. 19–21	Ps. ***5***; 6; (8) Zech. 6. 9–end Mark 10. 1–16	Ps. ***9***; 10† 1 Kings 1.32 - 2.4, 10–12 Acts 13.44 - 14.7
25 Wednesday	**Lancelot Andrewes, Bishop of Winchester, Spiritual Writer, 1626** *Sergei of Radonezh, Russian Monastic Reformer, Teacher, 1392* Ember Day*			
Gw *or* **Rw**	Com. Bishop *or* *esp.* Isa. 6. 1–8	Ezra 9. 5–9 *Canticle*: Song of Tobit *or* Ps. 103. 1–6 Luke 9. 1–6	Ps. 119. 1–32 Zech. ch. 7 Mark 10. 17–31	Ps. ***11***; 12; 13 1 Kings ch. 3 Acts 14. 8–end
26 Thursday	*Wilson Carlile, Founder of the Church Army, 1942*			
G		Hag. 1. 1–8 Ps. 149. 1–5 Luke 9. 7–9	Ps. 14; ***15***; 16 Zech. 8. 1–8 Mark 10. 32–34	Ps. 18† 1 Kings 4.29 - 5.12 Acts 15. 1–21
27 Friday	**Vincent de Paul, Founder of the Congregation of the Mission (Lazarists), 1660** Ember Day*			
Gw *or* **Rw**	Com. Religious *or* *also* 1 Cor. 1. 25–end Matt. 25. 34–40	Hag. 1.15b - 2.9 Ps. 43 Luke 9. 18–22	Ps. 17; ***19*** Zech. 8. 9–end Mark 10. 35–45	Ps. 22 1 Kings 6. 1, 11–28 Acts 15. 22–35
28 Saturday	Ember Day*			
G *or* **R**		Zech. 2. 1–5, 10–11 Ps. 125 *or Canticle*: Jer. 31. 10–13 Luke 9. 43b–45	Ps. 20; 21; ***23*** Zech. 9. 1–12 Mark 10. 46–end	Ps. ***24***; 25 1 Kings 8. 1–30 Acts 15.36 - 16.5 **ct** *or First EP of Michael and All Angels* Ps. 91 2 Kings 6. 8–17 Matt. 18. 1–6, 10 **W ct**
29 Sunday	**MICHAEL AND ALL ANGELS OR THE FIFTEENTH SUNDAY AFTER TRINITY (Proper 21)**			
W		Gen. 28. 10–17 *or* Rev. 12. 7–12 Ps. 103. 19–end Rev. 12. 7–12 *or* Heb. 1. 5–end John 1. 47–end	*MP*: Ps. 34; 150 Tobit 12. 6–end *or* Dan. 12. 1–4 Acts 12. 1–11	*EP*: Ps. 138; 148 Dan. 10. 4–end Rev. ch. 5
	or, for The Fifteenth Sunday after Trinity (Proper 21):			
G	*Track 1* Jer. 32. 1–3a, 6–15 Ps. 91. 1–6, 14–end (or 91. 11–end) 1 Tim. 6. 6–19 Luke 16. 19–end	*Track 2* Amos. 6. 1a, 4–7 Ps. 146 1 Tim. 6. 6–19 Luke 16. 19–end	Ps. 132 Isa. 48. 12–end Luke 11. 37–end	Ps. 134; 135 (*or* Ps. 135. 1–14) Neh. ch. 2 John 8. 31–38, 48–end
30 Monday	*Jerome, Translator of the Scriptures, Teacher, 420*			
G **DEL 26**		Zech. 8. 1–8 Ps. 102. 12–22 Luke 9. 46–50	Ps. 27; ***30*** Zech. ch. 10 Mark 11. 1–11	Ps. 26; ***28***; 29 1 Kings 8. 31–62 Acts 16. 6–24

*For Ember Day provision, see p. 11.

	Calendar and Holy Communion	Morning Prayer	Evening Prayer
G		Zech. 6. 9–end Mark 10. 1–16	1 Kings 1.32 – 2.4, 10–12 Acts 13.44 – 14.7
G		Zech. ch. 7 Mark 10. 17–31	1 Kings ch. 3 Acts 14. 8–end
	Cyprian, Bishop of Carthage, Martyr, 258		
Gr	Com. Martyr	Zech. 8. 1–8 Mark 10. 32–34	1 Kings 4.29 – 5.12 Acts 15. 1–21
G		Zech. 8. 9–end Mark 10. 35–45	1 Kings 6. 1, 11–28 Acts 15. 22–35
G		Zech. 9. 1–12 Mark 10. 46–end	1 Kings 8. 1–30 Acts 15.36 – 16.5 **ct** *or First EP of Michael and All Angels* (Ps. 91) 2 Kings 6. 8–17 John 1. 47–51 **W ct**
	MICHAEL AND ALL ANGELS		
W	Dan. 10. 10–19a Ps. 103. 17–22 Rev. 12. 7–12 Matt. 18. 1–10	Ps. 34; 150 Tobit 12. 6–end *or* Dan. 12. 1–4 Acts 12. 1–11	Ps. 138; 148 Gen. 28. 10–17 Rev. ch. 5
	or, for The Fifteenth Sunday after Trinity:		
G	Josh. 24. 14–25 Ps. 92. 1–6 Gal. 6. 11–end Matt. 6. 24–end	Ps. 132 Isa. 48. 12–end Luke 11. 37–end	Ps. 134; 135 (*or* Ps. 135. 1–14) Neh. ch. 2 John 8. 31–38, 48–end
	Jerome, Translator of the Scriptures, Teacher, 420		
Gw	Com. Doctor	Zech. ch. 10 Mark 11. 1–11	1 Kings 8. 31–62 Acts 16. 6–24

NOTES

October 2019

		Sunday Principal Service Weekday Eucharist	Third Service Morning Prayer	Second Service Evening Prayer
1 Tuesday	*Remigius, Bishop of Rheims, Apostle of the Franks, 533; Anthony Ashley Cooper, Earl of Shaftesbury, Social Reformer, 1885*			
G		Zech. 8. 20–end Ps. 87 Luke 9. 51–56	Ps. 32; ***36*** Zech. 11. 4–end Mark 11. 12–26	Ps. 33 1 Kings 8.63 – 9.9 Acts 16. 25–end
2 Wednesday				
G		Neh. 2. 1–8 Ps. 137. 1–6 Luke 9. 57–end	Ps. 34 Zech. 12. 1–10 Mark 11. 27–end	Ps. 119. 33–56 1 Kings 10. 1–25 Acts 17. 1–15
3 Thursday	*George Bell, Bishop of Chichester, Ecumenist, Peacemaker, 1958*			
G		Neh. 8. 1–12 Ps. 19. 7–11 Luke 10. 1–12	Ps. 37† Zech. ch. 13 Mark 12. 1–12	Ps. 39; ***40*** 1 Kings 11. 1–13 Acts 17. 16–end
4 Friday	**Francis of Assisi, Friar, Founder of the Friars Minor, 1226**			
Gw	Com. Religious *or* *also* Gal. 6. 14–end Luke 12. 22–34	Baruch 1. 15–end *or* Deut. 31. 7–13 Ps. 79. 1–9 Luke 10. 13–16	Ps. 31 Zech. 14. 1–11 Mark 12. 13–17	Ps. 35 1 Kings 11. 26–end Acts 18. 1–21
5 Saturday				
G		Baruch 4. 5–12, 27–29 *or* Josh. 22. 1–6 Ps. 69. 33–37 Luke 10. 17–24	Ps. 41; ***42***; 43 Zech. 14. 12–end Mark 12. 18–27	Ps. 45; ***46*** 1 Kings 12. 1–24 Acts 18.22 – 19.7 **ct** *or First EP of Dedication Festival*: Ps. 24 2 Chron. 7. 11–16 John 4. 19–29 **𝔚 ct**
6 Sunday	**THE SIXTEENTH SUNDAY AFTER TRINITY (Proper 22)**			
G	*Track 1* Lam. 1. 1–6 *Canticle*: Lam. 3. 19–26 *or* Ps. 137 (*or* 137. 1–6) 2 Tim. 1. 1–14 Luke 17. 5–10	*Track 2* Hab. 1. 1–4; 2. 1–4 Ps. 37. 1–9 2 Tim. 1. 1–14 Luke 17. 5–10	Ps. 141 Isa. 49. 13–23 Luke 12. 1–12	Ps. 142 Neh. 5. 1–13 John ch. 9
	or, if observed as Dedication Festival:			
𝔚		1 Chron. 29. 6–19 Ps. 122 Eph. 2. 19–end John 2. 13–22	*MP*: Ps. 48; 150 Hag. 2. 6–9 Heb. 10. 19–25	*EP*: Ps. 132 Jer. 7. 1–11 Luke 19. 1–10

	Calendar and Holy Communion	Morning Prayer	Evening Prayer	NOTES
	Remigius, Bishop of Rheims, Apostle of the Franks, 533			
Gw	Com. Bishop	Zech. 11. 4–end Mark 11. 12–26	1 Kings 8.63 – 9.9 Acts 16. 25–end	
G		Zech. 12. 1–10 Mark 11. 27–end	1 Kings 10. 1–25 Acts 17. 1–15	
G		Zech. ch. 13 Mark 12. 1–12	1 Kings 11. 1–13 Acts 17. 16–end	
G		Zech. 14. 1–11 Mark 12. 13–17	1 Kings 11. 26–end Acts 18. 1–21	
G		Zech. 14. 12–end Mark 12. 18–27	1 Kings 12. 1–24 Acts 18.22 – 19.7 **ct** *or First EP of Dedication Festival*: Ps. 24 2 Chron. 7. 11–16 John 4. 19–29 **𝔚 ct**	
	THE SIXTEENTH SUNDAY AFTER TRINITY			
G	1 Kings 17. 17–end Ps. 102. 12–17 Eph. 3. 13–end Luke 7. 11–17	Ps. 141 Isa. 49. 13–23 Luke 12. 1–12	Ps. 142 Neh. 5. 1–13 John ch. 9	
	or, if observed as Dedication Festival:			
𝔚	2 Chron. 7. 11–16 Ps. 122 1 Cor. 3. 9–17 *or* 1 Pet. 2. 1–5 Matt. 21. 12–16 *or* John 10. 22–29	Ps. 48; 150 Hag. 2. 6–9 Heb. 10. 19–25	Ps. 132 Jer. 7. 1–11 Luke 19. 1–10	

		Sunday Principal Service Weekday Eucharist	Third Service Morning Prayer	Second Service Evening Prayer
7 Monday				
G **DEL 27**		Jonah 1.1 - 2.2, 10 *Canticle*: Jonah 2. 2-4, 7 *or* Ps. 69. 1-6 Luke 10. 25-37	Ps. 44 Ecclus. 1. 1-10 *or* Ezek. 1. 1-14 Mark 12. 28-34	Ps. ***47***; 49 1 Kings 12.25 - 13.10 Acts 19. 8-20
8 Tuesday				
G		Jonah ch. 3 Ps. 130 Luke 10. 38-end	Ps. ***48***; 52 Ecclus. 1. 11-end *or* Ezek. 1.15 - 2.2 Mark 12. 35-end	Ps. 50 1 Kings 13. 11-end Acts 19. 21-end
9 Wednesday	*Denys, Bishop of Paris, and his Companions, Martyrs, c. 250; Robert Grosseteste, Bishop of Lincoln, Philosopher, Scientist, 1253*			
G		Jonah ch. 4 Ps. 86. 1-9 Luke 11. 1-4	Ps. 119. 57-80 Ecclus. ch. 2 *or* Ezek. 2.3 - 3.11 Mark 13. 1-13	Ps. ***59***; 60; (67) 1 Kings ch. 17 Acts 20. 1-16
10 Thursday	**Paulinus, Bishop of York, Missionary, 644** *Thomas Traherne, Poet, Spiritual Writer, 1674*			
Gw	Com. Missionary *or* *esp.* Matt. 28. 16-end	Mal. 3.13 - 4.2a Ps. 1 Luke 11. 5-13	Ps. 56; ***57***; (63†) Ecclus. 3. 17-29 *or* Ezek. 3. 12-end Mark 13. 14-23	Ps. 61; ***62***; 64 1 Kings 18. 1-20 Acts 20. 17-end
11 Friday	*Ethelburga, Abbess of Barking, 675; James the Deacon, Companion of Paulinus, 7th century*			
G		Joel 1. 13-15; 2. 1-2 Ps. 9. 1-7 Luke 11. 15-26	Ps. ***51***; 54 Ecclus. 4. 11-28 *or* Ezek. ch. 8 Mark 13. 24-31	Ps. 38 1 Kings 18. 21-end Acts 21. 1-16
12 Saturday	**Wilfrid of Ripon, Bishop, Missionary, 709** *Elizabeth Fry, Prison Reformer, 1845; Edith Cavell, Nurse, 1915*			
Gw	Com. Missionary *or* *esp.* Luke 5. 1-11 *also* 1 Cor. 1. 18-25	Joel 3. 12-end Ps. 97. 1, 8-end Luke 11. 27-28	Ps. 68 Ecclus. 4.29 - 6.1 *or* Ezek. ch. 9 Mark 13. 32-end	Ps. 65; ***66*** 1 Kings ch. 19 Acts 21. 17-36 **ct**
13 Sunday	**THE SEVENTEENTH SUNDAY AFTER TRINITY (Proper 23)**			
G	*Track 1* Jer. 29. 1, 4-7 Ps. 66. 1-11 2 Tim. 2. 8-15 Luke 17. 11-19	*Track 2* 2 Kings 5. 1-3, 7-15c Ps. 111 2 Tim. 2. 8-15 Luke 17. 11-19	Ps. 143 Isa. 50. 4-10 Luke 13. 22-30	Ps. 144 Neh. 6. 1-16 John 15. 12-end
14 Monday				
G **DEL 28**		Rom. 1. 1-7 Ps. 98 Luke 11. 29-32	Ps. 71 Ecclus. 6. 14-end *or* Ezek. 10. 1-19 Mark 14. 1-11	Ps. ***72***; 75 1 Kings ch. 21 Acts 21.37 - 22.21

	Calendar and Holy Communion	Morning Prayer	Evening Prayer	NOTES
G		Ecclus. 1. 1–10 *or* Ezek. 1. 1–14 Mark 12. 28–34	1 Kings 12.25 – 13.10 Acts 19. 8–20	
G		Ecclus. 1. 11–end *or* Ezek. 1.15 – 2.2 Mark 12. 35–end	1 Kings 13. 11–end Acts 19. 21–end	
	Denys, Bishop of Paris, Martyr, *c.* 250			
Gr	Com. Martyr	Ecclus. ch. 2 *or* Ezek. 2.3 – 3.11 Mark 13. 1–13	1 Kings ch. 17 Acts 20. 1–16	
G		Ecclus. 3. 17–29 *or* Ezek. 3. 12–end Mark 13. 14–23	1 Kings 18. 1–20 Acts 20. 17–end	
G		Ecclus. 4. 11–28 *or* Ezek. ch. 8 Mark 13. 24–31	1 Kings 18. 21–end Acts 21. 1–16	
G		Ecclus. 4.29 – 6.1 *or* Ezek. ch. 9 Mark 13. 32–end	1 Kings ch. 19 Acts 21. 17–36 **ct**	
	THE SEVENTEENTH SUNDAY AFTER TRINITY			
G	Prov. 25. 6–14 Ps. 33. 6–12 Eph. 4. 1–6 Luke 14. 1–11	Ps. 143 Isa. 50. 4–10 Luke 13. 22–30	Ps. 144 Neh. 6. 1–16 John 15. 12–end	
G		Ecclus. 6. 14–end *or* Ezek. 10. 1–19 Mark 14. 1–11	1 Kings ch. 21 Acts 21.37 – 22.21	

		Sunday Principal Service Weekday Eucharist	Third Service Morning Prayer	Second Service Evening Prayer
15 Tuesday	**Teresa of Avila, Teacher, 1582**			
Gw	Com. Teacher *or* *also* Rom. 8. 22–27	Rom. 1. 16–25 Ps. 19. 1–4 Luke 11. 37–41	Ps. 73 Ecclus. 7. 27–end *or* Ezek. 11. 14–end Mark 14. 12–25	Ps. 74 1 Kings 22. 1–28 Acts 22.22 - 23.11
16 Wednesday	*Nicholas Ridley, Bishop of London, and Hugh Latimer, Bishop of Worcester, Reformation Martyrs, 1555*			
G		Rom. 2. 1–11 Ps. 62. 1–8 Luke 11. 42–46	Ps. 77 Ecclus. 10. 6–8, 12–24 *or* Ezek. 12. 1–16 Mark 14. 26–42	Ps. 119. 81–104 1 Kings 22. 29–45 Acts 23. 12–end
17 Thursday	**Ignatius, Bishop of Antioch, Martyr, c. 107**			
Gr	Com. Martyr *or* *also* Phil. 3. 7–12 John 6. 52–58	Rom. 3. 21–30 Ps. 130 Luke 11. 47–end	Ps. 78. 1–39† Ecclus. 11. 7–28 *or* Ezek. 12. 17–end Mark 14. 43–52	Ps. 78. 40–end† 2 Kings 1. 2–17 Acts 24. 1–23 *or First EP of Luke* Ps. 33 Hos. 6. 1–3 2 Tim. 3. 10–end **R ct**
18 Friday	**LUKE THE EVANGELIST**			
R		Isa. 35. 3–6 *or* Acts 16. 6–12a Ps. 147. 1–7 2 Tim. 4. 5–17 Luke 10. 1–9	*MP*: Ps. 145; 146 Isa. ch. 55 Luke 1. 1–4	*EP*: Ps. 103 Ecclus. 38. 1–14 *or* Isa. 61. 1–6 Col. 4. 7–end
19 Saturday	**Henry Martyn, Translator of the Scriptures, Missionary in India and Persia, 1812**			
Gw	Com. Missionary *or* *esp.* Mark 16. 15–end *also* Isa. 55. 6–11	Rom. 4. 13, 16–18 Ps. 105. 6–10, 41–44 Luke 12. 8–12	Ps. ***76***; 79 Ecclus. 15. 11–end *or* Ezek. 14. 1–11 Mark 14. 66–end	Ps. 81; ***84*** 2 Kings 4. 1–37 Acts 25. 13–end **ct**
20 Sunday	**THE EIGHTEENTH SUNDAY AFTER TRINITY (Proper 24)**			
G	*Track 1* Jer. 31. 27–34 Ps. 119. 97–104 2 Tim. 3.14 - 4.5 Luke 18. 1–8	*Track 2* Gen. 32. 22–31 Ps. 121 2 Tim. 3.14 - 4.5 Luke 18. 1–8	Ps. 147 Isa. 54. 1–14 Luke 13. 31–end	Ps. [146]; 149 Neh. 8. 9–end John 16. 1–11
21 Monday				
G **DEL 29**		Rom. 4. 20–end *Canticle*: Benedictus 1–6 Luke 12. 13–21	Ps. ***80***; 82 Ecclus. 16. 17–end *or* Ezek. 14. 12–end Mark 15. 1–15	Ps. ***85***; 86 2 Kings ch. 5 Acts 26. 1–23
22 Tuesday				
G		Rom. 5. 12, 15, 17–end Ps. 40. 7–12 Luke 12. 35–38	Ps. 87; ***89. 1–18*** Ecclus. 17. 1–24 *or* Ezek. 18. 1–20 Mark 15. 16–32	Ps. 89. 19–end 2 Kings 6. 1–23 Acts 26. 24–end

	Calendar and Holy Communion	Morning Prayer	Evening Prayer	NOTES
G		Ecclus. 7. 27-end *or* Ezek. 11. 14-end Mark 14. 12-25	1 Kings 22. 1-28 Acts 22.22 - 23.11	
G		Ecclus. 10. 6-8, 12-24 *or* Ezek. 12. 1-16 Mark 14. 26-42	1 Kings 22. 29-45 Acts 23. 12-end	
	Etheldreda, Abbess of Ely, 679			
Gw	Com. Abbess	Ecclus. 11. 7-28 *or* Ezek. 12. 17-end Mark 14. 43-52	2 Kings 1. 2-17 Acts 24. 1-23 *or First EP of Luke* (Ps. 33) Hos. 6. 1-3 2 Tim. 3. 10-end **R ct**	
	LUKE THE EVANGELIST			
R	Isa. 35. 3-6 Ps. 147. 1-6 2 Tim. 4. 5-15 Luke 10. 1-9 *or* Luke 7. 36-end	(Ps. 145; 146) Isa. ch. 55 Luke 1. 1-4	(Ps. 103) Ecclus. 38. 1-14 *or* Isa. 61. 1-6 Col. 4. 7-end	
G		Ecclus. 15. 11-end *or* Ezek. 14. 1-11 Mark 14. 66-end	Ps. 81; ***84*** 2 Kings 4. 1-37 Acts 25. 13-end **ct**	
	THE EIGHTEENTH SUNDAY AFTER TRINITY			
G	Deut. 6. 4-9 Ps. 122 1 Cor. 1. 4-8 Matt. 22. 34-end	Ps. 147 Isa. 54. 1-14 Luke 13. 31-end	Ps. [146]; 149 Neh. 8. 9-end John 16. 1-11	
G		Ecclus. 16. 17-end *or* Ezek. 14. 12-end Mark 15. 1-15	Ps. ***85***; 86 2 Kings ch. 5 Acts 26. 1-23	
G		Ecclus. 17. 1-24 *or* Ezek. 18. 1-20 Mark 15. 16-32	2 Kings 6. 1-23 Acts 26. 24-end	

		Sunday Principal Service Weekday Eucharist	Third Service Morning Prayer	Second Service Evening Prayer
23 Wednesday				
G		Rom. 6. 12–18 Ps. 124 Luke 12. 39–48	Ps. 119. 105–128 Ecclus. 18. 1–14 *or* Ezek. 18. 21–32 Mark 15. 33–41	Ps. **91**; 93 2 Kings 9. 1–16 Acts 27. 1–26
24 Thursday				
G		Rom. 6. 19–end Ps. 1 Luke 12. 49–53	Ps. 90; **92** Ecclus. 19. 4–17 *or* Ezek. 20. 1–20 Mark 15. 42–end	Ps. 94 2 Kings 9. 17–end Acts 27. 27–end
25 Friday	*Crispin and Crispinian, Martyrs at Rome, c. 287*			
G		Rom. 7. 18–end Ps. 119. 33–40 Luke 12. 54–end	Ps. ***88***; (95) Ecclus. 19. 20–end *or* Ezek. 20. 21–38 Mark 16. 1–8	Ps. 102 2 Kings 12. 1–19 Acts 28. 1–16
26 Saturday	**Alfred the Great, King of the West Saxons, Scholar, 899** *Cedd, Abbot of Lastingham, Bishop of the East Saxons, 664**			
Gw	Com. Saint *or* *also* 2 Sam. 23. 1–5 John 18. 33–37	Rom. 8. 1–11 Ps. 24. 1–6 Luke 13. 1–9	Ps. 96; **97**; 100 Ecclus. 21. 1–17 *or* Ezek. 24. 15–end Mark 16. 9–end	Ps. 104 2 Kings 17. 1–23 Acts 28. 17–end **ct**
27 Sunday	**THE LAST SUNDAY AFTER TRINITY****			
G	*Track 1* Joel 2. 23–end Ps. 65 (*or* 65. 1–7) 2 Tim. 4. 6–8, 16–18 Luke 18. 9–14	*Track 2* Ecclus. 35. 12–17 *or* Jer. 14. 7–10, 19–end Ps. 84. 1–7 2 Tim. 4. 6–8, 16–18 Luke 18. 9–14	Ps. 119. 105–128 Isa. 59. 9–20 Luke 14. 1–14	Ps. 119. 1–16 Eccles. chs 11 & 12 2 Tim. 2. 1–7 *Gospel*: Matt. 22. 34–end *or First EP of Simon and Jude* Ps. 124; 125; 126 Deut. 32. 1–4 John 14. 15–26 **R ct**
	or, if being observed as Bible Sunday:			
G		Isa. 45. 22–end Ps. 119. 129–136 Rom. 15. 1–6 Luke 4. 16–24	Ps. 119. 105–128 1 Kings 22. 1–17 Rom. 15. 4–13 *or* Luke 14. 1–14	Ps. 119. 1–16 Jer. 36. 9–end Rom. 10. 5–17 *Gospel*: Matt. 22. 34–40 *or First EP of Simon and Jude* Ps. 124; 125; 126 Deut. 32. 1–4 John 14. 15–26 **R ct**
28 Monday	**SIMON AND JUDE, APOSTLES**			
R **DEL 30**		Isa. 28. 14–16 Ps. 119. 89–96 Eph. 2. 19–end John 15. 17–end	*MP*: Ps. 116; 117 Wisd. 5. 1–16 *or* Isa. 45. 18–end Luke 6. 12–16	*EP*: Ps. 119. 1–16 1 Macc. 2. 42–66 *or* Jer. 3. 11–18 Jude 1–4, 17–end

*Chad may be celebrated with Cedd on 26 October instead of 2 March.
**If the Dedication Festival is kept on this Sunday, use the provision given on 5 and 6 October.

	Calendar and Holy Communion	Morning Prayer	Evening Prayer
G		Ecclus. 18. 1–14 *or* Ezek. 18. 21–32 Mark 15. 33–41	2 Kings 9. 1–16 Acts 27. 1–26
G		Ecclus. 19. 4–17 *or* Ezek. 20. 1–20 Mark 15. 42–end	2 Kings 9. 17–end Acts 27. 27–end
	Crispin, Martyr at Rome, *c.* 287		
Gr	Com. Martyr	Ecclus. 19. 20–end *or* Ezek. 20. 21–38 Mark 16. 1–8	2 Kings 12. 1–19 Acts 28. 1–16
G		Ecclus. 21. 1–17 *or* Ezek. 24. 15–end Mark 16. 9–end	2 Kings 17. 1–23 Acts 28. 17–end **ct**
	THE NINETEENTH SUNDAY AFTER TRINITY		
G	Gen. 18. 23–32 Ps. 141. 1–9 Eph. 4. 17–end Matt. 9. 1–8	Ps. 119. 105–128 Isa. 59. 9–20 Luke 14. 12–24	Ps. 119. 1–16 Eccles. chs 11 & 12 2 Tim. 2. 1–7 *or First EP of Simon and Jude* Ps. 124; 125; 126 Deut. 32. 1–4 John 14. 15–26 **R ct**
	SIMON AND JUDE, APOSTLES		
R	Isa. 28. 9–16 Ps. 116. 11–end Jude 1–8 *or* Rev. 21. 9–14 John 15. 17–end	(Ps. 119. 89–96) Wisd. 5. 1–16 *or* Isa. 45. 18–end Luke 6. 12–16	(Ps. 119. 1–16) 1 Macc. 2. 42–66 *or* Jer. 3. 11–18 Eph. 2. 19–end

NOTES

			Sunday Principal Service Weekday Eucharist	Third Service Morning Prayer	Second Service Evening Prayer
29 Tuesday		**James Hannington, Bishop of Eastern Equatorial Africa, Martyr in Uganda, 1885**			
	Gr	Com. Martyr *or* *esp.* Matt. 10. 28–39	Rom. 8. 18–25 Ps. 126 Luke 13. 18–21	Ps. ***106***† (*or* 103) Ecclus. 22.27 – 23.15 *or* Ezek. 33. 1–20 John 13. 12–20	Ps. 107† 2 Kings 18. 1–12 Phil. 1. 12–end
30 Wednesday					
	G		Rom. 8. 26–30 Ps. 13 Luke 13. 22–30	Ps. 110; ***111***; 112 Ecclus. 24. 1–22 *or* Ezek. 33. 21–end John 13. 21–30	Ps. 119. 129–152 2 Kings 18. 13–end Phil. 2. 1–13
31 Thursday		*Martin Luther, Reformer, 1546*			
	G		Rom. 8. 31–end Ps. 109. 20–26, 29–30 Luke 13. 31–end	Ps. 113; ***115*** Ecclus. 24. 23–end *or* Ezek. 34. 1–16 John 13. 31–end	*First EP of All Saints* Ps. 1; 5 Ecclus. 44. 1–15 *or* Isa. 40. 27–end Rev. 19. 6–10 **W ct** *or, if All Saints is observed on 3 November*: Ps. 114; ***116***; 117 2 Kings 19. 1–19 Phil. 2. 14–end

November 2019

			Sunday Principal Service Weekday Eucharist	Third Service Morning Prayer	Second Service Evening Prayer
1 Friday		**ALL SAINTS' DAY**			
	W		Dan. 7. 1–3, 15–18 Ps. 149 Eph. 1. 11–end Luke 6. 20–31	*MP*: Ps. 15; 84; 149 Isa. ch. 35 Luke 9. 18–27	*EP*: Ps. 148; 150 Isa. 65. 17–end Heb. 11.32 – 12.2
		or, if the readings above are used on Sunday 3 November:			
	W		Isa. 56. 3–8 *or* 2 Esdras 2. 42–end Ps. 33. 1–5 Heb. 12. 18–24 Matt. 5. 1–12	*MP*: 111; 112; 117 Wisd. 5. 1–16 *or* Jer. 31. 31–34 2 Cor. 4. 5–12	*EP*: Ps. 145 Isa. 66. 20–23 Col. 1. 9–14
	R *or* **G**	*or, if kept as a feria*:	Rom. 9. 1–5 Ps. 147. 13–end Luke 14. 1–6	Ps. 139 Ecclus. 27.30 – 28.9 *or* Ezek. 34. 17–end John 14. 1–14	Ps. ***130***; 131; 137 2 Kings 19. 20–36 Phil. 3.1 – 4.1
2 Saturday		**Commemoration of the Faithful Departed (All Souls' Day)**			
	Rp *or* **Gp**	Lam. 3. 17–26, 31–33 *or* *or* Wisd. 3. 1–9 Ps. 23 *or* Ps. 27. 1–6, 16–end Rom. 5. 5–11 *or* 1 Pet. 1. 3–9 John 5. 19–25 *or* John 6. 37–40	Rom. 11. 1–2, 11–12, 25–29 Ps. 94. 14–19 Luke 14. 1, 7–11	Ps. 120; ***121***; 122 Ecclus. 28. 14–end *or* Ezek. 36. 16–36 John 14. 15–end	Ps. 118 2 Kings ch. 20 Phil. 4. 2–end **ct**

	Calendar and Holy Communion	Morning Prayer	Evening Prayer
G		Ecclus. 22.27 - 23.15 *or* Ezek. 33. 1–20 John 13. 12–20	2 Kings 18. 1–12 Phil. 1. 12–end
G		Ecclus. 24. 1–22 *or* Ezek. 33. 21–end John 13. 21–30	2 Kings 18. 13–end Phil. 2. 1–13
G		Ecclus. 24. 23–end *or* Ezek. 34. 1–16 John 13. 31–end	*First EP of All Saints* Ps. 1; 5 Ecclus. 44. 1–15 *or* Isa. 40. 27–end Rev. 19. 6–10 **W ct**
	ALL SAINTS' DAY		
W	Isa. 66. 20–23 Ps. 33. 1–5 Rev. 7. 2–4 [5–8] 9–12 Matt. 5. 1–12	Ps. 15; 84; 149 Isa. ch. 35 Luke 9. 18–27	Ps. 148; 150 Isa. 65. 17–end Heb. 11.32 - 12.2
	To celebrate All Souls' Day, see *Common Worship* provision.		
G		Ecclus. 28. 14–end *or* Ezek. 36. 16–36 John 14. 15–end	2 Kings ch. 20 Phil. 4. 2–end **ct**

NOTES

		Sunday Principal Service Weekday Eucharist	Third Service Morning Prayer	Second Service Evening Prayer
3 Sunday	**THE FOURTH SUNDAY BEFORE ADVENT**			
R *or* **G**		Isa. 1. 10–18 Ps. 32. 1–8 2 Thess. ch. 1 Luke 19. 1–10	Ps. 87 Job ch. 26 Col. 1. 9–14	Ps. 145 (*or* 145. 1–9) Lam. 3. 22–33 John 11. [1–31] 32–44
𝔚	*or ALL SAINTS' SUNDAY (see readings for 1 November throughout the day)*			
4 Monday				
R *or* **G** **DEL 31**		Rom. 11. 29–end Ps. 69. 31–37 Luke 14. 12–14	Ps. **2**; 146 *alt.* Ps. 123; 124; 125; ***126*** Isa. 1. 1–20 Matt. 1. 18–end	Ps. ***92***; 96; 97 *alt.* Ps. ***127***; 128; 129 Dan. ch. 1 Rev. ch. 1
5 Tuesday				
R *or* **G**		Rom. 12. 5–16 Ps. 131 Luke 14. 15–24	Ps. ***5***; 147. 1–12 *alt.* Ps. ***132***; 133 Isa. 1. 21–end Matt. 2. 1–15	Ps. 98; 99; ***100*** *alt.* Ps. (134); ***135*** Dan. 2. 1–24 Rev. 2. 1–11
6 Wednesday	*Leonard, Hermit, 6th century; William Temple, Archbishop of Canterbury, Teacher, 1944*			
R *or* **G**		Rom. 13. 8–10 Ps. 112 Luke 14. 25–33	Ps. ***9***; 147. 13–end *alt.* Ps. 119. 153–end Isa. 2. 1–11 Matt. 2. 16–end	Ps. 111; ***112***; 116 *alt.* Ps. 136 Dan. 2. 25–end Rev. 2. 12–end
7 Thursday	**Willibrord of York, Bishop, Apostle of Frisia, 739**			
Rw *or* **Gw**	Com. Missionary *or* *esp.* Isa. 52. 7–10 Matt. 28. 16–end	Rom. 14. 7–12 Ps. 27. 14–end Luke 15. 1–10	Ps. 11; ***15***; 148 *alt.* Ps. ***143***; 146 Isa. 2. 12–end Matt. ch. 3	Ps. 118 *alt.* Ps. ***138***; 140; 141 Dan. 3. 1–18 Rev. 3. 1–13
8 Friday	**The Saints and Martyrs of England**			
Rw *or* **Gw**	Isa. 61. 4–9 *or* *or* Ecclus. 44. 1–15 Ps. 15 Rev. 19. 5–10 John 17. 18–23	Rom. 15. 14–21 Ps. 98 Luke 16. 1–8	Ps. ***16***; 149 *alt.* Ps. 142; ***144*** Isa. 3. 1–15 Matt. 4. 1–11	Ps. 137; 138; ***143*** *alt.* Ps. 145 Dan. 3. 19–end Rev. 3. 14–end
9 Saturday	*Margery Kempe, Mystic, c. 1440*			
R *or* **G**		Rom. 16. 3–9, 16, 22–end Ps. 145. 1–7 Luke 16. 9–15	Ps. ***18. 31–end***; 150 *alt.* Ps. 147 Isa. 4.2 – 5.7 Matt. 4. 12–22	Ps. 145 *alt.* Ps. ***148***; 149; 150 Dan. 4. 1–18 Rev. ch. 4 **ct**
10 Sunday	**THE THIRD SUNDAY BEFORE ADVENT** (Remembrance Sunday)			
R *or* **G**		Job 19. 23–27a Ps. 17. 1–9 (*or* 17. 1–8) 2 Thess. 2. 1–5, 13–end Luke 20. 27–38	Ps. 20; 90 Isa. 2. 1–5 James 3. 13–end	Ps. 40 1 Kings 3. 1–15 Rom. 8. 31–end *Gospel*: Matt. 22. 15–22

	Calendar and Holy Communion	Morning Prayer	Evening Prayer	NOTES
	THE TWENTIETH SUNDAY AFTER TRINITY			
G	Prov. 9. 1–6 Ps. 145. 15–end Eph. 5. 15–21 Matt. 22. 1–14	Ps. 87 Job ch. 26 Luke 19. 1–10	Ps. 145 (*or* 145. 1–9) Lam. 3. 22–33 John 11. [1–31] 32–44	
G		Isa. 1. 1–20 Matt. 1. 18–end	Dan. ch. 1 Rev. ch. 1	
G		Isa. 1. 21–end Matt. 2. 1–15	Dan. 2. 1–24 Rev. 2. 1–11	
	Leonard, Hermit, 6th century			
Gw	Com. Abbot	Isa. 2. 1–11 Matt. 2. 16–end	Dan. 2. 25–end Rev. 2. 12–end	
G		Isa. 2. 12–end Matt. ch. 3	Dan. 3. 1–18 Rev. 3. 1–13	
G		Isa. 3. 1–15 Matt. 4. 1–11	Dan. 3. 19–end Rev. 3. 14–end	
G		Isa. 4.2 - 5.7 Matt. 4. 12–22	Dan. 4. 1–18 Rev. ch. 4 **ct**	
	THE TWENTY-FIRST SUNDAY AFTER TRINITY			
G	Gen. 32. 24–29 Ps. 90. 1–12 Eph. 6. 10–20 John 4. 46b–end	Ps. 20; 90 Isa. 2. 1–5 James 3. 13–end	Ps. 40 1 Kings 3. 1–15 Luke 20. 27–38	

Day			Sunday Principal Service Weekday Eucharist	Third Service Morning Prayer	Second Service Evening Prayer
11 Monday		**Martin, Bishop of Tours, *c.* 397**			
	Rw *or* **Gw** **DEL 32**	Com. Bishop *or* *also* 1 Thess. 5. 1–11 Matt. 25. 34–40	Wisd. 1. 1–7 *or* Titus 1. 1–9 Ps. 139. 1–9 *or* Ps. 24. 1–6 Luke 17. 1–6	Ps. 19; ***20*** *alt.* Ps. ***1***; 2; 3 Isa. 5. 8–24 Matt. 4.23 - 5.12	Ps. 34 *alt.* Ps. ***4***; 7 Dan. 4. 19–end Rev. ch. 5
12 Tuesday					
	R *or* **G**		Wisd. 2.23 - 3.9 *or* Titus 2. 1–8, 11–14 Ps. 34. 1–6 *or* Ps. 37. 3–5, 30–32 Luke 17. 7–10	Ps. ***21***; 24 *alt.* Ps. ***5***; 6; (8) Isa. 5. 25–end Matt. 5. 13–20	Ps. 36; ***40*** *alt.* Ps. ***9***; 10† Dan. 5. 1–12 Rev. ch. 6
13 Wednesday		**Charles Simeon, Priest, Evangelical Divine, 1836**			
	Rw *or* **Gw**	Com. Pastor *or* *esp.* Mal. 2. 5–7 *also* Col. 1. 3–8 Luke 8. 4–8	Wisd. 6. 1–11 *or* Titus 3. 1–7 Ps. 82 *or* Ps. 23 Luke 17. 11–19	Ps. ***23***; 25 *alt.* Ps. 119. 1–32 Isa. ch. 6 Matt. 5. 21–37	Ps. 37 *alt.* Ps. ***11***; 12; 13 Dan. 5. 13–end Rev. 7. 1–4, 9–end
14 Thursday		*Samuel Seabury, first Anglican Bishop in North America, 1796*			
	R *or* **G**		Wisd. 7.22 - 8.1 *or* Philemon 7–20 Ps. 119. 89–96 *or* Ps. 146. 4–end Luke 17. 20–25	Ps. ***26***; 27 *alt.* Ps. 14; ***15***; 16 Isa. 7. 1–17 Matt. 5. 38–end	Ps. 42; ***43*** *alt.* Ps. 18† Dan. ch. 6 Rev. ch. 8
15 Friday					
	R *or* **G**		Wisd. 13. 1–9 *or* 2 John 4–9 Ps. 19. 1–4 *or* Ps. 119. 1–8 Luke 17. 26–end	Ps. 28; ***32*** *alt.* Ps. 17; ***19*** Isa. 8. 1–15 Matt. 6. 1–18	Ps. 31 *alt.* Ps. 22 Dan. 7. 1–14 Rev. 9. 1–12
16 Saturday		**Margaret, Queen of Scotland, Philanthropist, Reformer of the Church, 1093** *Edmund Rich of Abingdon, Archbishop of Canterbury, 1240*			
	Rw *or* **Gw**	Com. Saint *or* *also* Prov. 31. 10–12, 20, 26–end 1 Cor. 12.13 - 13.3 Matt. 25. 34–end	Wisd. 18. 14–16; 19. 6–9 *or* 3 John 5–8 Ps. 105. 1–5, 35–42 *or* Ps. 112 Luke 18. 1–8	Ps. 33 *alt.* Ps. 20; 21; ***23*** Isa. 8.16 - 9.7 Matt. 6. 19–end	Ps. 84; ***86*** *alt.* Ps. ***24***; 25 Dan. 7. 15–end Rev. 9. 13–end **ct**
17 Sunday		**THE SECOND SUNDAY BEFORE ADVENT**			
	R *or* **G**		Mal. 4. 1–2a Ps. 98 2 Thess. 3. 6–13 Luke 21. 5–19	Ps. 132 1 Sam. 16. 1–13 Matt. 13. 44–52	Ps. [93]; 97 Dan. ch. 6 Matt. 13. 1–9, 18–23
18 Monday		**Elizabeth of Hungary, Princess of Thuringia, Philanthropist, 1231**			
	Rw *or* **Gw** **DEL 33**	Com. Saint *or* *esp.* Matt. 25. 31–end *also* Prov. 31. 10–end	Macc. 1. 10–15, 41–43, 54–57, 62–64 *or* Rev. 1. 1–4; 2. 1–5 Ps. 79. 1–5 *or* Ps. 1 Luke 18. 35–end	Ps. 46; ***47*** *alt.* Ps. 27; ***30*** Isa. 9.8 - 10.4 Matt. 7. 1–12	Ps. 70; ***71*** *alt.* Ps. 26; ***28***; 29 Dan. 8. 1–14 Rev. ch. 10

	Calendar and Holy Communion	Morning Prayer	Evening Prayer
	Martin, Bishop of Tours, *c.* 397		
Gw	Com. Bishop	Isa. 5. 8–24 Matt. 4.23 – 5.12	Dan. 4. 19–end Rev. ch. 5
G		Isa. 5. 25–end Matt. 5. 13–20	Dan. 5. 1–12 Rev. ch. 6
	Britius, Bishop of Tours, 444		
Gw	Com. Bishop	Isa. ch. 6 Matt. 5. 21–37	Dan. 5. 13–end Rev. 7. 1–4, 9–end
G		Isa. 7. 1–17 Matt. 5. 38–end	Dan. ch. 6 Rev. ch. 8
	Machutus, Bishop, Apostle of Brittany, *c.* 564		
Gw	Com. Bishop	Isa. 8. 1–15 Matt. 6. 1–18	Dan. 7. 1–14 Rev. 9. 1–12
G		Isa. 8.16 – 9.7 Matt. 6. 19–end	Dan. 7. 15–end Rev. 9. 13–end **ct**
	THE TWENTY-SECOND SUNDAY AFTER TRINITY		
G	Gen. 45. 1–7, 15 Ps. 133 Phil. 1. 3–11 Matt. 18. 21–end	Ps. 132 1 Sam. 16. 1–13 Matt. 13. 44–52	Ps. [93]; 97 Dan. ch. 6 Matt. 13. 1–9, 18–23
G		Isa. 9.8 – 10.4 Matt. 7. 1–12	Dan. 8. 1–14 Rev. ch. 10

NOTES

		Sunday Principal Service Weekday Eucharist	Third Service Morning Prayer	Second Service Evening Prayer
19 Tuesday	**Hilda, Abbess of Whitby, 680** *Mechtild, Béguine of Magdeburg, Mystic, 1280*			
Rw *or* **Gw**	Com. Religious *or* *esp.* Isa. 61.10 – 62.5	2 Macc. 6. 18–end *or* Rev. 3. 1–6, 14–31 Ps. 11 *or* Ps. 15 Luke 19. 1–10	Ps. 48; ***52*** *alt.* Ps. 32; ***36*** Isa. 10. 5–19 Matt. 7. 13–end	Ps. ***67***; 72 *alt.* Ps. 33 Dan. 8. 15–end Rev. 11. 1–14
20 Wednesday	**Edmund, King of the East Angles, Martyr, 870** *Priscilla Lydia Sellon, a Restorer of the Religious Life in the Church of England, 1876*			
R *or* **Gr**	Com. Martyr *or* *also* Prov. 20. 28; 21. 1–4, 7	2 Macc. 7. 1, 20–31 *or* Rev. ch. 4 Ps. 116. 10–end *or* Ps. 150 Luke 19. 11–28	Ps. ***56***; 57 *alt.* Ps. 34 Isa. 10. 20–32 Matt. 8. 1–13	Ps. 73 *alt.* Ps. 119. 33–56 Dan. 9. 1–19 Rev. 11. 15–end
21 Thursday				
R *or* **G**		1 Macc. 2. 15–29 *or* Rev. 5. 1–10 Ps. 129 *or* Ps. 149. 1–5 Luke 19. 41–44	Ps. 61; ***62*** *alt.* Ps. 37† Isa. 10.33 – 11.9 Matt. 8. 14–22	Ps. 74; ***76*** *alt.* Ps. 39; ***40*** Dan. 9. 20–end Rev. ch. 12
22 Friday	*Cecilia, Martyr at Rome, c. 230*			
R *or* **G**		1 Macc. 4. 36–37, 52–59 *or* Rev. 10. 8–11 Ps. 122 *or* Ps. 119. 65–72 Luke 19. 45–48	Ps. ***63***; 65 *alt.* Ps. 31 Isa. 11.10 – 12.end Matt. 8. 23–end	Ps. 77 *alt.* Ps. 35 Dan. 10.1 – 11.1 Rev. 13. 1–10
23 Saturday	**Clement, Bishop of Rome, Martyr, c. 100**			
R *or* **Gr**	Com. Martyr *or* *also* Phil. 3.17 – 4.3 Matt. 16. 13–19	1 Macc. 6. 1–13 *or* Rev. 11. 4–12 Ps. 124 *or* Ps. 144. 1–9 Luke 20. 27–40	Ps. 78. 1–39 *alt.* Ps. 41; ***42***; 43 Isa. 13. 1–13 Matt. 9. 1–17	Ps. 78. 40–end *alt.* Ps. 45; ***46*** Dan. ch. 12 Rev. 13. 11–end **ct** *or First EP of Christ the King* Ps. 99; 100 Isa. 10.33 – 11.9 1 Tim. 6. 11–16 **R** *or* **W ct**
24 Sunday	**CHRIST THE KING** The Sunday Next Before Advent			
R *or* **W**		Jer. 23. 1–6 Ps. 46 Col. 1. 11–20 Luke 23. 33–43	*MP*: Ps. 29; 110 Zech. 6. 9–end Rev. 11. 15–18	*EP*: Ps. 72 (*or* 72. 1–7) 1 Sam. 8. 4–20 John 18. 33–37
25 Monday	*Catherine of Alexandria, Martyr, 4th century; Isaac Watts, Hymn Writer, 1748*			
R *or* **G** **DEL 34**		Dan. 1. 1–6, 8–20 *Canticle*: Bless the Lord Luke 21. 1–4	Ps. 92; ***96*** *alt.* Ps. 44 Isa. 14. 3–20 Matt. 9. 18–34	Ps. ***80***; 81 *alt.* Ps. ***47***; 49 Isa. 40. 1–11 Rev. 14. 1–13

	Calendar and Holy Communion	Morning Prayer	Evening Prayer	NOTES
G		Isa. 10. 5–19 Matt. 7. 13–end	Dan. 8. 15–end Rev. 11. 1–14	
	Edmund, King of the East Angles, Martyr, 870			
Gr	Com. Martyr	Isa. 10. 20–32 Matt. 8. 1–13	Dan. 9. 1–19 Rev. 11. 15–end	
G		Isa. 10.33 – 11.9 Matt. 8. 14–22	Dan. 9. 20–end Rev. ch. 12	
	Cecilia, Martyr at Rome, c. 230			
Gr	Com. Virgin Martyr	Isa. 11.10 – 12.end Matt. 8. 23–end	Dan. 10.1 – 11.1 Rev. 13. 1–10	
	Clement, Bishop of Rome, Martyr, *c.* 100			
Gr	Com. Martyr	Isa. 13. 1–13 Matt. 9. 1–17	Dan. ch. 12 Rev. 13. 11–end	
			ct	
	THE SUNDAY NEXT BEFORE ADVENT To celebrate Christ the King, see *Common Worship* provision.			
G	Jer. 23. 5–8 Ps. 85. 8–end Col. 1. 13–20 John 6. 5–14	Ps. 29; 110 Zech. 6. 9–end Rev. 11. 15–18	Ps. 72 (*or* 72. 1–7) 1 Sam. 8. 4–20 John 18. 33–37	
	Catherine of Alexandria, Martyr, 4th century			
Gr	Com. Virgin Martyr	Isa. 14. 3–20 Matt. 9. 18–34	Isa. 40. 1–11 Rev. 14. 1–13	

		Sunday Principal Service Weekday Eucharist	Third Service Morning Prayer	Second Service Evening Prayer
26 Tuesday				
R *or* **G**		Dan. 2. 31–45 *Canticle*: Benedicite 1–3 Luke 21. 5–11	Ps. ***97***; 98; 100 *alt*. Ps. ***48***; 52 Isa. ch. 17 Matt. 9.35 – 10.15	Ps. 99; ***101*** *alt*. Ps. 50 Isa. 40. 12–26 Rev. 14.14 – 15.end
27 Wednesday				
R *or* **G**		Dan. 5. 1–6, 13–14, 16–17, 23–28 *Canticle*: Benedicite 4–5 Luke 21. 12–19	Ps. 110; 111; ***112*** *alt*. Ps. 119. 57–80 Isa. ch. 19 Matt. 10. 16–33	Ps. 121; ***122***; 123; 124 *alt*. Ps. ***59***; 60; (67) Isa. 40.27 – 41.7 Rev. 16. 1–11
28 Thursday				
R *or* **G**		Dan. 6. 12–end *Canticle*: Benedicite 6–8a Luke 21. 20–28	Ps. ***125***; 126; 127; 128 *alt*. Ps. 56; ***57***; (63†) Isa. 21. 1–12 Matt. 10.34 – 11.1	Ps. 131; 132; ***133*** *alt*. Ps. 61; ***62***; 64 Isa. 41. 8–20 Rev. 16. 12–end
29 Friday				
R *or* **G**		Dan. 7. 2–14 *Canticle*: Benedicite 8b–10a Luke 21. 29–33	Ps. 139 *alt*. Ps. ***51***; 54 Isa. 22. 1–14 Matt. 11. 2–19	Ps. ***146***; 147 *alt*. Ps. 38 Isa. 41.21 – 42.9 Rev. ch. 17 *or First EP of Andrew the Apostle* Ps. 48 Isa. 49. 1–9a 1 Cor. 4. 9–16 **R ct**
	Day of Intercession and Thanksgiving for the Missionary Work of the Church			
		Isa. 49. 1–6; 52. 7–10; Mic. 4. 1–5 Acts 17. 12–end; 2 Cor. 5.14 – 6.2; Eph. 2. 13–end Ps. 2; 46; 47 Matt. 5. 13–16; 28. 16–end; John 17. 20–end		
30 Saturday	**ANDREW THE APOSTLE**			
R		Isa. 52. 7–10 Ps. 19. 1–6 Rom. 10. 12–18 Matt. 4. 18–22	*MP*: Ps. 47; 147. 1–12 Ezek. 47. 1–12 *or* Ecclus. 14. 20–end John 12. 20–32	*EP*: Ps. 87; 96 Zech. 8. 20–end John 1. 35–42

December 2019

1 Sunday	**THE FIRST SUNDAY OF ADVENT** *CW Year A begins*			
P		Isa. 2. 1–5 Ps. 122 Rom. 13. 11–end Matt. 24. 36–44	Ps. 44 Micah 4. 1–7 1 Thess. 5. 1–11	Ps. 9 (*or* 9. 1–8) Isa. 52. 1–12 Matt. 24. 15–28

	Calendar and Holy Communion	Morning Prayer	Evening Prayer
G		Isa. ch. 17 Matt. 9.35 - 10.15	Isa. 40. 12–26 Rev. 14.14 - 15.end
G		Isa. ch. 19 Matt. 10. 16–33	Isa. 40.27 - 41.7 Rev. 16. 1–11
G		Isa. 21. 1–12 Matt. 10.34 - 11.1	Isa. 41. 8–20 Rev. 16. 12–end
G		Isa. 22. 1–14 Matt. 11. 2–19	Isa. 41.21 - 42.9 Rev. ch. 17 *or First EP of Andrew the Apostle* (Ps. 48) Isa. 49. 1–9a 1 Cor. 4. 9–16 **R ct**

To celebrate the Day of Intercession and Thanksgiving for the Missionary Work of the Church, see *Common Worship* provision.

ANDREW THE APOSTLE

R	Zech. 8. 20–end Ps. 92. 1–5 Rom. 10. 9–end Matt. 4. 18–22	(Ps. 47; 147. 1–12) Ezek. 47. 1–12 *or* Ecclus. 14. 20–end John 12. 20–32	(Ps. 87; 96) Isa. 52. 7–10 John 1. 35–42

THE FIRST SUNDAY IN ADVENT

P	Advent 1 Collect until Christmas Eve		
	Mic. 4. 1–4, 6–7 Ps. 25. 1–9 Rom. 13. 8–14 Matt. 21. 1–13	Ps. 44 Isa. 2. 1–5 1 Thess. 5. 1–11	Ps. 9 (*or* 9. 1–8) Isa. 52. 1–12 Matt. 24. 15–28

NOTES

		Sunday Principal Service Weekday Eucharist	Third Service Morning Prayer	Second Service Evening Prayer
2 Monday	Daily Eucharistic Lectionary Year 2 begins			
P		Isa. 4. 2–end Ps. 122 Matt. 8. 5–11	Ps. ***50***; 54 *alt.* Ps. ***1***; 2; 3 Isa. 25. 1–9 Matt. 12. 1–21	Ps. 70; ***71*** *alt.* Ps. ***4***; 7 Isa. 42. 18–end Rev. ch. 19
3 Tuesday	*Francis Xavier, Missionary, Apostle of the Indies, 1552*			
P		Isa. 11. 1–10 Ps. 72. 1–4, 18–19 Luke 10. 21–24	Ps. ***80***; 82 *alt.* Ps. ***5***; 6; (8) Isa. 26. 1–13 Matt. 12. 22–37	Ps. ***74***; 75 *alt.* Ps. ***9***; 10† Isa. 43. 1–13 Rev. ch. 20
4 Wednesday	*John of Damascus, Monk, Teacher, c. 749; Nicholas Ferrar, Deacon, Founder of the Little Gidding Community, 1637*			
P		Isa. 25. 6–10a Ps. 23 Matt. 15. 29–37	Ps. 5; ***7*** *alt.* Ps. 119. 1–32 Isa. 28. 1–13 Matt. 12. 38–end	Ps. 76; ***77*** *alt.* Ps. ***11***; 12; 13 Isa. 43. 14–end Rev. 21. 1–8
5 Thursday				
P		Isa. 26. 1–6 Ps. 118. 18–27a Matt. 7. 21, 24–27	Ps. ***42***; 43 *alt.* Ps. 14; ***15***; 16 Isa. 28. 14–end Matt. 13. 1–23	Ps. ***40***; 46 *alt.* Ps. 18† Isa. 44. 1–8 Rev. 21. 9–21
6 Friday	**Nicholas, Bishop of Myra, c. 326**			
Pw	Com. Bishop *or* *also* Isa. 61. 1–3 1 Tim. 6. 6–11 Mark 10. 13–16	Isa. 29. 17–end Ps. 27. 1–4, 16–17 Matt. 9. 27–31	Ps. ***25***; 26 *alt.* Ps. 17; ***19*** Isa. 29. 1–14 Matt. 13. 24–43	Ps. 16; ***17*** *alt.* Ps. 22 Isa. 44. 9–23 Rev. 21.22 - 22.5
7 Saturday	**Ambrose, Bishop of Milan, Teacher, 397**			
Pw	Com. Teacher *or* *also* Isa. 41. 9b–13 Luke 22. 24–30	Isa. 30. 19–21, 23–26 Ps. 146. 4–9 Matt. 9.35 - 10.1, 6–8	Ps. ***9***; (10) *alt.* Ps. 20; 21; ***23*** Isa. 29. 15–end Matt. 13. 44–end	Ps. ***27***; 28 *alt.* Ps. ***24***; 25 Isa. 44.24 - 45.13 Rev. 22. 6–end **ct**
8 Sunday	**THE SECOND SUNDAY OF ADVENT**			
P		Isa. 11. 1–10 Ps. 72. 1–7, 18–19 (*or* 72. 1–7) Rom. 15. 4–13 Matt. 3. 1–12	Ps. 80 Amos ch. 7 Luke 1. 5–20	Ps. 11; [28] 1 Kings 18. 17–39 John 1. 19–28
9 Monday				
P		Isa. ch. 35 Ps. 85. 7–end Luke 5. 17–26	Ps. 44 *alt.* Ps. 27; ***30*** Isa. 30. 1–18 Matt. 14. 1–12	Ps. ***144***; 146 *alt.* Ps. 26; ***28***; 29 Isa. 45. 14–end 1 Thess. ch. 1
10 Tuesday				
P		Isa. 40. 1–11 Ps. 96. 1, 10–end Matt. 18. 12–14	Ps. ***56***; 57 *alt.* Ps. 32; ***36*** Isa. 30. 19–end Matt. 14. 13–end	Ps. ***11***; 12; 13 *alt.* Ps. 33 Isa. ch. 46 1 Thess. 2. 1–12

	Calendar and Holy Communion	Morning Prayer	Evening Prayer	NOTES
P		Isa. 25. 1-9 Matt. 12. 1-21	Isa. 42. 18-end Rev. ch. 19	
P		Isa. 26. 1-13 Matt. 12. 22-37	Isa. 43. 1-13 Rev. ch. 20	
P		Isa. 28. 1-13 Matt. 12. 38-end	Isa. 43. 14-end Rev. 21. 1-8	
P		Isa. 28. 14-end Matt. 13. 1-23	Isa. 44. 1-8 Rev. 21. 9-21	
	Nicholas, Bishop of Myra, c. 326			
Pw	Com. Bishop	Isa. 29. 1-14 Matt. 13. 24-43	Isa. 44. 9-23 Rev. 21.22 - 22.5	
P		Isa. 29. 15-end Matt. 13. 44-end	Isa. 44.24 - 45.13 Rev. 22. 6-end **ct**	
	THE SECOND SUNDAY IN ADVENT			
P	2 Kings 22. 8-10; 23. 1-3 Ps. 50. 1-6 Rom. 15. 4-13 Luke 21. 25-33	Ps. 80 Amos ch. 7 Luke 1. 5-20	Ps. 11; [28] 1 Kings 18. 17-39 Matt. 3. 1-12	
P		Isa. 30. 1-18 Matt. 14. 1-12	Isa. 45. 14-end 1 Thess. ch. 1	
P		Isa. 30. 19-end Matt. 14. 13-end	Isa. ch. 46 1 Thess. 2. 1-12	

		Sunday Principal Service Weekday Eucharist	Third Service Morning Prayer	Second Service Evening Prayer
11 Wednesday	Ember Day*			
P		Isa. 40. 25-end Ps. 103. 8-13 Matt. 11. 28-end	Ps. ***62***; 63 *alt.* Ps. 34 Isa. ch. 31 Matt. 15. 1-20	Ps. ***10***; 14 *alt.* Ps. 119. 33-56 Isa. ch. 47 1 Thess. 2. 13-end
12 Thursday				
P		Isa. 41. 13-20 Ps. 145. 1, 8-13 Matt. 11. 11-15	Ps. 53; ***54***; 60 *alt.* Ps. 37† Isa. ch. 32 Matt. 15. 21-28	Ps. 73 *alt.* Ps. 39; ***40*** Isa. 48. 1-11 1 Thess. ch. 3
13 Friday	**Lucy, Martyr at Syracuse, 304** *Samuel Johnson, Moralist, 1784* Ember Day*			
Pr	Com. Martyr *or* *also* Wisd. 3. 1-7 2 Cor. 4. 6-15	Isa. 48. 17-19 Ps. 1 Matt. 11. 16-19	Ps. 85; ***86*** *alt.* Ps. 31 Isa. 33. 1-22 Matt. 15. 29-end	Ps. 82; ***90*** *alt.* Ps. 35 Isa. 48. 12-end 1 Thess. 4. 1-12
14 Saturday	**John of the Cross, Poet, Teacher, 1591** Ember Day*			
Pw	Com. Teacher *or* *esp.* 1 Cor. 2. 1-10 *also* John 14. 18-23	Ecclus. 48. 1-4, 9-11 *or* 2 Kings 2. 9-12 Ps. 80. 1-4, 18-19 Matt. 17. 10-13	Ps. 145 *alt.* Ps. 41; ***42***; 43 Isa. ch. 35 Matt. 16. 1-12	Ps. 93; ***94*** *alt.* Ps. 45; ***46*** Isa. 49. 1-13 1 Thess. 4. 13-end **ct**
15 Sunday	**THE THIRD SUNDAY OF ADVENT**			
P		Isa. 35. 1-10 Ps. 146. 4-10 *or Canticle*: Magnificat James 5. 7-10 Matt. 11. 2-11	Ps. 68. 1-19 Zeph. 3. 14-end Phil. 4. 4-7	Ps. 12; [14] Isa. 5. 8-end Acts 13. 13-41 *Gospel*: John 5. 31-40
16 Monday				
P		Num. 24. 2-7, 15-17 Ps. 25. 3-8 Matt. 21. 23-27	Ps. 40 *alt.* Ps. 44 Isa. 38. 1-8, 21-22 Matt. 16. 13-end	Ps. 25; ***26*** *alt.* Ps. ***47***; 49 Isa. 49. 14-25 1 Thess. 5. 1-11
17 Tuesday	O Sapientia** *Eglantyne Jebb, Social Reformer, Founder of 'Save the Children', 1928*			
P		Gen. 49. 2, 8-10 Ps. 72. 1-5, 18-19 Matt. 1. 1-17	Ps. ***70***; 74 *alt.* Ps. ***48***; 52 Isa. 38. 9-20 Matt. 17. 1-13	Ps. ***50***; 54 *alt.* Ps. 50 Isa. ch. 50 1 Thess. 5. 12-end
18 Wednesday				
P		Jer. 23. 5-8 Ps. 72. 1-2, 12-13, 18-end Matt. 1. 18-24	Ps. ***75***; 96 *alt.* Ps. 119. 57-80 Isa. ch. 39 Matt. 17. 14-21	Ps. 25; ***82*** *alt.* Ps. ***59***; 60; (67) Isa. 51. 1-8 2 Thess. ch. 1

*For Ember Day provision, see p. 11.
**The Evening Prayer readings from the Additional Weekday Lectionary (see p. 121) may be used from 17 to 23 December.

	Calendar and Holy Communion	Morning Prayer	Evening Prayer	NOTES
P		Isa. ch. 31 Matt. 15. 1–20	Isa. ch. 47 1 Thess. 2. 13–end	
P		Isa. ch. 32 Matt. 15. 21–28	Isa. 48. 1–11 1 Thess. ch. 3	
	Lucy, Martyr at Syracuse, 304			
Pr	Com. Virgin Martyr	Isa. 33. 1–22 Matt. 15. 29–end	Isa. 48. 12–end 1 Thess. 4. 1–12	
P		Isa. ch. 35 Matt. 16. 1–12	Isa. 49. 1–13 1 Thess. 4. 13–end **ct**	
	THE THIRD SUNDAY IN ADVENT			
P	Isa. ch. 35 Ps. 80. 1–7 1 Cor. 4. 1–5 Matt. 11. 2–10	Ps. 68. 1–19 Zeph. 3. 14–end James 5. 7–10	Ps. 12; [14] Isa. 5. 8–end Acts 13. 13–41	
	O Sapientia			
P		Isa. 38. 1–8, 21–22 Matt. 16. 13–end	Isa. 49. 14–25 1 Thess. 5. 1–11	
P		Isa. 38. 9–20 Matt. 17. 1–13	Isa. ch. 50 1 Thess. 5. 12–end	
	Ember Day			
P	Ember CEG	Isa. ch. 39 Matt. 17. 14–21	Isa. 51. 1–8 2 Thess. ch. 1	

		Sunday Principal Service Weekday Eucharist	Third Service Morning Prayer	Second Service Evening Prayer
19 Thursday				
P		Judg. 13. 2–7, 24–end Ps. 71. 3–8 Luke 1. 5–25	Ps. 144; ***146*** Zeph. 1.1 – 2.3 Matt. 17. 22–end	Ps. 10; ***57*** Isa. 51. 9–16 2 Thess. ch. 2
20 Friday				
P		Isa. 7. 10–14 Ps. 24. 1–6 Luke 1. 26–38	Ps. ***46***; 95 Zeph. 3. 1–13 Matt. 18. 1–20	Ps. ***4***; 9 Isa. 51. 17–end 2 Thess. ch. 3
21 Saturday*				
P		Zeph. 3. 14–18 Ps. 33. 1–4, 11–12, 20–end Luke 1. 39–45	Ps. ***121***; 122; 123 Zeph. 3. 14–end Matt. 18. 21–end	Ps. 80; ***84*** Isa. 52. 1–12 Jude **ct**
22 Sunday	**THE FOURTH SUNDAY OF ADVENT**			
P		Isa. 7. 10–16 Ps. 80. 1–8, 18–20 (*or* 80. 1–8) Rom. 1. 1–7 Matt. 1. 18–end	Ps. 144 Micah 5. 2–5a Luke 1. 26–38	Ps. 113; [126] 1 Sam. 1. 1–20 Rev. 22. 6–end *Gospel*: Luke 1. 39–45
23 Monday				
P		Mal. 3. 1–4; 4. 5–end Ps. 25. 3–9 Luke 1. 57–66	Ps. 128; 129; ***130***; 131 Mal. 1. 1, 6–end Matt. 19. 1–12	Ps. 89. 1–37 Isa. 52.13 – 53.end 2 Pet. 1. 1–15
24 Tuesday	**CHRISTMAS EVE**			
P		*Morning Eucharist* 2 Sam. 7. 1–5, 8–11, 16 Ps. 89. 2, 19–27 Acts 13. 16–26 Luke 1. 67–79	Ps. ***45***; 113 Mal. 2. 1–16 Matt. 19. 13–15	Ps. 85 Zech. ch. 2 Rev. 1. 1–8
25 Wednesday	**CHRISTMAS DAY**			
𝔴	*Any of the following sets of readings may be used on the evening of Christmas Eve and on Christmas Day. Set III should be used at some service during the celebration.*	*I* Isa. 9. 2–7 Ps. 96 Titus 2. 11–14 Luke 2. 1–14 [15–20] *II* Isa. 62. 6–end Ps. 97 Titus 3. 4–7 Luke 2. [1–7] 8–20 *III* Isa. 52. 7–10 Ps. 98 Heb. 1. 1–4 [5–12] John 1. 1–14	*MP*: Ps. ***110***; 117 Isa. 62. 1–5 Matt. 1. 18–end	*EP*: Ps. 8 Isa. 65. 17–25 Phil. 2. 5–11 *or* Luke 2. 1–20 *if it has not been used at the principal service of the day*

*Thomas the Apostle may be celebrated on 21 December instead of 3 July.

	Calendar and Holy Communion	Morning Prayer	Evening Prayer	NOTES
P		Zeph. 1.1 - 2.3 Matt. 17. 22-end	Isa. 51. 9-16 2 Thess. ch. 2	
	Ember Day			
P	Ember CEG	Zeph. 3. 1-13 Matt. 18. 1-20	Isa. 51. 17-end 2 Thess. ch. 3 *or First EP of Thomas* (Ps. 27) Isa. ch. 35 Heb. 10.35 - 11.1 **R ct**	
	THOMAS THE APOSTLE Ember Day			
R	Job 42. 1-6 Ps. 139. 1-11 Eph. 2. 19-end John 20. 24-end	(Ps. 92; 146) 2 Sam. 15. 17-21 *or* Ecclus. ch. 2 John 11. 1-16	(Ps. 139) Hab. 2. 1-4 1 Pet. 1. 3-12	
	THE FOURTH SUNDAY IN ADVENT			
P	Isa. 40. 1-9 Ps. 145. 17-end Phil. 4. 4-7 John 1. 19-28	Ps. 144 Micah 5. 2-5a Luke 1. 26-38	Ps. 113; [126] 1 Sam. 1. 1-20 Rev. 22. 6-end	
P		Mal. 1. 1, 6-end Matt. 19. 1-12	Isa. 52.13 - 53.end 2 Pet. 1. 1-15	
	CHRISTMAS EVE			
P	Collect (1) Christmas Eve (2) Advent 1 Mic. 5. 2-5a Ps. 24 Titus 3. 3-7 Luke 2. 1-14	Mal. 2. 1-16 Matt. 19. 13-15	Zech. ch. 2 Rev. 1. 1-8	
	CHRISTMAS DAY			
𝔚	Isa. 9. 2-7 Ps. 98 Heb. 1. 1-12 John 1. 1-14	Ps. 110; 117 Isa. 62. 1-5 Matt. 1. 18-end	Ps. 8 Isa. 65. 17-25 Phil. 2. 5-11 *or* Luke 2. 1-20	

		Sunday Principal Service Weekday Eucharist	Third Service Morning Prayer	Second Service Evening Prayer
26 Thursday	**STEPHEN, DEACON, FIRST MARTYR**			
R		2 Chron. 24. 20–22 *or* Acts 7. 51–end Ps. 119. 161–168 Acts 7. 51–end *or* Gal. 2. 16b–20 Matt. 10. 17–22	*MP*: Ps. ***13***; 31. 1–8; 150 Jer. 26. 12–15 Acts ch. 6	*EP*: Ps. 57; ***86*** Gen. 4. 1–10 Matt. 23. 34–end
27 Friday	**JOHN, APOSTLE AND EVANGELIST**			
W		Exod. 33. 7–11a Ps. 117 1 John ch. 1 John 21. 19b–end	*MP*: Ps. ***21***; 147. 13–end Exod. 33. 12–end 1 John 2. 1–11	*EP*: Ps. 97 Isa. 6. 1–8 1 John 5. 1–12
28 Saturday	**THE HOLY INNOCENTS**			
R		Jer. 31. 15–17 Ps. 124 1 Cor. 1. 26–29 Matt. 2. 13–18	*MP*: Ps. ***36***; 146 Baruch 4. 21–27 *or* Gen. 37. 13–20 Matt. 18. 1–10	*EP*: Ps. 123; ***128*** Isa. 49. 14–25 Mark 10. 13–16
29 Sunday	**THE FIRST SUNDAY OF CHRISTMAS**			
W		Isa. 63. 7–9 Ps. 148 (*or* 148. 7–end) Heb. 2. 10–end Matt. 2. 13–end	Ps. 105. 1–11 Isa. 35. 1–6 Gal. 3. 23–end	Ps. 132 Isa. 49. 7–13 Phil. 2. 1–11 *Gospel*: Luke 2. 41–52
30 Monday				
W		1 John 2. 12–17 Ps. 96. 7–10 Luke 2. 36–40	Ps. 111; 112; ***113*** Jonah ch. 2 Col. 1. 15–23	Ps. ***65***; 84 Isa. 59. 1–15a John 1. 19–28
31 Tuesday	*John Wyclif, Reformer, 1384*			
W		1 John 2. 18–21 Ps. 96. 1, 11–end John 1. 1–18	Ps. 102 Jonah chs 3 & 4 Col. 1.24 - 2.7	Ps. ***90***; 148 Isa. 59. 15b–end John 1. 29–34 *or First EP of The Naming of Jesus* Ps. 148 Jer. 23. 1–6 Col. 2. 8–15 **ct**

	Calendar and Holy Communion	Morning Prayer	Evening Prayer	NOTES
	STEPHEN, DEACON, FIRST MARTYR			
R	Collect (1) Stephen (2) Christmas 2 Chron. 24. 20–22 Ps. 119. 161–168 Acts 7. 55–end Matt. 23. 34–end	(Ps. 13; 31. 1–8; 150) Jer. 26. 12–15 Acts ch. 6	(Ps. 57; 86) Gen. 4. 1–10 Matt. 10. 17–22	
	JOHN, APOSTLE AND EVANGELIST			
W	Collect (1) John (2) Christmas Exod. 33. 18–end Ps. 92. 11–end 1 John ch. 1 John 21. 19b–end	(Ps. 21; 147. 13–end) Exod. 33. 7–11a 1 John 2. 1–11	(Ps. 97) Isa. 6. 1–8 1 John 5. 1–12	
	THE HOLY INNOCENTS			
R	Collect (1) Innocents (2) Christmas Jer. 31. 10–17 Ps. 123 Rev. 14. 1–5 Matt. 2. 13–18	(Ps. 36; 146) Baruch 4. 21–27 *or* Gen. 37. 13–20 Matt. 18. 1–10	(Ps. 124; 128) Isa. 49. 14–25 Mark 10. 13–16	
	THE SUNDAY AFTER CHRISTMAS DAY			
W	Isa. 62. 10–12 Ps. 45. 1–7 Gal. 4. 1–7 Matt. 1. 18–end	Ps. 105. 1–11 Isa. 35. 1–6 Gal. 3. 23–end	Ps. 132 Isa. 49. 7–13 Phil. 2. 1–11	
W		Jonah ch. 2 Col. 1. 15–23	Isa. 59. 1–15a John 1. 19–28	
	Silvester, Bishop of Rome, 335			
W	Com. Bishop	Jonah chs 3 & 4 Col. 1.24 - 2.7	Isa. 59. 15b–end John 1. 29–34 *or First EP of The Circumcision of Christ* (Ps. 148) Jer. 23. 1–6 Col. 2. 8–15 **ct**	

The *Common Worship* Additional Weekday Lectionary

The Additional Weekday Lectionary provides two readings on a one-year cycle for each day (except for Sundays, Principal Feasts and Holy Days, Festivals and Holy Week). They 'stand alone' and are intended particularly for use in those churches and cathedrals that attract occasional rather than regular congregations. The Additional Weekday Lectionary has been designed to complement rather than replace the existing Weekday Lectionary. Thus a church with a regular congregation in the morning and a congregation made up mainly of visitors in the evening would continue to use the Weekday Lectionary in the morning but might choose to use this Additional Weekday Lectionary for Evening Prayer.

Psalms are not provided, since the Weekday Lectionary already offers a variety of approaches with regard to psalmody. This Lectionary is not intended for use at the Eucharist; the Daily Eucharistic Lectionary is already authorized for that purpose.

On Sundays, Principal Feasts, other Principal Holy Days, Festivals, and in Holy Week, where no readings are provided in this table, the lectionary provision in the main part of this volume should be used.

December 2018

Date		Old Testament	New Testament
2	S	THE FIRST SUNDAY OF ADVENT	
3	M	Mal. 3. 1–6	Matt. 3. 1–6
4	Tu	Zeph. 3. 14–end	I Thess. 4. 13–end
5	W	Isa. 65.17 – 66.2	Matt. 24. 1–14
6	Th	Mic. 5. 2–5a	John 3. 16–21
7	F	Isa. 66. 18–end	Luke 13. 22–30
8	Sa	Mic. 7. 8–15	Rom. 15.30 – 16.7, 25–end
9	S	THE SECOND SUNDAY OF ADVENT	
10	M	Jer. 7. 1–11	Phil. 4. 4–9
11	Tu	Dan. 7. 9–14	Matt. 24. 15–28
12	W	Amos 9. 11–end	Rom. 13. 8–14
13	Th	Jer. 23. 5–8	Mark 11. 1–11
14	F	Jer. 33. 14–22	Luke 21. 25–36
15	Sa	Zech. 14. 4–11	Rev. 22. 1–7
16	S	THE THIRD SUNDAY OF ADVENT	
17	M	Ecclus. 24. 1–9 *or* Prov. 8. 22–31	I Cor. 2. 1–13
18	Tu	Exod. 3. 1–6	Acts 7. 20–36
19	W	Isa. 11. 1–9	Rom. 15. 7–13
20	Th	Isa. 22. 21–23	Rev. 3. 7–13
21	F	Num. 24. 15b–19	Rev. 22. 10–21
22	Sa	Jer. 30. 7–11a	Acts 4. 1–12
23	S	THE FOURTH SUNDAY OF ADVENT	
24	M	*At Evening Prayer the readings for Christmas Eve are used. At other services, the following readings are used:* Isa. 29. 13–18	I John 4. 7–16
25	Tu	**CHRISTMAS DAY**	
26	W	STEPHEN	
27	Th	JOHN THE EVANGELIST	
28	F	THE HOLY INNOCENTS	
29	Sa	Mic. 1. 1–4; 2. 12–13	Luke 2. 1–7
30	S	THE FIRST SUNDAY OF CHRISTMAS	
31	M	Eccles. 3. 1–13	Rev. 21. 1–8

January 2019

Date		Old Testament	New Testament
1	Tu	**NAMING AND CIRCUMCISION OF JESUS**	
2	W	Isa. 66. 6–14	Matt. 12. 46–50
3	Th	Deut. 6. 4–15	John 10. 31–end
4	F	Isa. 63. 7–16	Gal. 3.23 – 4.7
5	Sa	*At Evening Prayer the readings for the Eve of Epiphany are used. At other services, the following readings are used:* Isa. ch. 12	2 Cor. 2. 12–end
6	S	**THE EPIPHANY**	
7	M	Gen. 25. 19–end	Eph. 1. 1–6
8	Tu	Joel 2. 28–end	Eph. 1. 7–14
9	W	Prov. 8. 12–21	Eph. 1. 15–end
10	Th	Gen. 19. 15–29	Eph. 2. 1–10
11	F	Gen. 17. 1–14	Eph. 2. 11–end
12	Sa	*At Evening Prayer the readings for the Eve of the Baptism of Christ are used. At other services, the following readings are used:* I Kings 10. 1–13	Eph. 3. 14–end
13	S	THE BAPTISM OF CHRIST (The Second Sunday of Epiphany)	
14	M	Isa. 41. 14–20	John 1. 29–34
15	Tu	Exod. 17. 1–7	Acts 8. 26–end
16	W	Exod. 15. 1–19	Col. 2. 8–15
17	Th	Zech. 6. 9–15	I Pet. 2. 4–10
18	F	Isa. 51. 7–16	Gal. 6. 14–18
19	Sa	Lev. 16. 11–22	Heb. 10. 19–25
20	S	THE THIRD SUNDAY OF EPIPHANY	
21	M	I Kings. 17. 8–16	Mark 8. 1–10
22	Tu	I Kings 19. 1–9a	Mark 1. 9–15
23	W	I Kings 19. 9b–18	Mark 9. 2–13
24	Th	Lev. 11. 1–8, 13–19, 41–45	Acts 10. 9–16
25	F	THE CONVERSION OF PAUL	
26	Sa	Gen. 35. 1–15	Acts 10. 44–end
27	S	THE FOURTH SUNDAY OF EPIPHANY	
28	M	Ezek. 37. 15–end	John 17. 1–19
29	Tu	Ezek. 20. 39–44	John 17. 20–end
30	W	Neh. 2. 1–10	Rom. 12. 1–8
31	Th	Deut. 26. 16–end	Rom. 14. 1–9

February 2019

Date		Old Testament	New Testament
1	F	Lev. 19. 9–28	Rom. 15. 1–7
2	Sa	**THE PRESENTATION** *or* Jer. 33. 1–11 *or, where The Presentation is celebrated on Sunday 3 February, First EP of The Presentation*	I Pet. 5. 5b–end
3	S	THE FIFTH SUNDAY BEFORE LENT (*or The Presentation*)	
4	M	Isa. 42. 10–21	Luke 1. 5–25
5	Tu	I Sam. 4. 12–end	Luke 1. 57–80
6	W	Baruch ch. 5 *or* Hag. 1. 1–11	Mark 1. 1–11
7	Th	Isa. ch. 35	Matt. 11. 2–19
8	F	2 Sam. 11. 1–17	Matt. 14. 1–12
9	Sa	Isa. 43. 15–21	Acts 19. 1–10
10	S	THE FOURTH SUNDAY BEFORE LENT	
11	M	Gen. 1. 26–end	Mark 10. 1–16
12	Tu	Ruth 1. 1–18	I John 3. 14–end
13	W	I Sam. 1. 19b–end	Luke 2. 41–end
14	Th	Gen. 47. 1–12	Eph. 3. 14–end
15	F	2 Sam. 1. 17–end	Rom. 8. 28–end
16	Sa	Song of Sol. 2. 8–end	I Cor. ch. 13
17	S	THE THIRD SUNDAY BEFORE LENT	
18	M	Exod. 23. 1–13	James 2. 1–13
19	Tu	Deut. 10. 12–end	Heb. 13. 1–16
20	W	Isa. 58. 6–end	Matt. 25. 31–end
21	Th	Isa. 42. 1–9	Luke 4. 14–21
22	F	Amos 5. 6–15	Eph. 4. 25–end
23	Sa	Amos 5. 18–24	John 2. 13–22
24	S	THE SECOND SUNDAY BEFORE LENT	
25	M	Isa. 61. 1–9	Mark 6. 1–13
26	Tu	Isa. 52. 1–10	Rom. 10. 5–21
27	W	Isa. 52.13 – 53.6	Rom. 15. 14–21
28	Th	Isa. 53. 4–12	2 Cor. 4. 1–10

March 2019

Date		Old Testament	New Testament
1	F	Zech. 8. 16–end	Matt. 10. 1–15
2	Sa	Jer. 1. 4–10	Matt. 10. 16–22
3	S	THE SUNDAY NEXT BEFORE LENT	
4	M	2 Kings 2. 13–22	3 John
5	Tu	Judges 14. 5–17	Rev. 10. 4–11

6	W	**ASH WEDNESDAY**	
7	Th	Gen. 2. 7–end	Heb. 2. 5–end
8	F	Gen. 4. 1–12	Heb. 4. 12–end
9	Sa	2 Kings 22. 11–end	Heb. 5. 1–10
10	S	THE FIRST SUNDAY OF LENT	
11	M	Gen. 6. 11–end; 7. 11–16	Luke 4. 14–21
12	Tu	Deut. 31. 7–13	1 John 3. 1–10
13	W	Gen. 11. 1–9	Matt. 24. 15–28
14	Th	Gen. 13. 1–13	1 Pet. 2. 13–end
15	F	Gen. 21. 1–8	Luke 9. 18–27
16	Sa	Gen. 32. 22–32	2 Pet. 1. 10–end
17	S	THE SECOND SUNDAY OF LENT	
18	M	1 Chron. 21. 1–17	1 John 2. 1–8
19	Tu	JOSEPH OF NAZARETH	
20	W	Job. 1. 1–22	Luke 21.34 – 22.6
21	Th	2 Chron. 29. 1–11	Mark 11. 15–19
22	F	Exod. 19. 1–9a	1 Pet. 1. 1–9
23	Sa	Exod. 19. 9b–19	Acts 7. 44–50
24	S	THE THIRD SUNDAY OF LENT	
25	M	**THE ANNUNCIATION**	
26	Tu	Exod. 15. 22–27	Heb. 10. 32–end
27	W	Gen. 9. 8–17	1 Pet. 3. 18–end
28	Th	Dan. 12. 5–end	Mark 13. 21–end
29	F	Num. 20. 1–13	1 Cor. 10. 23–end
30	Sa	Isa. 43. 14–end	Heb. 3. 1–15
31	S	THE FOURTH SUNDAY OF LENT **(Mothering Sunday)**	

April 2019

1	M	2 Kings 24.18 – 25.7	1 Cor. 15. 20–34
2	Tu	Jer. 13. 12–19	Acts 13. 26–35
3	W	Jer. 13. 20–27	1 Pet. 1.17 – 2.3
4	Th	Jer. 22. 11–19	Luke 11. 37–52
5	F	Jer. 17. 1–14	Luke 6. 17–26
6	Sa	Ezra ch. 1	2 Cor. 1. 12–19
7	S	THE FIFTH SUNDAY OF LENT **(Passiontide begins)**	
8	M	Joel 2. 12–17	2 John
9	Tu	Isa. 58. 1–14	Mark 10. 32–45
10	W	Joel 36. 1–12	John 14. 1–14
11	Th	Jer. 9. 17–22	Luke 13. 31–35
12	F	Lam. 5. 1–3, 19–22	John 12. 20–26
13	Sa	Job 17. 6–end	John 12. 27–36
14	S	PALM SUNDAY	
		HOLY WEEK	
21	S	**EASTER DAY** THE FOURTH SUNDAY OF EASTER	
22	M	Isa. 54. 1–14	Rom. 1. 1–7
23	Tu	Isa. 51. 1–11	John 5. 19–29
24	W	Isa. 26. 1–19	John 20. 1–10
25	Th	Isa. 43. 14–21	Rev. 1. 4–end
26	F	Isa. 42. 10–17	1 Thess. 5. 1–11
27	Sa	Job 14. 1–14	John 21. 1–14
28	S	THE SECOND SUNDAY OF EASTER	
29	M	GEORGE (transferred from 23 April)	
30	Tu	MARK (transferred from 25 April)	

May 2019

1	W	PHILIP AND JAMES	
2	Th	Jonah ch. 2	Mark 4. 35–end
3	F	Gen. 6. 9–end	1 Pet. 3. 8–end
4	Sa	1 Sam. 2. 1–8	Matt. 28. 8–15
5	S	THE THIRD SUNDAY OF EASTER	
6	M	Exod. 24. 1–11	Rev. ch. 5
7	Tu	Lev. 19. 9–18, 32–end	Matt. 5. 38–end
8	W	Gen. 3. 8–21	1 Cor. 15. 12–28
9	Th	Isa. 33. 13–22	Mark 6. 47–end
10	F	Neh. 9. 6–17	Rom. 5. 12–end
11	Sa	Isa. 61.10 – 62.5	Luke 24. 1–12
12	S	THE FOURTH SUNDAY OF EASTER	
13	M	Jer. 31. 10–17	Rev. 7. 9–end
14	Tu	MATTHIAS	
		Where Matthias is celebrated on 24 February:	
		Job 31. 13–23	Matt. 7. 1–12
15	W	Gen. 2. 4b–9	1 Cor. 15. 35–49
16	Th	Prov. 28. 3–end	Mark 10. 17–31
17	F	Eccles. 12. 1–8	Rom. 6. 1–11
18	Sa	1 Chron. 29. 10–13	Luke 24. 13–35
19	S	THE FIFTH SUNDAY OF EASTER	
20	M	Gen. 15. 1–18	Rom. 4. 13–end
21	Tu	Deut. 8. 1–10	Matt. 6. 19–end
22	W	Hos. 13. 4–14	1 Cor. 15. 50–end
23	Th	Exod. 3. 1–15	Mark 12. 18–27
24	F	Ezek. 36. 33–end	Rom. 8. 1–11
25	Sa	Isa. 38. 9–20	Luke 24. 33–end
26	S	THE SIXTH SUNDAY OF EASTER	
27	M	Prov. 4. 1–13	Phil. 2. 1–11
28	Tu	Isa. 32. 12–end	Rom. 5. 1–11
29	W	*At Evening Prayer the readings for the Eve of Ascension Day are used. At other services, the following readings are used:*	
		Isa. 43. 1–13	Titus 2.11 – 3.8
30	Th	**ASCENSION DAY**	
31	F	THE VISITATION	
		Where The Visitation is celebrated on 2 July:	
		Exod. 35.30 – 36.1	Gal. 5. 13–end

June 2019

1	Sa	Num. 11. 16–17, 24–29	1 Cor. ch. 2
2	S	THE SEVENTH SUNDAY OF EASTER (Sunday after Ascension Day)	
3	M	Num. 27. 15–end	1 Cor. ch. 3
4	Tu	1 Sam. 10. 1–10	1 Cor. 12. 1–13
5	W	1 Kings 19. 1–18	Matt. 3. 13–end
6	Th	Ezek. 11. 14–20	Matt. 9.35 – 10.20
7	F	Ezek. 36. 22–28	Matt. 12. 22–32
8	Sa	*At Evening Prayer the readings for the Eve of Pentecost are used. At other services, the following readings are used:*	
		Mic. 3. 1–8	Eph. 6. 10–20
9	S	**PENTECOST** (Whit Sunday)	
10	M	Gen. 12. 1–9	Rom. 4. 13–end
11	Tu	BARNABAS	
12	W	Gen. ch. 15	Rom. 4. 1–8
13	Th	Gen. 22. 1–18	Heb. 11. 8–19
14	F	Isa. 51. 1–8	John 8. 48–end
15	Sa	*At Evening Prayer the readings for the Eve of Trinity Sunday are used. At other services, the following readings are used:*	
		Ecclus. 44. 19–23	James 2. 14–26
		or Josh. 2. 1–15	
16	S	**TRINITY SUNDAY**	
17	M	Exod. 2. 1–10	Heb. 11. 23–31
18	Tu	Exod. 2. 11–end	Acts 7. 17–29
19	W	Exod. 3. 1–12	Acts 7. 30–38
20	Th	*Day of Thanksgiving for the Institution of the Holy Communion (Corpus Christi), or, where Corpus Christi is celebrated as a Lesser Festival:*	
		Exod. 6. 1–13	John 9. 24–38
21	F	Exod. 34. 1–10	Mark 7. 1–13
22	Sa	Exod. 34. 27–end	2 Cor. 3. 7–end
23	S	THE FIRST SUNDAY AFTER TRINITY	
24	M	THE BIRTH OF JOHN THE BAPTIST	
25	Tu	Gen. 41. 15–40	Mark 13. 1–13
26	W	Gen. 42. 17–end	Matt. 18. 1–14
27	Th	Gen. 45. 1–15	Acts 7. 9–16
28	F	Gen. 47. 1–12	1 Thess. 5. 12–end
29	Sa	PETER AND PAUL	
30	S	THE SECOND SUNDAY AFTER TRINITY	

July 2019

1	M	Isa. ch. 32	James 3. 13–end
2	Tu	Prov. 3. 1–18	Matt. 5. 1–12
3	W	THOMAS	
		Where Thomas is celebrated on 21 December:	
		Judg. 6. 1–16	Matt. 5. 13–24
4	Th	Jer. 6. 9–15	1 Tim. 2. 1–6
5	F	1 Sam. 16. 14–end	John 14. 15–end
6	Sa	Isa. 6. 1–9	Rev. 19. 9–end

7	S	**THE THIRD SUNDAY AFTER TRINITY**	
8	M	Exod. 13. 13b–end	Luke 15. 1–10
9	Tu	Prov. 1. 20–end	James 5. 13–end
10	W	Isa. 5. 8–24	James 1. 17–25
11	Th	Isa. 57. 14–end	John 13. 1–17
12	F	Jer. 15. 15–end	Luke 16. 19–31
13	Sa	Isa. 25. 1–9	Acts 2. 22–33
14	S	**THE FOURTH SUNDAY AFTER TRINITY**	
15	M	Exod. 20. 1–17	Matt. 6. 1–15
16	Tu	Prov. 6. 6–19	Luke 4. 1–14
17	W	Isa. 24. 1–15	1 Cor. 6. 1–11
18	Th	Job ch. 7	Matt. 7. 21–29
19	F	Jer. 20. 7–end	Matt. 27. 27–44
20	Sa	Job ch. 28	Heb. 11.32 – 12.2
21	S	**THE FIFTH SUNDAY AFTER TRINITY**	
22	M	**MARY MAGDALENE**	
23	Tu	Prov. 9. 1–12	2 Thess. 2.13 – 3.5
24	W	Isa. 26. 1–9	Rom. 8. 12–27
25	Th	**JAMES**	
26	F	2 Sam. 5. 1–12	Matt. 27. 45–56
27	Sa	Hos. 11. 1–11	Matt. 28. 1–7
28	S	**THE SIXTH SUNDAY AFTER TRINITY**	
29	M	Exod. 40. 1–16	Luke 14. 15–24
30	Tu	Prov. 11. 1–12	Mark 12. 38–44
31	W	Isa. 33. 2–10	Phil. 1. 1–11

August 2019

1	Th	Job ch. 38	Luke 18. 1–14
2	F	Job 42. 1–6	John 3. 1–15
3	Sa	Eccles. 9. 1–11	Heb. 1. 1–9
4	S	**THE SEVENTH SUNDAY AFTER TRINITY**	
5	M	Num. 23. 1–12	1 Cor. 1. 10–17
6	Tu	**THE TRANSFIGURATION**	
7	W	Isa. 49. 8–13	2 Cor. 8. 1–11
8	Th	Hos. ch. 14	John 15. 1–17
9	F	2 Sam. 18. 18–end	Matt. 27. 57–66
10	Sa	Isa. 55. 1–7	Mark 16. 1–8
11	S	**THE EIGHTH SUNDAY AFTER TRINITY**	
12	M	Joel 3. 16–21	Mark 4. 21–34
13	Tu	Prov. 12. 13–end	John 1. 43–51
14	W	Isa. 55. 8–end	2 Tim. 2. 8–19
15	Th	**THE BLESSED VIRGIN MARY**	
		Where the Blessed Virgin Mary is celebrated on 8 September:	
		Isa. 38. 1–8	Mark 5. 21–43
16	F	Jer. 14. 1–9	Luke 8. 4–15
17	Sa	Eccles. 5. 10–19	1 Tim. 6. 6–16
18	S	**THE NINTH SUNDAY AFTER TRINITY**	
19	M	Josh. 1. 1–9	1 Cor. 9. 19–end
20	Tu	Prov. 15. 1–11	Matt. 15. 21–28
21	W	Isa. 49. 1–7	1 John 1
22	Th	Prov. 27. 1–12	John 15. 12–27
23	F	Isa. 59. 8–end	Mark 15. 6–20
24	Sa	**BARTHOLOMEW**	
25	S	**THE TENTH SUNDAY AFTER TRINITY**	
26	M	Judg. 13. 1–23	Luke 10. 38–42
27	Tu	Prov. 15. 15–end	Gal. 2. 15–end
28	W	Isa. 45. 1–7	Eph. 4. 1–16
29	Th	Jer. 16. 1–15	Luke 12. 35–48
30	F	Jer. 18. 1–11	Heb. 1. 1–9
31	Sa	Jer. 26. 1–19	Eph. 3. 1–13

September 2019

1	S	**THE ELEVENTH SUNDAY AFTER TRINITY**	
2	M	Ruth 2. 1–13	Luke 10. 25–37
3	Tu	Prov. 16. 1–11	Phil. 3. 4b–end
4	W	Deut. 11. 1–21	2 Cor. 9. 6–end
5	Th	Ecclus. ch. 2 *or* Eccles. 2. 12–25	John 16. 1–15
6	F	Obad. 1–10	John 19. 1–16
7	Sa	2 Kings 2. 11–14	Luke 24. 36–end
8	S	**THE TWELFTH SUNDAY AFTER TRINITY**	
9	M	1 Sam. 17. 32–50	Matt. 8. 14–22
10	Tu	Prov. 17. 1–15	Luke 7. 1–17
11	W	Jer. 5. 20–end	2 Pet. 3. 8–end
12	Th	Dan. 2. 1–23	Luke 10. 1–20
13	F	Dan. 3. 1–28	Rev. ch. 15
14	Sa	**HOLY CROSS DAY**	
15	S	**THE THIRTEENTH SUNDAY AFTER TRINITY**	
16	M	2 Sam. 7. 4–17	2 Cor. 5. 1–10
17	Tu	Prov. 18. 10–21	Rom. 14. 10–end
18	W	Judg. 4. 1–10	Rom. 1. 8–17
19	Th	Isa. 49. 14–end	John 16. 16–24
20	F	Job 9. 1–24	Mark 15. 21–32
21	Sa	**MATTHEW**	
22	S	**THE FOURTEENTH SUNDAY AFTER TRINITY**	
23	M	Hag. ch. 1	Mark 7. 9–23
24	Tu	Prov. 21. 1–18	Mark 6. 30–44
25	W	Hos. 11. 1–11	1 John 4. 9–end
26	Th	Lam. 3. 34–48	Rom. 7. 14–end
27	F	1 Kings 19. 4–18	1 Thess. ch. 3
28	Sa	Ecclus. 4. 11–28 *or* Deut. 29. 2–15	2 Tim. 3. 10–end
29	S	**MICHAEL AND ALL ANGELS** *OR* **THE FIFTEENTH SUNDAY AFTER TRINITY**	
30	M	Wisd. 6. 12–21 *or* Job 12. 1–16	Matt. 15. 1–9

October 2019

1	Tu	Prov. 8. 1–11	Luke 6. 39–end
2	W	Prov. 2. 1–15	Col. 1. 9–20
3	Th	Baruch 3. 14–end *or* Gen. 1. 1–13	John 1. 1–18
4	F	Ecclus. 1. 1–20 *or* Deut. 7. 7–16	1 Cor. 1. 18–end
5	Sa	Wisd. 9. 1–12 *or* Jer. 1. 4–10	Luke 2. 41–end
6	S	**THE SIXTEENTH SUNDAY AFTER TRINITY**	
7	M	Gen. 21. 1–13	Luke 1. 26–38
8	Tu	Ruth 4. 7–17	Luke 2. 25–38
9	W	2 Kings 4. 1–7	John 2. 1–11
10	Th	2 Kings 4. 25b–37	Mark 3. 19b–35
11	F	Judith 8. 9–17, 28–36 *or* Ruth 1. 1–18	John 19. 25b–30
12	Sa	Exod. 15. 19–27	Acts 1. 6–14
13	S	**THE SEVENTEENTH SUNDAY AFTER TRINITY**	
14	M	Exod. 19. 16–end	Heb. 12. 18–end
15	Tu	1 Chron. 16. 1–13	Rev. 11. 15–end
16	W	1 Chron. 29. 10–19	Col. 3. 12–17
17	Th	Neh. 8. 1–12	1 Cor. 14. 1–12
18	F	**LUKE**	
19	Sa	Dan. 6. 6–23	Rev. 12. 7–12
20	S	**THE EIGHTEENTH SUNDAY AFTER TRINITY**	
21	M	2 Sam. 22. 4–7, 17–20	Heb. 7.26 – 8.6
22	Tu	Prov. 22. 17–end	2 Cor. 12. 1–10
23	W	Hos. ch. 14	James 2. 14–26
24	Th	Isa. 24. 1–15	John 16. 25–33
25	F	Jer. 14. 1–9	Luke 23. 44–56
26	Sa	Zech. 8. 14–end	John 20. 19–end
27	S	**THE LAST SUNDAY AFTER TRINITY**	
28	M	**SIMON AND JUDE**	
29	Tu	1 Sam. 4. 12–end	Luke 1. 57–80
30	W	Baruch ch. 5 *or* Hag. 1. 1–11	Mark 1. 1–11
31	Th	*At Evening Prayer the readings for the Eve of All Saints are used. At other services, the following readings are used:*	
		Isa. ch. 35	Matt. 11. 2–19

November 2019

1	F	**ALL SAINTS' DAY**	
		or, where All Saints' Day is celebrated on Sunday 3 November:	
		2 Sam. 11. 1–17	Matt. 14. 1–12
2	Sa	Isa. 43. 15–21	Acts 19. 1–10
3	S	**THE FOURTH SUNDAY BEFORE ADVENT**	
4	M	Esther 3. 1–11; 4. 7–17	Matt. 18. 1–10

5	Tu	Ezek. 18. 21–end	Matt. 18. 12–20
6	W	Prov. 3. 27–end	Matt. 18. 21–end
7	Th	Exod. 23. 1–9	Matt. 19. 1–15
8	F	Prov. 3. 13–18	Matt. 19. 16–end
9	Sa	Deut. 28. 1–6	Matt. 20. 1–16
10	S	**THE THIRD SUNDAY BEFORE ADVENT**	
11	M	Isa. 40. 21–end	Rom. 11. 25–end
12	Tu	Ezek. 34. 20–end	John 10. 1–18
13	W	Lev. 26. 3–13	Titus 2. 1–10
14	Th	Hos. 6. 1–6	Matt. 9. 9–13
15	F	Mal. ch. 4	John 4. 5–26
16	Sa	Mic. 6. 6–8	Col. 3. 12–17
17	S	**THE SECOND SUNDAY BEFORE ADVENT**	
18	M	Mic. 7. 1–7	Matt. 10. 24–39
19	Tu	Hab. 3. 1–19a	1 Cor. 4. 9–16
20	W	Zech. 8. 1–13	Mark 13. 3–8
21	Th	Zech. 10. 6–end	1 Pet. 5. 1–11
22	F	Mic. 4. 1–5	Luke 9. 28–36
23	Sa	*At Evening Prayer the readings for the Eve of Christ the King are used. At other services, the following readings are used:*	
		Exod. 16. 1–21	John 6. 3–15
24	S	**CHRIST THE KING** (The Sunday next before Advent)	
25	M	Jer. 30. 1–3, 10–17	Rom. 12. 9–21
26	Tu	Jer. 30. 18–24	John 10. 22–30
27	W	Jer. 31. 1–9	Matt. 15. 21–31
28	Th	Jer. 31. 10–17	Matt. 16. 13–end
29	F	Jer. 31. 31–37	Heb. 10. 11–18
30	Sa	**ANDREW**	

December 2019

1	S	**THE FIRST SUNDAY OF ADVENT**	
2	M	Mal. 3. 1–6	Matt. 3. 1–6
3	Tu	Zeph. 3. 14–end	1 Thess. 4. 13–end
4	W	Isa. 65.17 – 66.2	Matt. 24. 1–14
5	Th	Mic. 5. 2–5a	John 3. 16–21
6	F	Isa. 66. 18–end	Luke 13. 22–30
7	Sa	Mic. 7. 8–15	Rom. 15.30 – 16.7, 25–end
8	S	**THE SECOND SUNDAY OF ADVENT**	
9	M	Jer. 7. 1–11	Phil. 4. 4–9
10	Tu	Dan. 7. 9–14	Matt. 24. 15–28
11	W	Amos 9. 11–end	Rom. 13. 8–14
12	Th	Jer. 23. 5–8	Mark 11. 1–11
13	F	Jer. 33. 14–22	Luke 21. 25–36
14	Sa	Zech. 14. 4–11	Rev. 22. 1–7
15	S	**THE THIRD SUNDAY OF ADVENT**	
16	M	Isa. 40. 1–11	Matt. 3. 1–12
17	Tu	Ecclus. 24. 1–9 *or* Prov. 8. 22–31	1 Cor. 2. 1–13
18	W	Exod. 3. 1–6	Acts 7. 20–36
19	Th	Isa. 11. 1–9	Rom. 15. 7–13
20	F	Isa. 22. 21–23	Rev. 3. 7–13
21	Sa	Num. 24. 15b–19	Rev. 22. 10–21
22	S	**THE FOURTH SUNDAY OF ADVENT**	
23	M	Isa. 7. 10–15	Matt. 1. 18–23
24	Tu	*At Evening Prayer the readings for Christmas Eve are used. At other services, the following readings are used:*	
		Isa. 29. 13–18	1 John 4. 7–16
25	W	**CHRISTMAS DAY**	
26	Th	**STEPHEN**	
27	F	**JOHN THE EVANGELIST**	
28	Sa	**THE HOLY INNOCENTS**	
29	S	**THE FIRST SUNDAY OF CHRISTMAS**	
30	M	Isa. 9. 2–7	John 8. 12–20
31	Tu	Eccles. 3. 1–13	Rev. 21. 1–8

CALENDAR 2019

JANUARY						
Su	..	E	B	E^3	E^4	..
M	..	7	14	21	28	..
Tu	1	8	15	22	29	..
W	2	9	16	23	30	..
Th	3	10	17	24	31	..
F	4	11	18	25	..	..
Sa	5	12	19	26	..	..

FEBRUARY						
Su	..	L^{-5}	L^{-4}	L^{-3}	L^{-2}	..
M	..	4	11	18	25	..
Tu	..	5	12	19	26	..
W	..	6	13	20	27	..
Th	..	7	14	21	28	..
F	1	8	15	22	..	..
Sa	Pr	9	16	23	..	..

MARCH						
Su	..	L^{-1}	L^1	L^2	L^3	L^4
M	..	4	11	18	An	..
Tu	..	5	12	19	26	..
W	..	A	13	20	27	..
Th	..	7	14	21	28	..
F	1	8	15	22	29	..
Sa	2	9	16	23	30	..

APRIL						
Su	..	L^5	P	E	E^2	..
M	1	8	15	22	29	..
Tu	2	9	16	23	30	..
W	3	10	17	24	..	..
Th	4	11	M	25	..	..
F	5	12	G	26	..	..
Sa	6	13	20	27	..	..

MAY						
Su	..	E^3	E^4	E^5	E^6	..
M	..	6	13	20	27	..
Tu	..	7	14	21	28	..
W	1	8	15	22	29	..
Th	2	9	16	23	A	..
F	3	10	17	24	31	..
Sa	4	11	18	25	..	..

JUNE						
Su	..	E^7	W	T	T^1	T^2
M	..	3	10	17	24	..
Tu	..	4	11	18	25	..
W	..	5	12	19	26	..
Th	..	6	13	20	27	..
F	..	7	14	21	28	..
Sa	1	8	15	22	29	..

JULY						
Su	..	T^3	T^4	T^5	T^6	..
M	1	8	15	22	29	..
Tu	2	9	16	23	30	..
W	3	10	17	24	31	..
Th	4	11	18	25	..	..
F	5	12	19	26	..	..
Sa	6	13	20	27	..	..

AUGUST						
Su	..	T^7	T^8	T^9	T^{10}	..
M	..	5	12	19	26	..
Tu	..	6	13	20	27	..
W	..	7	14	21	28	..
Th	1	8	15	22	29	..
F	2	9	16	23	30	..
Sa	3	10	17	24	31	..

SEPTEMBER						
Su	T^{11}	T^{12}	T^{13}	T^{14}	T^{15}	..
M	2	9	16	23	30	..
Tu	3	10	17	24	..	..
W	4	11	18	25	..	..
Th	5	12	19	26	..	..
F	6	13	20	27	..	..
Sa	7	14	21	28	..	..

OCTOBER						
Su	..	T^{16}	T^{17}	T^{18}	T^L	..
M	..	7	14	21	28	..
Tu	1	8	15	22	29	..
W	2	9	16	23	30	..
Th	3	10	17	24	31	..
F	4	11	18	25	..	..
Sa	5	12	19	26	..	..

NOVEMBER						
Su	..	A^{-4}	A^{-3}	A^{-2}	A^{-1}	..
M	..	4	11	18	25	..
Tu	..	5	12	19	26	..
W	..	6	13	20	27	..
Th	..	7	14	21	28	..
F	AS	8	15	22	29	..
Sa	2	9	16	23	30	..

DECEMBER						
Su	A	A^2	A^3	A^4	X^1	..
M	2	9	16	23	30	..
Tu	3	10	17	24	31	..
W	4	11	18	X	..	..
Th	5	12	19	26	..	..
F	6	13	20	27	..	..
Sa	7	14	21	28	..	..

A = Ash Wednesday, Ascension, Advent
A^- = Before Advent
A^{-4} = also All Saints, 2020, and 2019 (if trans.)

A^{-1} = Christ the King
An = Annunciation
AS = All Saints
B = Baptism
E = Epiphany, Easter

G = Good Friday
L = Lent
L^- = Before Lent

CALENDAR 2020

JANUARY						
Su	..	X^2	B	E^2	E^3	..
M	..	E	13	20	27	..
Tu	..	7	14	21	28	..
W	1	8	15	22	29	..
Th	2	9	16	23	30	..
F	3	10	17	24	31	..
Sa	4	11	18	25	..	..

FEBRUARY						
Su	..	Pr	L^{-3}	L^{-2}	L^{-1}	..
M	..	3	10	17	24	..
Tu	..	4	11	18	25	..
W	..	5	12	19	A	..
Th	..	6	13	20	27	..
F	..	7	14	21	28	..
Sa	1	8	15	22	29	..

MARCH						
Su	L^1	L^2	L^3	L^4	L^5	..
M	2	9	16	23	30	..
Tu	3	10	17	24	31	..
W	4	11	18	An	..	..
Th	5	12	19	26	..	..
F	6	13	20	27	..	..
Sa	7	14	21	28	..	..

APRIL						
Su	..	P	E	E^2	E^3	..
M	..	6	13	20	27	..
Tu	..	7	14	21	28	..
W	1	8	15	22	29	..
Th	2	M	16	23	30	..
F	3	G	17	24	..	..
Sa	4	11	18	25	..	..

MAY						
Su	..	E^4	E^5	E^6	E^7	W
M	..	4	11	18	25	..
Tu	..	5	12	19	26	..
W	..	6	13	20	27	..
Th	..	7	14	A	28	..
F	1	8	15	22	29	..
Sa	2	9	16	23	30	..

JUNE						
Su	..	T	T^1	T^2	T^3	..
M	1	8	15	22	29	..
Tu	2	9	16	23	30	..
W	3	10	17	24	..	..
Th	4	11	18	25	..	..
F	5	12	19	26	..	..
Sa	6	13	20	27	..	..

JULY						
Su	..	T^4	T^5	T^6	T^7	..
M	..	6	13	20	27	..
Tu	..	7	14	21	28	..
W	1	8	15	22	29	..
Th	2	9	16	23	30	..
F	3	10	17	24	31	..
Sa	4	11	18	25	..	..

AUGUST						
Su	..	T^8	T^9	T^{10}	T^{11}	T^{12}
M	..	3	10	17	24	31
Tu	..	4	11	18	25	..
W	..	5	12	19	26	..
Th	..	6	13	20	27	..
F	..	7	14	21	28	..
Sa	1	8	15	22	29	..

SEPTEMBER						
Su	..	T^{13}	T^{14}	T^{15}	T^{16}	..
M	..	7	14	21	28	..
Tu	1	8	15	22	29	..
W	2	9	16	23	30	..
Th	3	10	17	24	..	..
F	4	11	18	25	..	..
Sa	5	12	19	26	..	..

OCTOBER						
Su	..	T^{17}	T^{18}	T^{19}	T^L	..
M	..	5	12	19	26	..
Tu	..	6	13	20	27	..
W	..	7	14	21	28	..
Th	1	8	15	22	29	..
F	2	9	16	23	30	..
Sa	3	10	17	24	31	..

NOVEMBER						
Su	AS	A^{-3}	A^{-2}	A^{-1}	A	..
M	2	9	16	23	30	..
Tu	3	10	17	24	..	..
W	4	11	18	25	..	..
Th	5	12	19	26	..	..
F	6	13	20	27	..	..
Sa	7	14	21	28	..	..

DECEMBER						
Su	..	A^2	A^3	A^4	X^1	..
M	..	7	14	21	28	..
Tu	1	8	15	22	29	..
W	2	9	16	23	30	..
Th	3	10	17	24	31	..
F	4	11	18	X	..	..
Sa	5	12	19	26	..	..

L^{-5} = also Presentation, 2019 (if trans.)
M = Maundy Thursday
P = Palm Sunday
Pr = Presentation

T = Trinity
(T^{15} = also Michael and All Angels, 2019)
(T^{19} = also Luke, 2020)
T^L = Last Sunday after Trinity

W = Pentecost (Whit Sunday)
X = Christmas
(X^1 = also John, 2020)